# A HISTORY OF
# THE CHURCH OF ENGLAND
## 1945-1980

BY THE SAME AUTHOR

Lancelot Andrewes, 1555–1626
The Bond of Church and State
How the Church of England Works
George Abbot: The Unwanted Archbishop
Sermons and Society

# A HISTORY OF
# THE CHURCH
# OF ENGLAND
## 1945-1980

Paul A. Welsby

OXFORD UNIVERSITY PRESS
1984

Oxford University Press, Walton Street, Oxford OX2 6DP
London Glasgow New York Toronto
Delhi Bombay Calcutta Madras Karachi
Kuala Lumpur Singapore Hong Kong Tokyo
Nairobi Dar es Salaam Cape Town
Melbourne Auckland
and associated companies in
Beirut Berlin Ibadan Mexico City Nicosia

Oxford is a trade mark of Oxford University Press

Published in the United States
by Oxford University Press, New York

© Paul A. Welsby 1984

British Library Cataloguing in Publication Data
Welsby, Paul A.
A history of the Church of England, 1945-1980.
1. Church of England—History
I. Title
283'.42   BX5101
ISBN 0-19-213231-8

Library of Congress Cataloging in Publication Data
Welsby, Paul A.
A history of the Church of England, 1945-1980.
Bibliography: p.
Includes index.
1. Church of England—History—20th century.
2. Anglican Communion—England—History—20th century.
3. England—Church history—20th century. I. Title.
BX5101.W44 1984   283'.42   83-13114
ISBN 0-19-213231-8

Typeset by DMB (Typesetting), Oxford
and printed in Great Britain
at the University Press, Oxford

*To*
JAMES

# FOREWORD
## by the
## ARCHBISHOP OF CANTERBURY

DURING THE period which forms the subject of Canon Welsby's *History of the Church of England*, Anglicans have frequently displayed an uncertainty about the identity of their Church and confusion about the proper direction for its development.

Some Anglicans have continued to be loyal to the idea of a National Church, expressing and confirming the ill-defined but still strong religious convictions of the English people. Others have wanted a Church which would mark out its boundaries more sharply and which was more rigorous in its demands on those who claimed membership. Still others have tried to urge the Church to be the radical conscience and sometimes the disturber of the nation.

All the while, hopes for wider Christian unity have engendered a debate about whether the Church of England had greater affinities with Roman Catholicism or with the Churches of the Reformation.

In the eighties, I detect a new appreciation of the Anglican tradition and a new confidence in the creative potential of the Church of England. It is vital, however, that confidence does not degenerate into cocksure and exclusive attitudes, bred out of an ignorance of our past failures and limitations as a Church. It has always been a vital element in our self-understanding that the Church of England is a *part* of the one, holy, catholic, and apostolic Church. Anglicans have not sought to identify themselves as the one true Church, but as an authentic heir of the catholic and apostolic faith, yearning for the union of all Christians in Christ's own Church. Sober historical scholarship checks the growth of the kind of romantic fantasies about ourselves which are a threat, both to a proper humility and to a respectful estimate of other religious traditions.

In some of his previous works, Canon Welsby has enriched our understanding of the seventeenth century. Now we are further in his debt for his survey of the modern, post-war period of church history. He does not make any rash judgements. He is scrupulously fair and balanced. He gives a lucid presentation of material which cannot fail to give Anglicans a better understanding of where the Church of England now stands. In his scholarly restraint and care, Canon Welsby has produced a book which is itself a good example of the best traditions of Anglican sound learning.

This history deserves to be read and studied as Anglicans ponder the nature of the contribution they make to the great Christian centuries to come.

*Lambeth Palace*                                           +ROBERT CANTUAR
*August 1983*

# PREFACE

THE WRITING of contemporary history can be a hazardous enterprise. Each of the readers of such a work, having lived through the same events, has certain expectations which he may well find unfulfilled, for what appears of significance to him may not be seen in that way by another reader or by the author. Moreover, contemporary events are too close for any reliable analysis of their significance in the larger perspective of history. This is aggravated when, as in this case, the author himself participated in some of these events. Consequently, it is unwise to pass more than provisional judgements on trends and events. I have tried to approach the period 1945-80 as a historian would approach any other period. In a sense, however, this is an impossible task. In approaching the history of the sixteenth or the nineteenth century sufficient time has elapsed to enable the historian to distinguish what was significant and what was not and this, in turn, enables him to make a judicious selection of the material to be incorporated. Lacking this perspective of time makes the selection of material for contemporary history particularly difficult. Yet I believe the story ought to be told because it covers years in which both Church and State have undergone rapid and far-reaching changes, an appreciation of which is essential for understanding the present. The years 1945-80 saw many revolutions in the life of the nation and to these and to the rapidly increasing secularization of those years, the Church of England, which by its very nature is largely conservative, did remarkably well to respond as it did. If it failed to do better, that was because the problems were too complex and too many to be coped with in any simple or dramatic way.

I have divided this work into three periods. There is a certain arbitrariness in this because events cannot be neatly marshalled into watertight compartments, but it has the advantage of convenience provided one recognizes flexibility in such a framework. There can, in fact, be little doubt that the fifties, the sixties, and the seventies each possessed its own characteristics. It so happened that these three periods also coincide approximately with the primacies of Geoffrey Fisher, Michael Ramsay and Donald Coggan.

I would like to express my gratitude to the Archbishop of Canterbury for his kindness in writing the foreword to this book. In acknowledging the assistance which many people have given me, I would like particularly to thank the Provost of Southwark (The Very Revd David Edwards) for reading the typescript and making many valuable suggestions, and the Bishop of Rochester (Dr David Say) for answering many questions, for lending me numerous reports and other papers and for giving me insights born out of his experience as a bishop for nearly twenty-five years. I would also like to thank Mr Bernard Palmer, editor of the *Church Times*, for granting me facilities for research among the back editions of that paper, Mrs Brenda Hoff of Church House Library and Miss J. M. Owen of Sion College Library. The staff of the General Synod has been most helpful, particularly Mr Derek Pattinson (Secretary-General), Mr Brian Hanson (Legal Adviser), Canon Robert Waddington (Board of Education), Canon M. A. Reardon and Miss Daphne Fraser (Board of Mission and Unity), Mr Giles Ecclestone (formerly of the Board of Social Responsibility) and Mr John Miles (Chief Information Officer). The following have been kind enough to answer my requests for information: Lord Coggan of Sissinghurst, formerly Archbishop of Canterbury, the Rt Revd and Rt Hon Gerald Ellison, formerly Bishop of London, the Rt Revd Oliver Tomkins, formerly Bishop of Bristol, the Rt Revd Cyril Bowles, Bishop of Derby, the Rt Revd Ross Hook, Chief of Staff to the present Archbishop of Canterbury, the Very Revd Edward Carpenter, Dean of Westminster, the Very Revd John Arnold, Dean of Rochester, Canon C. O. Buchanan, Principal of St. John's College, Nottingham, the Revd David Collyer, Dr Lionel Dakers, Director of the Royal School of Church Music, Mrs J. A. Farnill, formerly Central Secretary of the Mothers' Union, Canon J. G. Hunter, the Ven Robert Jeffrey, Canon Professor Douglas Jones, Professor J. D. McClean, and Prebendary F. C. Tyler. The Rt Revd Cuthbert Bardsley, formerly Bishop of Coventry, the Rt Revd Mervyn Stockwood, formerly Bishop of Southwark, Canon L. W. Chidzey, Canon Bryan Green, and Canon John Poulton gave me much useful information about the report *Towards the Conversion of England* (1945), and the inauguration of the Archbishops' Council for Evangelism. Finally, I would acknowledge my greatest debt—to my wife, who has cheerfully tolerated my moods of preoccupation during the three years' gestation of this work, who has given me constant encouragement, and who spent many hours correcting the typescript.

*Rochester*                                          PAUL A. WELSBY
*May 1983*

# CONTENTS

## Part I. 1945-1959

# PART I

# 1945-1959

# 1

# RECONSTRUCTION

There is now a whole demon-ridden world to be reordered and everything of stability and high purpose which man can find will be needed for the task.

Geoffrey Fisher: *Enthronement Sermon*, 1945

It would have been to be wished...that at the end of so long a struggle the several Powers might have enjoyed some repose, without forming calculations that always augment the risks of war; but the tone and conduct of Russia have disappointed this hope and forced upon us fresh considerations.

Castlereagh to the Duke of Wellington, 1814

## 1. A New Era and a New Archbishop

ON 8 May 1945 people danced in the streets as victory in Europe was proclaimed and a new era dawned for a war-weary Britain. The country looked forward to a new order in which the hopes and aspirations which had been nourished and articulated during the war years would be realized. 1945 marked also the beginning of a new era for the Church of England. In January Geoffrey Fisher was appointed ninety-ninth Archbishop of Canterbury and on 19 April, with due splendour and ceremony, was enthroned in Canterbury Cathedral. When the fanfare of trumpets following his installation in the chair of St. Augustine had died away and *Te Deum* had been sung, the new archbishop preached his enthronement sermon which Charles Smyth asserted 'historians will recognise as a key-document of his Primacy'.[1] Of the Church of England, Dr Fisher said that

its distinguishing characteristic is that in loyalty to Christ it endeavours to hold together in due proportion, truths which, though essential to the fulness of the Gospel of Christ, are through the fraility of man's

[1] *The Church and the Nation*, 1962, Foreword.

spirit not easily combined—fidelity to the apostolic faith, and freedom in its apprehension and application; liberty of the spirit and obedience to the disciplined life of the Church; the corporate unity of a divinely constituted people of God, and the free response of each man in his own person to the grace and guidance of the Holy Spirit.... It is the conviction and justification of this Church of England that Christ means us to essay this difficult comprehension to hold together within our communion of the Catholic Church what may not be put asunder without grievous injury, and to present, as far as we may, the whole-ness of the Gospel of God.

He followed this classic statement of the genius of the Church of England by enumerating the tasks which lay before the Church in the post-war world. First, there was 'a whole demon-ridden world to be re-ordered'. Secondly, 'the Church has much to put in order if it is faithfully to serve the nation'. Thirdly, there was the task of seeking unity with other churches so that 'in God's good time we may stand wholly together in the one Body of Christ'. Finally, the Church of England had given birth to 'the far-flung Anglican Communion'.[2] It will be seen how far these four themes were to be characteristic of the primacy of Geoffrey Fisher.

On that Spring day, amid the beauty, the colour, and the joy of the great service in Canterbury Cathedral, the minds of many recalled the very different scene in the previous November when, on a grey drizzling day, the wind swirling the autumn leaves, similar representatives of Church and State gathered for the funeral service of Archbishop William Temple. It is no exag-geration to describe William Temple's death at the age of sixty-three, after holding the archbishopric for only two years, as a grievous blow to the Church of England, a shock to the whole nation and, indeed, to the whole world. 'We are burying the hopes of the Church of England', reflected Joseph McCulloch at his funeral service.[3] Temple was a man who was listened to with respect by many in authority in Church and State and was loved by the common man, who regarded him as both champion and friend. He possessed exceptional intellectual power and pro-phetic insight. He was able to hold in synthesis theology, phil-osophy, politics, and economics and from this combination emerged his grasp of the nature of the Christian social principles

[2] Ibid., pp. 14-15.    [3] Quoted in Edward Carpenter, *Cantuar*, 1971, p. 487.

which ought to guide the Church and which he set forth in his immensely popular Penguin book, *Christianity and Social Order*.[4] He persuaded many Christians that faith demanded a concern with the affairs of the world. He appeared to be the ideal leader for the Church at a time when many of the principles which he saw as leading to action in the fields of housing, health, education, and social welfare seemed to be on the verge of being put into practical operation as the war drew to its close. Temple's intellectual stature was combined with goodness and humility and a great capacity for friendship, while for twenty years he had been an outstanding figure in the ecumenical movement. Never had an appointment to the archbishopric of Canterbury been so universally acclaimed as that of William Temple and, because expectations were so high, it is understandable that his death was viewed in catastrophic terms. With hindsight, however, we may have reservations. He was essentially a prophet and he prophesied in the lean years when the voice of a prophet was needed, but the post-war years were of necessity a time when the Church had to wrestle with its own administrative and financial problems and even Temple's greatest admirers would not have regarded him as an efficient administrator. Again, would Temple have been at home in the vastly changed world that was to emerge after the War? Would he have really understood the moral, social, and political tensions and struggles which were to mark the fifties? Dr Alec Vidler has pointed out that Temple's life 'could hardly have run more smoothly or successfully', that being such a unified and integrated person limited his appeal to those who were not unified and integrated, that he 'seems to have been free from any torture or tension'.[5] In Dr Vidler's view these characteristics were limitations which would have blunted his effectiveness in the post-war world. Certainly many of Temple's philosophical and theological ideas failed to endure and the Christian socialism he proclaimed was soon to recede into the background, partly because of the absence of a theology which would give sanction and imperative to Christian social thinking. Perhaps Bishop Hensley Henson, a caustic prelate of a previous gener-

---

[4] 1942. Republished, 1976.
[5] 'The Limitations of William Temple', in *Theology*, January 1976.

ation, was correct when he wrote: 'I could but reflect on the Archbishop's good fortune on being called away precisely at the juncture when popular hopes were fresh and full, before the chill of reaction had chastened enthusiasm and the exasperation of disillusionment had replaced the exultation of success.'[6]

After Temple's death two months elapsed before the name of his successor was announced. The delay caused considerable indignation and moved Archbishop Garbett of York to describe it as fast becoming a scandal. 'We are like a government without a Prime Minister.'[7] The reason was certainly due to the preoccupation of the Prime Minister, Winston Churchill, with the problems of the war and his lack of interest in episcopal appointments. There were three bishops widely recognized as candidates for the primacy. The first was Cyril Garbett himself, a wise counsellor and statesman, a man of vast experience and with the capacity for hard work. He was sixty-nine, however, and contemplating retirement and, young in spirit though he was, the strains of the post-war years would require a younger man. As he himself said to Archbishop Lord Lang, 'what is really out of the question is a man who will be 70 next year going to Canterbury...it would be absurd'.[8]

Secondly, there was Mervyn Haigh, Bishop of Winchester, not well-known but intellectually powerful, a brilliant administrator and very influential in the central councils of the Church. Because of his earlier close connection with Archbishop Davidson he knew more than anyone the special difficulties and responsibilities of a Primate. When in 1928 Bishop Winnington-Ingram had wanted him to be Bishop of Stepney, Davidson had said that 'Haigh could have been Archbishop of Canterbury tomorrow'.[9] It is known that his name was seriously considered and that he was invited to lunch at 10, Downing Street.[10] He was fifty-eight but his health was precarious and he would not have survived long in the demanding office of Primate. Indeed, his health deteriorated so rapidly that seven years later he was compelled to resign. Moreover, Haigh's biographer points to a strain

---

[6] *Retrospect of an Unimportant Life*, Vol.III, 1950, p. 276.
[7] Quoted, Charles Smyth, *Cyril Foster Garbett*, 1959, p. 296.
[8] Ibid., p. 296.
[9] F. R. Barry, *Mervyn Haigh*, 1964, p. 190.
[10] Ibid.

of chronic indecision in him which 'might have brought the
Lambeth machinery to a standstill'.[11]

The third candidate, and in the eyes of many the strongest,
was George Bell, Bishop of Chichester. Aged sixty-one he was a
figure of international importance, well known for his outspoken pronouncements during the war, for his work for the
ecumenical movement and for his world-wide contacts, particularly with Church leaders in Germany. A capable administrator
and a devoted pastor, he was wise and saintly, a patron of the
arts and a person of great humanity. It was not the first time
that his name had been canvassed for the office, for when Randall Davidson had retired in 1928 some people, such as Dean
Inge of St. Paul's, considered that Bell, then Dean of Canterbury, would have been a good choice to succeed him.[12] The
appointment of an Archbishop of Canterbury, however, is not
solely a matter of concern to the Church but one in which the
Church-State relationship operates and in 1945 George Bell was
*persona non grata* to the Prime Minister and to many members
of the government. This is hardly surprising in view of Bell's
outspoken pronouncements during the war. In face of the
government's insistence on the unconditional surrender of Germany, Bell had constantly pleaded for a negotiated peace. He
had urged the government to relax its blockade of German-
occupied Europe in order to avoid famine. He regarded the stra-
tegic bombing of German cities, 'deliberately to attack civilians,
quite irrespective of whether or not they are actively contributing to the war effort', as 'a wrong deed, whether done by the
Nazis or by ourselves'.[13] Moreover, as Dr Jasper has pointed out,
Bell's pertinacity could grow to a point at which his influence
on others suffered—'he could appear to be just obstinate or
harbouring bees in his bonnet'.[14] Charles Smyth judged that
'Bell of Chichester...was by nature a protagonist, and seemed to
make every subject controversial when he spoke on it',[15] and

[11] Ibid., p. 191.
[12] Ronald C. D. Jasper, *George Bell*, 1967, p. 53. Cf. also Kenneth Slack, *George Bell*, 1971.
[13] Ibid., p. 276. Bell was not entirely alone in his views. Bishop Barnes of Birmingham, from a pacifist point of departure, shared many of them. Cf. John Barnes, *Ahead
of his Time: Bishop Barnes of Birmingham*, 1979, pp. 359-60.
[14] Op. cit., p. 285.
[15] *Cyril Foster Garbett*, p. 434.

Lord Longford in a BBC appreciation of Bell at the time of the latter's death in 1958 spoke of those who differed from him finding him 'so terribly irritating, and so acutely provocative in public, although for the most part they had an enormous respect for him in his private life'.[16]

There can be no doubt that his outspoken criticisms of the government, many of them in the House of Lords, virtually destroyed Bell's chances of becoming archbishop. Dr A. C. Don, a former Dean of Westminster, wrote in his diary: 'The Prime Minister admires courage and deplores indiscretion; and George Bell has been both courageous and indiscreet in his speeches about the war....He has paid the penalty of his con-scientious opposition to the more fire-eating patriots in the House of Lords.'[17] In his biography of Brendan Bracken, Minister of Information and a personal friend of Churchill, Andrew Boyle said that Bracken 'would cheerfully have silenced or dethroned' Bell 'for daring to raise his voice against the wickedness of the R.A.F. bomber offensive'. He then made the point that 'since Churchill suffered from a characteristic allergy even to discussing episcopal appointments he was content to underwrite the opinionated decisions of his court favourite, Brendan'.[18] Churchill knew little about the Church of England and there can be no doubt that he would have been influenced by Bracken's view of Bell which in this case coincided with that of many of his colleagues. There is some evidence that Bell's name was put before Churchill by Lord Halifax,[19] but Bell had his eyes wide open. 'I have no illusions about Churchill's atti-tude to me', he wrote to Liddell Hart in November 1944. 'He is the last man to put me in any position of greater influence.'[20] Ten years later he was asked by Archbishops Fisher and Garbett to accept nomination to succeed Garbett at York. Launcelot Mason says that 'he privately hoped that this appointment might be regarded as something of a vindication of his speeches during the war'.[21] Nothing further was heard about it. In 1963

[16] Quoted, Jasper, op. cit., p. 286.
[17] Quoted, Jasper, op. cit., p. 285.
[18] Andrew Boyle, *Poor Dear Brendan*, 1974, pp. 289-90.
[19] Donald MacKinnon in a letter in *Crucible*, July 1969, p. 124.
[20] Quoted Jasper, op. cit., p. 286.
[21] '"Soldiers" and Bishop Bell', in *Crucible*, March 1969, p. 36.

Professor Donald MacKinnon was to maintain that 'the historian of the Church of England may yet recognise that the worst misfortune to befall its leadership at the end of the war was less the premature death of William Temple than his succession by Fisher of London and not by Bell of Chichester'.[22]

On 2 January 1945 Geoffrey Fisher, Bishop of London, was nominated as the new archbishop. If this came as a surprise to some people it was because hitherto he had taken little part in national life and was therefore virtually unknown. Others might concern themselves with national issues and world affairs; Fisher devoted his energies to the particular job he was called to do. His appointment would have caused no surprise to his predecessor, for William Temple saw him as his natural successor. 'I must give up in time to let Geoffrey have his whack',[23] was a comment he made when discussing plans for retirement. After an outstandingly successful career at Oxford, Fisher had been a master at Marlborough College and at the age of twenty-seven had succeeded William Temple as headmaster of Repton. His apprenticeship for high ecclesiastical office had been served as Bishop of Chester from 1932 to 1939, when he had been translated to London. To that diocese he brought order out of administrative chaos, spending much time in drawing up rules and regulations which were duly presented to each clergyman. In this way he did much to heal the chronic divisions of churchmanship in the diocese, although among some dissentients his regulations had little effect. In the central affairs of the Church he had taken a leading part in changing the policy of the Church Commissioners which led to an increase in their annual income and thus to the provision of more realistic stipends for the clergy. It was he too who had been instrumental in establishing what came to be known as the Churches' Main Committee, an ecumenical body whose origins lay in dealing with government departments over war damage, but which in time became the agent through which the Churches made representations to the government on a wide range of issues. It was in these ways that Geoffrey Fisher revealed his talents as a brilliant administrator and an indefatigable worker. In this respect he was the man for the time as the post-war Church set about the mighty tasks of administrative and financial reform, and of meeting the challenges of war damage, the creation of new housing estates and the need for adequate pastoral ministrations. Although he possessed a first-class brain, his interests were not predominantly academic. His approach to problems was pragmatic and his outlook was practical. He once said: 'I have never tried to think out a considered plan of what I ought to follow; I have just gone forward and taken up each task, or group of tasks, as they appeared to demand attention, and no doubt there came to be some kind of pattern forming in my mind into which they fitted.'[24] This was certainly true of some of his activities but in some respects he did himself less than justice. His remarks in his enthronement service about the ecumenical movement, his Cambridge Sermon in 1946,[25] his unceasing work for the improvement of the stipends of the clergy,[26] and—whatever one's view of its wisdom—his unremitting attention to the reform of canon law,[27] reveal evidence of considered long-term plans in more than one field. Other qualities which Fisher brought to the primacy were his good humour and friendliness which, coupled with freedom from pomposity, enabled him to be at ease with people of all classes. A man of impeccable honesty in thought and speech, he could become formidable when occasion demanded and he did not suffer fools gladly. His self-confidence and self-assurance, the apparent ease with which he was able to make up his mind, produced a poise and resilience which enabled him to cope with complicated and tense situations. He possessed a phenomenal memory, a clear and logical mind, an eye for detail and a remarkable understanding of people. He was an excellent speaker, an able financier and a brilliant chairman. On the other hand, he always found it difficult to forget that he was no longer a headmaster and never took easily to any questioning of established authority. While not being illiberal, he was impatient of rebellion and was unable to understand rebels. The contrast with his predecessor was great, but each was a man for his time. One of the obituary notices after his death in 1972 pointed out that 'Fisher, without possessing Temple's

[24] Quoted in William Purcell, *Fisher of Lambeth*, 1969, p. 149.
[25] Cf. below, p. 78.
[26] Cf. below, p. 30.
[27] Cf. below, pp. 41ff.

particular gifts, was able to supply what his predecessor lacked. The hand of providence can be seen in giving the Church an administrator when the work of the prophet was done.'[28]

Such was the man who succeeded to the primacy of the Church of England. We have already noted the merits of some of his colleagues—Cyril Garbett who, as Archbishop of York was to prove a loyal and able colleague, Mervyn Haigh and George Bell. Kenneth Kirk, pastor, administrator, and scholar, whose contribution to the study of moral theology was outstanding, was Bishop of Oxford[29] and A. J. Rawlinson, an acute theologian whose service to the Church has been undervalued, was Bishop of Derby. Then there was Christopher Chavasse,[30] the doughty Evangelical Bishop of Rochester, F. R. Barry of Southwell,[31] F. A. Cockin of Bristol and Spencer Leeson of Peterborough.[32] When to these are added the names of Edward Wynne of Ely, Richard Parsons of Hereford, Joseph Hunkin of Truro[33] and Leslie Hunter of Sheffield,[34] it was a formidable team which the new archbishop was to lead. Fisher himself was succeeded at London by William Wand, the Bishop of Bath and Wells. Possessed of tireless energy and a disciplined devotional life, he was a scholar with the ability to communicate his scholarship to the non-academic. Before he became an English diocesan he had been Archbishop of Brisbane and had been offered the see of Bath and Wells by Winston Churchill because Brendan Bracken had noticed a patriotic booklet he had published in Australia not long before the fall of Singapore, entitled *Has Britain Let Us Down?* It was Brendan Bracken who, taking him out to lunch, asked Wand whether he would be prepared to go to London.[35]

[28] *Church Times*, 22 September 1972.
[29] Cf. E. W. Kemp, *Life and Letters of Kenneth Escott Kirk*, 1959.
[30] Cf. Selwyn Gummer, *The Chavasse Twins*, 1963.
[31] Cf. Frank West, *F.R.B.—A Portrait of Bishop Russell Barry*, 1980; F. R. Barry, *Period of My Life*, 1970.
[32] Cf. below, p. 23, and *Spencer Leeson; A Memoir*, by some of his friends, 1958.
[33] Cf. A. Dunstan and J. S. Peart-Binns, *Cornish Bishop: a Biography of J. W. Hunkin*, 1977.
[34] Cf. Mary Walton, *History of the Diocese of Sheffield*, 1981, Part 2, Chap. 1.
[35] Andrew Boyle, op. cit., p. 291. Cf. J. W. C. Wand, *Changeful Page*, 1965.

## 2. The Aftermath of Victory

Geoffrey Fisher was enthroned on 19 April. The next day the Russian armies reached Berlin and the end of the war in Europe was in sight. On 8 May the Germans surrendered and four months later the war in the Far East was over. After six years of war an exhausted Europe faced the gigantic task of post-war reconstruction. When Bishop Bell visited Germany in 1946 he noted that 'there is hardly any town of any size which has not been reduced, either wholly or in part, to ruins by the bombing and the shelling', while Berlin 'is like an inferno in ruins'.[36] In addition to material reconstruction there was the task of reconstituting the whole fabric of political, economic, and social life. There were an estimated 12,500,000 refugees and displaced persons in western Europe, 10,000 damaged or destroyed Church buildings and 2,000 pastor's houses, parish halls, and other Church premises seriously damaged. Of particular concern to Christians was the isolation, spiritual desolation, and persecution of clergy and congregations of all communions during the previous six years.

Material reconstruction and the resettlement of refugees and displaced persons was the responsibility of the United Nations Relief and Rehabilitation Administration (UNRRA), but in the year before the war ended there had emerged in Great Britain, America, and many neutral countries Christian Reconstruction in Europe, concerned with spiritual recovery and the rebuilding of Church life in Europe. This organization collaborated with the department of Reconstruction and Inter-Church Aid set up by the emerging World Council of Churches in Geneva. It became the task of this department to discover from the Churches in Europe the extent of the war damage and their most urgent needs. This information was communicated to the national Committees for Christian Reconstruction, which appealed to their member Churches for resources. In February 1945 the Church Assembly had accepted on behalf of the Church of England the responsibility of contributing £250,000 (regarded in those days as a 'very high' sum) towards the national appeal for £1 million, the sum to be divided between the dioceses. Churchpeople were urged to regard this not primarily as a finan-

---

[36] Quoted, Jasper, op. cit., p. 295.

cial contribution but as a gesture of brotherhood and solidarity between Christians in Great Britain and those on the Continent. The money was used for training ordinands and for ministering to prisoners of war. Equipment of every kind was made available and there were scholarships for ordinands from other countries to study theology in colleges in Great Britain.

With his international outlook, his human concern and his special contact with the German Church leaders, Bishop Bell was intensely active in the reconstruction of Europe. He had a particular concern for the millions of starving and homeless refugees wandering about Germany and he was able to arrange for a deputation of twenty Church leaders of all denominations, led by the Archbishop of York, to discuss matters with the Prime Minister, who assured the deputation that everything possible would be done and welcomed any support the Churches could give by educating public opinion. With this in mind, Bell arranged for a motion to be put to the Convocations deploring the forceful expulsion by the Russians of German families from East Germany, Poland, Czechoslovakia and Hungary, in contrast to the British and American policy of the repatriation of displaced persons. The motion asked the British Government to continue to make representations to the government of Russia and the other Communist countries.[37]

Bishop Bell paid a visit to Germany to study the situation at first-hand and in October 1946, with a representative delegation, he toured the British Zone. The delegates produced a report, *The Task of the Churches in Germany*, which emphasized the need to give enhanced status to the Religious Affairs Branch of the Control Commission so that it could ensure that adequate facilities for public worship, for education, and for training for the ministry were available to the German Churches. In November of that year Bell reported at length on the visit to the House of Lords and called for 'a change in policy, a change in attitude and a new basis of confidence'. Germany must be given the opportunity to help herself, she must be treated as a single economic unit, the process of de-Nazification should be

---

[37] Ibid., p. 293.

ended, and Germans must be given more responsibility in their own internal affairs.[38]

The conviction that victory had brought peace to the world was soon seen to be a fond delusion. The machinery of the United Nations, on which such high hopes had been placed, worked slowly and was hamstrung by the veto, and the comradeship of nations in time of war gave place to fear and suspicion. The greatest blow was the grim deterioration in the relationship between Russia and the other two great powers, and, as Europe became divided into two hostile camps, the spectacle of war once again loomed on the horizon. The position in Berlin symbolized the growing tension, when Russia blockaded the city in 1948 and deprived it of food and other necessities of life thus evoking the amazing achievement of the allied air-lift. Communist governments were firmly in control in the countries of Eastern Europe, and in Germany the post-war refugee problem was swelled by an enormous influx of displaced persons escaping from East Germany. In the Far East in 1950 Southern Korea was invaded by the Communists and the Russians refused to help the United Nations to bring to an end this act of unprovoked aggression. In China the Communist Party established the People's Republic. Thus, the post-war period was marked by a hardening of world relationships on ideological lines and the 'cold war', greatly aggravated by the announcement in 1949 that an atomic explosion had occurred in the Soviet Union. When the cold war was at its height Bishop Bell, with the approval of Archbishop Fisher, initiated a series of discussions on Anglican attitudes to Communism and published in 1953 conclusions which condemned Communism for its atheism, its inhumanity, and its insidious propaganda.[39]

There were grave signs of a concentrated attack on religious freedom in Eastern Europe. In 1949 Bishop Ordas, Lutheran Bishop of Budapest, and Cardinal Mindszenty were arrested. Both had refused to accept government policy with regard to the Church's schools and had used legislative means to oppose it. 'We are witnessing a deadly struggle between the Christian faith and the Christian Church on the one side', said the Archbishop

---

[38] Ibid., pp. 304-5.
[39] D. M. MacKinnon (ed.), *Christian Faith and Communist Faith*, 1953.

of Canterbury, 'and, on the other, a Communism which will not tolerate any form of the Christian Church unless it be subservient to the State.'[40] The Cardinal was sentenced to life-long imprisonment. In Bulgaria a number of Protestant pastors were imprisoned for several months before being tried and sentenced. In Czechoslovakia violent propaganda and accusations of treason were directed against the bishops and clergy, including Archbishop Beran of Prague. In 1950 Archbishop Fisher spoke of the danger of Russia and the threat of Communism. 'The dominant spiritual feature of our time is the tremendous and highly-organised assault upon the faith and freedom of the Christian Church.'[41] Three years later concern was expressed about the Church struggle in East Germany, about persecution in Poland and about attacks on the Orthodox Church in Yugoslavia.[42] In 1950 the International Department of the British Council of Churches prepared a booklet documenting the official attitude of Communist governments towards the Churches.[43] The documents and facts, presented with the minimum of comment, spoke for themselves. In 1954 the Church Assembly debated a motion on the Churches of Europe under Communist governments and the period saw the publication of a spate of books and pamphlets on religion and Communism. Little attention was paid to the Communist views of Dr Hewlett Johnson, the Dean of Canterbury, whose naivety and uncritical outlook led him to make such extreme claims for the virtues of Communism that his judgement was open to grave question. Nevertheless, on more than one occasion the Archbishop of Canterbury was obliged to repudiate his opinions openly.

### 3. The Emergence of the Welfare State

In England itself the years 1945 and 1946 saw a people emerging from five years of war during which their lives had been disrupted and many hardships had been endured. The armed forces had experienced the slaughter and the hardships of combat. Civilians at home had endured shortages and the strain of

---

[40] *Chronicle of Convocation*, January 1949.
[41] Ibid., September 1950.
[42] Ibid., October 1953.
[43] J. B. Barrow and H. M. Waddams, *Communism and the Churches; A Documentation.*

bombing and working long hours in difficult conditions. Amidst the weariness and lowering of vitality the celebrations of victory engendered feelings of relief and elation. The first few years after the war were a time of endeavour and hope in which difficulties could be faced because of optimism for a future which would be marked by the banishment of poverty and insecurity, a new national unity and the end of industrial tensions. There was much talk of building 'a new Britain' and the dawn of 'a new world'.

In July 1945 the first General Election for ten years was held, as the result of which the Labour Party secured a spectacular victory. The new Government, built around a number of remarkable men—Clement Attlee, Ernest Bevin, Stafford Cripps, Herbert Morrison, Hugh Dalton—was convinced that central control was necessary for social planning and social justice. Two far-reaching pieces of legislation were embarked upon to secure this end. First, between 1946 and 1949, there was the nationalization of the Bank of England, gas, electricity, coal, and transport. Secondly, a series of Acts of Parliament established what came to be called 'the Welfare State'. The Education Act had already become law in 1944 and, under the Labour Government, the National Insurance Act (1946) brought the whole population into a comprehensive scheme covering maternity, sickness, unemployment, retirement, and death—'from the cradle to the grave'—and the National Health Service Act (1946) provided a free medical service for all and nationalized the former voluntary hospitals.

Because a great number of the reforms advocated by Christians since the end of the First World War were embodied in the welfare legislation, it is not surprising that the Welfare State was accepted by the Church as a whole. 'Christians should welcome the Welfare State', wrote Archbishop Garbett. 'It is the embodiment of the principle "Bear ye one another's burdens and so fulfil the law of Christ". In bringing relief to the poor, giving food to the hungry, finding work for the unemployed, caring for the children and the aged, and providing healing for the sick it is carrying on the work of Christ.'[44] The Bishop of London, Dr Wand, described the Welfare State as 'an expression at the

---

[44] Cyril Garbett, *In An Age of Revolution*, 1952, p. 151.

national level of the humanitarian work of the Church',[45] and
Canon Roger Lloyd of Winchester declared that 'in the Bible,
and therefore in Christian theology, there is every warrant for
believing that a reasonable degree of material security is part of
God's desire for every one of His human creatures'.[46] Churchmen such as Cyril Garbett, however, were never prone to allow
enthusiasm to obscure reality and they were not blind to the
dangers against which Christians should be on their guard. For
Garbett these were two. The first was that the Welfare State
'might easily become a State concerned only with physical and
mental well-being, while the spiritual needs of its citizens are
neglected'.[47] Time would reveal the truth of this danger, particularly after 1960 when the Welfare State operated in an
affluent society and when, at the same time, many people
began to learn that material prosperity did not automatically
produce happiness. The second danger was 'that the Welfare
State might weaken the sense of personal responsibility'.[48] Once
again, time was to show that Garbett was as farsighted as ever,
for some of the malaise of the seventies was due to the unwilling-
ness of many people to accept personal responsibility, assuming that the State possessed a bottomless purse out of which
could be extracted unlimited public spending which would
serve as a substitute for hard work and personal responsibility.
In fact, as Canon Lloyd pointed out, 'the Welfare State seems at
once splendidly idealistic and at the same time both innocent
and naive'. Its idealism lay in its assumption of 'a high standard
of morality for the whole nation...· It makes a characteristic act
of faith that we will all try to give as much as we get, that we will
all work hard to increase the national wealth and then take out
of it our fair share, and no more.' The innocence and naivity lay
in an optimistic estimate of human nature, particularly as the
system itself was 'a form of social organisation so particularly
easy to exploit'.[49] Nevertheless, the defects of the Welfare State
were of minor significance compared with the social and economic conditions to which many were exposed before the war.

[45] J. W. C. Wand, *God and Goodness*, 1947, p. 56.
[46] Roger Lloyd, *The Church and the Artisan Today*, 1952, p. 32.
[47] Garbett, op. cit., p. 152.
[48] Ibid.
[49] Roger Lloyd, op. cit., p. 31. Cf. also A. R. Vidler, 'The Welfare State: A Christian
View', in *Theology*, December 1952, reprinted in *Essays in Liberality*, 1957.

'With all its limitations', wrote Garbett, 'the Welfare State is more Christian both in spirit and in actual practice than a state which confined itself to the protection of its citizens from violence, and its poor from actual starvation, but did nothing to feed the hungry, to clothe the naked, or to restore those who had fallen by the way.'[50]

## 4. Health and Education

There were two aspects of the Welfare State in which the Church was particularly involved. In the first place, the National Health Service had important effects on the provision of the spiritual ministrations for hospital patients. Hospital authorities were instructed to provide for the spiritual needs of patients and staff and to arrange duties to enable the staff to attend religious services. A chaplain (or chaplains) was to be appointed to every hospital, either full-time or part-time, to be paid by the hospital.[51] The existence of a hospital chaplain was no new thing; the change that occurred in 1948 was that the chaplain's position in the hospital was officially recognized, that his importance was emphasized, and that the State was prepared to pay him for his work.

It was in the field of education that the partnership of Church and State was to be most clearly demonstrated. For centuries the Church had been the main instrument of education in this country and until 1870 there was little education other than that provided by the Church or through foundations created by pious churchmen. In 1870 the State began to establish a national system of education and the story of education since then has been one of continual growth of State education in which the Church has been a prominent and influential partner. The outstanding feature of the settlement achieved by the Education Act of 1944 was the spirit of harmony and co-operation between the Churches, quite unlike the bitterness and rivalry which had characterized the relationship between them on educational matters in the previous hundred years. Much of the credit for this must go to the understanding, sympathy, and patience of

---

[50] Garbett, op. cit., p. 153.
[51] Ministry of Health Circular RHB(48)76, 1948.

Archbishop William Temple,[52] together with the valuable contribution made by the Anglican National Society[53] through
regular meetings over a number of years of a Joint Conference of
representatives of the Society and representatives of the Free
Churches. In 1939 the Church Assembly passed a Measure
establishing in every diocese an education committee with statutory powers. This was an extremely wise move in view of the
forthcoming educational developments, for it meant that each
diocese had a body with the necessary authority and status to
co-operate with the local education authority in promoting
plans for the reorganization of education.

So far as the Church was concerned the most important provisions of the Act were two. First, the dual system of education
was retained. There were to be two classes of schools, county and
voluntary. The latter were to be divided into controlled and
aided schools. In controlled schools the Ministry of Education
and the Local Education Authority were to undertake complete
responsibility for the school, in return for which the Church
forfeited its right to appoint teachers and had only a third of the
places on the board of management. Religious instruction was to
be based on an agreed syllabus, although parents might request
that their children receive specific Church of England teaching
for not more than two periods a week in school hours. In aided
schools the Church was to pay half the cost of structural repairs
and improvements, while the Ministry would produce the other
half. In these schools the Church was to have two-thirds of the
places on the board of management and the right to appoint all
teachers. Church of England teaching was to be given to all,
subject to a conscience clause.

Secondly, there was to be a daily act of worship and regular
religious teaching in all State-maintained schools, subject to the
rights of conscience of parents and teachers. The content of
religious teaching in State schools, and for most days in voluntary controlled schools, was to be based on an agreed syllabus—

[52] Cf. Lord Butler, 'William Temple and Educational Reform', in *The Art of
Memory*, 1982, pp. 143ff.
[53] Founded in 1811. Under the Society's direction thousands of new schools had been
built, with the result that between 1820 and 1834 the number of children in schools
doubled. Cf. H. J. Burgess and P. A. Welsby, *A Short History of the National Society,
1811-1961*, 1961.

agreed, that is, between representatives of all denominations (other than the Roman Catholic Church), of the teachers and of the local education authority.

The Church of England welcomed the Act. Dr Spencer Leeson, Rector of St. Mary's, Southampton, and later to play a leading part in the Church's educational work, was delivering the Bampton Lectures when the Bill was being debated in Parliament. In the course of these he welcomed the Bill for 'requiring a continuation of worship and instruction in the State schools'.[54] F. R. Braley declared that the Church 'ought to regard the Act as a great victory for Christian principles—a sure and certain proof that the work of the Church has not been such a failure as many people represent it to be'.[55] On the other hand, secularists like Harold Laski expressed the view that, by pressing for compulsory religious education and worship, the Churches were 'announcing that they have exhausted their religious vitality and desire to be no more than an arm of the state's police power'.[56]

The first task facing each local education authority was the preparation of a development plan for its area which, among other things, would show which Church schools it was prepared to use. Inevitably, the managers of some schools were presented with building demands which were impossible to meet. Again, one of the most disturbing and unforseen features of the new Act was the large number of village schools scheduled for closure because they were regarded as financially uneconomic and educationally inefficient. In spite of the Government's request that local education authorities should give special consideration to village schools on the ground that closure could disrupt village life and community, over a thousand such schools, the majority of them Anglican, had disappeared by 1955. With regard to the major provisions of the Act, managers of Church schools were strongly recommended to opt for aided status wherever possible, but when controlled status was inevitable incumbents were encouraged to seize the opportunities under the Act to accept

---

[54] Spencer Leeson, *Christian Education*, 1947. E. R. Norman has described these lectures as 'the finest statement of the Church of England's view of education written this century'—*The Church and Society, 1770-1970*, 1976, p. 402.

[55] *The School without the Parson*, 1945, pp. 7f.

[56] Quoted F. A. Iremonger, *William Temple*, p. 577.

responsibility for Church teaching in those schools. The new agreed syllabuses were generally welcomed as they began to be published and as it was seen that non-denominational was not synonymous with non-doctrinal teaching.

The Act raised the gravest of financial problems for the Church because the Ministry's requirements went beyond anything the Church had anticipated. Everywhere existing schools fell far short of the high standards demanded. The problem was aggravated by the fact that within a few years of the passing of the Act the school population increased by half a million and further increases lay ahead. At first everyone was so shocked by the astronomical figures that they found it difficult to think constructively at all. The shock was the greater because it coincided with a period of acute inflation in which building costs more than trebled those of pre-war years. It coincided also with the unprecedented load of financial responsibility caused by the vast restoration work following the war and the need to increase the stipends of the clergy. Clearly, not all the demands could be met and the number of Church schools diminished considerably. Alongside this there emerged the growing conviction that the aided schools that remained, if they were to become financially viable, could no longer be regarded as solely a parochial concern. As it was in the interest of the Church as a whole to continue to play its part in the educational system of the country, so it was reasonable to expect financial aid to come from a wider source than the local parish. Consequently, in 1949 the National Society, in co-operation with Mr J. L. B. Todhunter of the Ministry of Education and with the approval of the Ministry, sponsored a scheme for financing aided schools on a diocesan basis. It was a form of co-operative venture, known as the Barchester Scheme, whereby managers could agree to be assessed to pay into a diocesan fund contributions for the rebuilding, improvement, and maintenance of their school, such contributions being augmented by certain central educational resources of the diocese.

Immense efforts were made to save as many schools as possible. There was genuine concern on the part of the main political parties at the scale of voluntary school commitments and a desire to ease the financial burden. Accordingly, the Government attempted to alleviate the hardship within the framework of the existing settlement. A new Act, passed in 1953, made grants available for building aided schools in new housing areas and, in order to maintain the balance of the existing settlement, local authorities were also empowered to build new controlled schools. Further stimulus was given in 1958 when the Church Commissioners were given authority to make payments from their funds for grants and loans for school building. It was the Education Act of 1959, however, which changed the financial situation and brought confidence where before there had been depression. The Act raised the Exchequer grant for aided schools from a half to three-quarters and introduced a new grant of three-quarters of the cost of building new aided secondary schools where it could be shown that they could provide substantially for children at existing primary schools. The Church was thus able to build new secondary schools, which it had not been able to do under the 1944 Act.

By 1959 it was possible to assess the school situation so far as the Church of England was concerned. It had lost more than 10% of its schools but what is most noteworthy is the fact that, in spite of the heavy financial obstacles, 3,000 Anglican schools were able to choose aided status. The situation varied from diocese to diocese. Some dioceses, particularly those covering rural areas, had deliberately chosen controlled status, but in Lancashire and London, where Churchmen were particularly concerned to maintain a fully denominational atmosphere, the proportion of aided schools was larger. The vigour, the tenacity, and the shrewdness of Anglican Churchmen in preserving the Church's witness in the field of education cannot be over-estimated.

The Church training colleges for teachers, many of which, like the schools, were hampered by obsolete buildings, were another source of financial anxiety. The Government was prepared to meet half the capital expenditure required for new buildings or for bringing existing buildings up to the required standard, and thereafter to cover all maintenance costs. As the Church was determined to maintain its numerical and proportional contribution to the training of teachers to meet the educational expansion, very heavy expenditure was required. The massive financial operation was made possible largely by loans from the Church's Central Board of Finance and by 1958 the Church was training one quarter of all training college students. No sooner had the Church coped with these overwhelming problems, however, than the Government announced its intention to expand teacher training by 12,000 places by 1962, following the extension in 1957 of the teacher training course from two to three years. This faced the Church with the task of providing 3,000 new places and would involve building at least one new college. The estimated cost to the Church of this latest expansion was £1¼ million. The Central Board of Finance made the necessary provision and with this money existing colleges were greatly expanded and two new colleges were built at Lancaster and Canterbury. Thus, in the period from 1946 to 1962 diocesan and central Church funds supported the colleges to the extent of some £3,135,000, which enabled them to expand from a group providing about 3,500 places to one providing just under 10,000.

There were two reasons why the Church was prepared to invest such vast resources in teacher training. First, the Church's training colleges represented the only direct stake which the Church had in the vast and growing influential sphere of higher education. Secondly, the colleges sent into the nation's schools a stream of teachers educated in a Christian atmosphere where Anglican worship and instruction were an integral part of college life.

Two names are to be honoured for their contribution to enabling the Church to grapple so successfully with post-war educational demands. The first is Spencer Leeson who, as headmaster of Merchant Taylors' School and of Winchester College, had worked in the field of education for many years. He became Bishop of Peterborough in 1949, the first Churchman since the Reformation to become a bishop within ten years of his ordination. He was the first chairman of the Schools Council of the Church of England and in that capacity he knew intimately the problems of Church schools and worked unceasingly to secure their future. 'The sheer weight of his enthusiasm moved mountains of prejudice and apathy: and the schools saved for the Church are a monument of his ability, courage and faith.'[57] The second name is that of Robert Stopford who, as Moderator of the Church Training Colleges after the war, greatly assisted in

---

[57] *Spencer Leeson: A Memoir*, by some of his friends, 1958, p. 140.

solving the problems facing the colleges. From 1952 to 1955 he was General Secretary of the National Society and Secretary of the Schools Council and later, when he had become a bishop, was chairman of the Board of Education.

## 5. Dark Clouds at Home and Abroad

Post-war aspirations included the banishment of poverty and insecurity and the establishment of a new national unity, but these were soon mocked by the resurgence of old insecurities and the acquisitiveness of individuals and groups. Disillusionment and frustration began to emerge as the years of austerity and rationing continued until 1954. Hard work and a united people were essential for the speedy reconstruction of the nation, but a natural weariness settled over the people and class suspicion and industrial unrest dissipated energies and distracted attention from the main task. The nationalization measures not only failed to usher in the age of industrial peace and prosperity, but produced even greater discontent and inefficiency. 1947 and 1948 saw the 'Winter crisis', with power cuts and coal rationing, and in 1948 a dock strike cost the country millions of pounds and created widespread bitterness. People appeared unable or unwilling to realize that social change had to be worked for and paid for and the result was that the nation faced an economic crisis as the balance of payments deteriorated, production flagged, the pound was devalued and the country found itself still living on credit and reserves. While the economic fortunes of the nation declined, wages, incomes, and profits soared.

Thus, by 1950—a year which saw a serious rise in prices—the optimism of 1945 had evaporated. The Festival of Britain in 1951 seemed to many to be but 'a whistling in the dark'. Certainly the Festival was a celebration of the nation's confidence in its future, yet there was something symbolic in the unveiling of this future against the back-cloth of a city of bomb-sites and boarded-up windows, a flagging economy and international tension. Similarly, the Coronation of Queen Elizabeth II in 1953, although it witnessed to the continuity of history and the divine basis of monarchy, had as its background the same bomb sites together with high taxes and a balance of payments crisis, while beneath the surface of national and imperial solidarity lay the old animosities and the intractable realities of economics.

The disillusionment and frustration at home was fuelled by the menacing clouds on the international horizon as, faced with the apparent paralysis of the United Nations, the country watched the disintegration of relations between Russia and the Western Powers, the growing threat of Communism and the dangers of atomic warfare. Since 1949, when the Soviet Union exploded its first atomic bomb, the fear of a new and horrific war had begun to trouble the minds of men as they foresaw the escalation of armaments and the horror of nuclear warfare hovering over the future of world civilization.

The Churches were very much aware of the moral problems raised by the discovery of atomic energy and the use of the atomic bomb. In 1945, the year in which the first atomic bomb had been dropped on Hiroshima, the British Council of Churches had appointed a commission to consider these issues and in the following year published its report[58] which presented an admirable balance between a sound theology and a realistic attitude to political practicalities, while one of its characteristics was the note of urgency which it struck time after time. The ethical crux was the Christian attitude to war in the modern age, which differed from that of previous eras in that atomic warfare introduced the new dimension of widespread and indiscriminate destruction. Some members of the Commission believed that in no circumstances should a Christian support the use of atomic weapons, but others argued that technical advances and new weapons could not alter the Christian responsibility for defending the fundamental rights and liberties of men and institutions, and the possession of atomic weapons might be the only sufficient deterrent to a would-be aggressor. The Commission had no solution to offer to the dilemma of renunciation or possession of these weapons and believed that this represented the present divided mind of the Church. When the Church Assembly appointed a body to consider the BCC report it revealed a similar division of opinion. This report,[59] however, declared the *use* of nuclear weapons to be immoral, yet argued

---

[58] *The Era of Atomic Power*, 1946. In 1959 the BCC published a further report on the subject—*Christians and Atomic War* which was followed by *The Valley of Decision: The Christian Dilemma in the Nuclear Age*, by T. R. Milford, 1960.
[59] *The Church and the Atom*, 1948.

that the retention of such armaments was morally justifiable. This judgement was based on the traditional concept of the 'just war' and the responsibility of a government for the safety of its citizens. The report went so far as to agree that in certain circumstances defensive 'necessity' might justify the use of atomic weapons against an unscrupulous aggressor. The report was criticized for its lack of realism and for the absence of any sense of urgency. In debate Bishop Bell maintained that the report and its recommendations might have been written and signed by men of good will who were not Christian believers and it was pointed out that in a long chapter on 'Morality and Warfare' the name of Christ was not once mentioned. The recommendation that 'necessity' might justify the use of atomic weapons against an unscrupulous aggressor was criticized for implying that 'necessity knows no law'. Dr Bell considered 'that the Report fails to give guidance which the Church needs as a Church, which the public needs, and which the pilots, scientists and politicians need from the Church—it fails to give distinctively Christian help'.[60]

The issues raised by nuclear weapons were far from being the concern only of moralists and theologians. Many Christian clergy and laymen, by no means all of them pacifists, were deeply concerned and in 1958 the Campaign for Nuclear Disarmament (CND) was launched under the chairmanship of Canon John Collins[61] of St. Paul's Cathedral, with the object of calling upon Britain to declare that, regardless of what others might do, she intended to abandon the use of nuclear power for military purposes. It supported the first Aldermaston March on Good Friday 1958, organized by the Direct Action Committee against Nuclear Weapons. It was not a specifically Christian body and included such well-known figures as Bertrand Russell, J. B. Priestley and Kingsley Martin. It became the largest political mass movement outside the political parties and its importance lay in its enabling the apparently powerless to try to influence those who administered power to use their efforts to transform the impulses of destruction into enterprises of construction. It provided an outlet for the corporate expression of frustration and horror which many people felt at the waste of resources and

[60] *Church Assembly: Report of Proceedings*, Autumn Session, 1948, p. 397.
[61] Cf. L. John Collins, *Faith Under Fire*, 1966.

energies in the manufacture of weapons of destruction, at the risk to health entailed in their manufacture and testing, and at the unspeakable horror at the possibility of unlimited nuclear warfare. The weakness of the Campaign was the impression given 'that there is a simple and straightforward method of removing the sources of international conflict and of abolishing nuclear weapons which politicians are too obtuse to perceive or too irresponsible to pursue'.[62]

Between 1958 and 1960 the Campaign grew and in 1959 the Aldermaston March was organized by CND itself and its route reversed so that it ended in London where the six or seven thousand marchers were joined by a huge crowd in Trafalgar Square. The next year it was estimated that some twenty thousand took part. The marches continued to be held in subsequent years, but after 1966 much dissension broke out in the ranks of CND. Bertrand Russell, the President of CND, believed that civil disobedience was necessary if governments were to be made to act and he established the Committee of 100 to organize civil disobedience on a large scale. After many difficult negotiations CND reaffirmed its official policy against direct action and accepted the resignation of Russell. By the time the Committee of 100 collapsed it had inflicted a great deal of damage on CND and diminished support for it.

[62] Editorial in *Theology*, June 1959.

# 2

# PUTTING THE HOUSE
# IN ORDER

Unless the Church of England is prepared energeti-
cally to set its house in order, it will not only lose,
in a critical hour, an opportunity of leadership, it
will also experience the impoverishment of spirit
which follows a great refusal.

*Putting our House in Order*, 1941

## 1. Out of the Ashes

WHILE THE nation was meeting the challenge caused by war
damage and the need for a vast increase in the housing supply,
the Church of England was faced with the restoration of bombed
churches, parsonages, and church halls and with the provision of
buildings for the new housing areas. In the diocese of London,
out of 700 churches, only seventy had remained unscathed by
bombing and many had been completely destroyed,[1] and this was
paralleled throughout the big cities. Again, over one million new
houses were built by the Labour Government before 1951, and
between that date and 1954 Mr Harold Macmillan exceeded the
promised target of 300,000 houses a year, so that by 1955 the
Conservatives had equipped the country with more than a million
new houses. The emergence of vast new housing estates, in addition to the need to cope with war-damage, posed problems of
considerable magnitude for the Church of England. A series of
Measures[2] passed by the Church Assembly facilitated a solution
to the problem and made possible schemes of reorganization, the
creation of new parishes, the union of benefices and the holding
of benefices in plurality, and enabled the Church Commissioners to make grants or loans in respect of Church buildings.

---

[1] J. W. C. Wand, *Changeful Page*, 1965, p. 183.
[2] *New Parishes Measure*, 1943; *Reorganisation Areas Measure*, 1944; *Pastoral Reorganisation Measure*, 1949; *Benefice (Suspension of Presentation) Measures*, 1947,
1949, 1952; *New Housing Areas (Church Buildings) Measure*, 1954.

The scale of the problem can be illustrated from the diocese of Rochester. Between 1944 and 1954 the population of the diocese increased from 600,000 to more than a million. Well over a hundred churches, halls, and parsonages had been severely damaged during the war and in one deanery only three out of fourteen churches could be used at all. Apart from payments from the War Damage Commission, the money for restoration and reorganization was raised in the diocese. This amounted to a quarter of a million pounds, to which was added £80,000 from the central account of the Great Appeal Fund launched in the diocese in 1944. By 1952 this stage of reconstruction was completed, but in 1955 the diocese embarked on a ten-year extension scheme as a result of which twenty-one new churches, sixteen parsonages, and sixteen church halls were built at the cost of one and three quarter million pounds. This is one example, to be paralleled throughout the Church, of the magnitude of the reconstruction problem and the determination of churchmen to grapple with it.

Special problems were associated with the City of London, where there were forty-six parish churches and a correspondingly high amount of war damage in an area which had become largely non-residential. In 1952 the City of London (Guild Churches) Act, followed by a further Act in 1960, enabled the Bishop of London to designate certain churches in the City of London as Guild Churches to serve the non-residential population of the City. The forty-six parish churches were reduced to twenty-four and, of the remainder, sixteen were chosen to be Guild Churches. The incumbent had no territorial responsibility and no statutory obligation to hold Sunday services. His ministry was to the City workers, but he was also expected to have some specialist qualification whereby he and his church could serve the Church as a whole. For example, the Church of St. Ethelburga, Bishopsgate, became a centre for the Church's ministry of healing, and St. Benet's, Paul's Wharf, was to minister to the Welsh congregation in and about the City. This was the vision of Bishop Wand and the Ven. O. Gibbs-Smith, Archdeacon of London, both of whom believed that in this way 'the City may become a great laboratory in which new methods of ministry, new spiritual expedients, and new pastoral techniques may be tried out for the benefit of the Church as a whole'.[3] It is doubt-

[3] Bishop Wand, quoted in Roger Lloyd, *The Church of England, 1900-1965*, 1966, p. 530.

ful if the scheme ever fulfilled these hopes and expectations.

## 2.  Men, Money, and the Ministry

We have seen the brave efforts made by the Church to tackle the problems arising from the devastation of the war years and the rapid growth of new housing areas. The problems were aggravated by the declining number of clergy and by the need to pay a realistic salary to those who were available. Much credit must go to Archbishop Fisher for his untiring efforts to increase the remuneration of the clergy. Until 1948 two bodies had been responsible for the stipends of the clergy. The first was the Ecclesiastical Commissioners, established as a permanent body in 1836, which augmented the endowment income of poorer benefices. They became 'a clearing house for most of the administrative problems of the Church, and particularly those concerned with the cure of souls'.[4] The second was Queen Anne's Bounty,[5] which had been established in 1704 for the purpose of augmenting the maintenance of the poorer clergy. By the end of the war, however, the Bounty was engaged in paying out very small sums to one parish or another and in 1948 it was amalgamated with the Ecclesiastical Commissioners to form a body to be known as the Church Commissioners. This ensured a more united policy on clergy stipends and was followed by a review of the general financial operations of the Church Commissioners. Traditionally all the Commissioners' money was invested in gilt-edged securities, which in the post-war world was a wasteful policy. They now began to invest in industrial and commercial shares, which yielded a considerably higher return and this marked the beginning of the rise in the level of stipends. At the same time an appeal was made to the laity for new giving and in these ways the parochial clergy were rescued from severe financial hardship, although their stipends still remained meagre and inflation was to overtake the best efforts of the Commissioners.

With the conscription of young men into the Forces, the war years saw a dramatic fall in the number of men ordained, while

[4] H. W. Bradfield, *The Church's Property*, 1944, p. 15. Cf. also *Number One Millbank: The Story of the Ecclesiastical Commissioners*, by J. R. Brown, n.d. and G. F. A. Best, *Temporal Pillars*, 1964.

[5] Cf. A. Savidge, *The Foundation and Early Years of Queen Anne's Bounty*, 1955.

the normal loss by death and retirement continued. For example, in the large diocese of London no more than two or three men had been ordained at each ordination in the three years before the war ended. Between 1938 and 1949 the number of curates at work in Manchester declined from 141 to 54, in Liverpool from 158 to 58, in Sheffield from 106 to 43, and in Birmingham from 178 to 38.[6] Whereas in 1940 the total number of ordinations had been 562, this had fallen to 158 by the end of the war. After the war numbers gradually increased so that in 1950 they had risen to 419 and in 1956 to 481. The consequence of the drastic decline between 1940 and 1945 and the tardiness of the increase in post-war years was to become seriously apparent in the nine-teen-sixties and subsequent decades. In April 1946 the arch-bishops made an appeal for £600,000 towards £650,000 required for training War Service ordinands—for some 5,000 ex-service men had offered themselves as candidates and it was agreed that no lack of financial provision should prevent their ordination.

By long tradition the selection of candidates for ordination and proposals for their training had been a matter for individual diocesan bishops. The Central Advisory Council of Training for the Ministry (CACTM), established in 1912, watched the supply of ordinands and was concerned with the best methods of testing and training, with the recognition and inspection of theological colleges and with attempting to ensure some uni-formity in standards of selection and training throughout the Church. During the war the disparity of standards of selection and the haphazard methods whereby candidates secured accep-tance were criticized.[7] Some candidates applied to a bishop, others to the principal of a theological college and others to CACTM. Because of the inequality of standards some candi-dates would 'shop around' until they found a bishop or prin-cipal who would accept them. To remedy these deficiencies the position of the Central Advisory Council was greatly strength-ened and its scope enlarged. A national system of selection was established which has operated ever since. All candidates under the age of forty were required by the bishops to attend a selec-

---

[6] G. F. Townley, 'The Supply and Distribution of Assistant Curates', in *Theology*, December 1948.

[7] E.g., *Training for the Ministry: Final Report of the Archbishops' Commission*, 1944, p. 26.

tion conference, the selectors being chosen from a panel of people nominated by the bishops themselves. At the conclusion of a conference the selectors were to make a recommendation to the candidate's bishop that the candidate be accepted for training, either at once or conditionally; they might recommend that he should *not* be accepted, or that, for various reasons, his acceptance be deferred. The bishop, having considered the selector's advice, would make the final decision. The type of training would vary in accordance with age, background, and experience. If the candidate was under twenty-five a university degree was normally required, followed by two years at a theological college. Between the ages of twenty-one and thirty the training would take the form of a three-year course at a theological college, and for those between the age of thirty and forty a two-year course at a theological college. In the case of men over forty the length and type of course was to be determined by the bishop. In 1952 a new college was established at Worcester, with Canon C. B. Armstrong as its warden, for the training of men over forty and in 1959 Rochester Theological College was founded by Dean William Stannard for the training of men over thirty. A notable contribution to the training of selected ordinands was made by Dr A. R. Vidler at Windsor from 1946 to 1956.[8] A number of preliminary courses became available for those who had left school without the General Certificate of Education. Greystoke in Cumberland and Ponsborne Vicarage in Hertfordshire provided tuition in GCE subjects and Brasted Place in Kent, which came into existence through the generosity of the Revd and Mrs David Stewart-Smith, provided a course for specially selected non-graduates whose education had been interrupted or limited or had lain in predominatingly technical fields. The Society of the Sacred Mission at Kelham and the Leeds Hostel of the Community of the Resurrection, also provided preliminary courses. In an increasing number of dioceses in the nineteen-fifties provision was being made for post-ordination training, so that by the sixties it had become a recognized part of the life of a newly ordained curate during his first three years.

---

[8] 'Training Doves', editorial in *Theology*, October 1956. Cf. A. R. Vidler, *Scenes from a Clerical Life*, 1977, pp. 140ff.

Throughout the forties and fifties recruitment to the ordained ministry remained the cause of grave concern. There were many reasons for the failure of recruitment. The prevailing secular character of post-war society and its increasingly scientific and technological character left little room in the minds of many for a spiritual dimension. The attraction of scientific studies and their practical application, together with an educational system which encouraged the view that scientific progress would meet the total needs of man and cure the ills of the world, led young men to seek their careers in those fields. Fewer homes and schools brought before boys the possibility of the ordained ministry as a career. With the advent of the Welfare State and the proliferation of caring professions, men whose compassion and care would once have found their fulfilment in the ordained ministry turned to social work which neither required the unconditional commitment of ordination nor possessed of its financial disincentives. Again, in an era which witnessed an egalitarian social swing in society, the Church was still identified in the popular mind with the maintenance of the traditional order of society in England. Some would-be ordinands were critical of what they regarded as the inefficiency of the Church and its evident reluctance to reform its own administration. The anomalies of the Church's financial arrangements, the burden of large parsonage houses, the growing inadequacy of the parochial system to meet new needs—all these factors acted as deterrents. Other influences were ignorance of the nature of a clergyman's work, his apparent absorption with money-raising and his concern with a pious in-group. The unfairness of much of this picture may be acknowledged, but it was one which many appeared to possess. Finally, some young men with a scientific education suspected the intellectual integrity of Christians and recoiled from clerical dogmatism which they felt to be intellectually dishonest. On the other hand, there were others who accused the Church of lacking authority so that the trumpet gave an uncertain sound. To counter all these objections every effort was made to portray the ordained ministry as a challenge and to emphasize the need and the worthwhileness of the opportunity. Nevertheless, recruitment remained tardy. We have seen that between 1945 and 1960 numbers rose steadily, but not sufficiently to replace the number of those retiring or dying or to cope with the increasing population.

## 3. The Urban Church

The new housing estates were built with little provision for community and the people who moved into them had no roots there and possessed very little sense of 'belonging'. There was little awareness of neighbourhood based on tradition, family, and kindred. The unity of life and work was non-existent and such relationships as people made were often outside the place they lived—at work, at school, or where they found their leisure. So often the place in which they lived was the dormitory to which they returned from work at the end of each day, and from which they set out in the evening and at weekends to enjoy their leisure. Many were reluctant to meet their neighbours and when efforts were made to encourage community they had little interest. Moreover, there was a high mobility rate which militated even further against this sense of 'belonging'. Where there is no community the Church cannot be an integral part of what does not exist, with the result that the traditional role of the parson as the *persona* of the place becomes meaningless. His acceptance in such areas depended greatly upon his personal gifts. It was also difficult in such places for the Church to find committed lay leadership and so the task of building up a strong Christian presence was a task fraught with difficulties. The need to cope with baptisms, marriages, and funerals, and the pastoral care attendant on these events, were as much as— if not more than—the parish priest had time and energy to sustain. It is remarkable how so many of the clergy coped and remained confident in a situation which objectively was an impossible one.

To meet situations of this kind some notable experiments were made. In 1944 Ernest Southcott was appointed vicar of Halton, a large parish containing five estates, and twelve years later he wrote of his work there in a book significantly entitled, *The Parish Comes Alive*. His strategy was theologically based, starting with the desire to exhibit the fulness of Christian initiation—an initiation into a teaching, worshipping, and caring community. The Parish Communion on Sunday became the focus of worship, with a great deal of lay participation which was unusual in that period, alongside a weekly parish meeting to formulate and monitor parish policy and to develop the fellowship of the Eucharist. 'House Churches' were established with the object of meeting people where they were. These started as meetings for discussion and bible study but it gradually became clear that what was needed was the celebration of Holy Communion in these groups. Through the house church the clergy met over a thousand people and it was discovered that the house church made the parish church more, rather than less, used.[9]

Another remarkable piece of work was done by Alan Ecclestone at Holy Trinity, Darnall, Sheffield. This was a parish of 14,000 in an industrial city where in 1942 the communicants numbered twenty-two. Once again the heart of the revival lay in the Parish Communion and the parish meeting, both being regarded as interrelated parts of a single activity. At the parish Communion great use was made of visual aids to bring home to worshippers the concerns of the Church at the time. This concern had to be translated into action and one of the results was that the parish meeting took the first steps to bring into existence a local Community Association and to provide the first officers to secure its development. It encouraged people to devote time to social work with the elderly and to participate in public meetings and deputations on such questions as nuclear warfare and world peace. What began to emerge at Darnall was a more disciplined fellowship, aware of its tasks in the local community and much more capable of understanding what the Bible had to say to the Church and to the world.[10] It may be of some significance that Ernest Southcott was prepared to spend seventeen years at Halton and Alan Ecclestone twenty-three years at Darnall.

If clergy and laity were attempting to meet the situation where people lived, there was also a task be done in the places where many of them worked. The post-war period, therefore, saw the development of industrial mission, so that by the mid-sixties there were seventy full-time industrial chaplains and many more part-time chaplains. A number of experiments had

[9] Cf. E. Southcott, op. cit.; Eric James, 'What is going on at Halton', in *Theology*, February 1957, pp. 61ff.

[10] Alan Ecclestone, 'Experiment in the Parish', in *Theology*, October 1958, pp. 398ff.

already been made, some by Christians working in industry, some by ordained ministers and some by both working together. The Industrial Christian Fellowship, which was primarily a lay movement, had been in existence since 1919. In many places of work groups of Christians met together regularly for prayer and mutual support in order that they might witness better to the faith in their place of work and parochial clergy made efforts to exercise a pastoral ministry in relation to the industries in their locality. It was, however, the Sheffield Industrial Mission, under the leadership of E. R. Wickham, which pioneered the direct involvement of the Church in industry. It began in 1944 with a selected and trained group of clergy operating as a team in the steel works, making contact with men at all levels and at the same time working out the theological and social implications of their work.[11]

The main aim of industrial mission has been, not to convert individuals, but to engage in dialogue with both employers and employees.[12] The result has been that industrial chaplains have become involved in the field of education and training and, through their contact with various industrial groups, have been able to influence decisions which affect the workers. On occasion some of them have been called upon to mediate between unions and management. The role has to be earned by the chaplain and it is as he meets men regularly, as individuals and in groups, that he becomes accepted by both men and management. It is unfortunate that so many of the parochial clergy have been reluctant to recognize the importance of the work of the industrial chaplains. If the parish is no longer always the natural unit for expressing community, then the office, factory, or industrial complex where people work will provide the sense of community which they will not find elsewhere. To this community of work the parish priest has no right of access, nor may he possess the knowledge required to meet the situation. Thus, if the Church is to reach people it can do so only by penetrating the work community as well as the parish community. Moreover, because the industrial population is so large, because its influence upon culture, politics, and morals is so immense, and because the

---

[11] Mary Walton, *History of the Diocese of Sheffield,* 1981, pp. 77, 88, 133ff.
[12] Cf. E. R. Wickham, *Church and People in an Industrial City,* 1957, pp. 246ff.

lives of people are largely shaped by forces operating in the places where they work, it is crucial that the Church should have something to say about those factors and should have a ministry to industrial and commercial structures. This can be done effectively only by those whose knowledge comes from within those structures.

Most of the work of industrial mission is locally inspired and organized. It is true that as early as 1923 a Social and Industrial Commission of the Church Assembly was constituted, to be replaced in 1951 by the Social and Industrial Council. In the post-war years the Council produced a number of valuable reports and surveys, one of which was *The National Church and the Social Order*, published in 1956. It contained a full and valuable account of the principles that governed the attitude of the Church of England towards the social order; it identified leading questions facing the Church in the field of the Welfare State; and it commented on such issues as the rewards for work, the development of technology and its effects upon both industry and society. It was a severely academic document and exuded an atmosphere far removed from the harsh realities of the shop floor, the board room, or the union meeting. A much more direct approach to the relationship between the Church and industry was provided in a document published in 1958 by the British Council of Churches.[13] This work was thoroughly theological but anchored firmly in the empirical situation. It called for a doctrine of creation as strong as the doctrine of redemption and raised a question which became crucial in the sixties and seventies. Does the Church, through its representative clergy and laity, take Christ into a world from which he is absent or does it go into the world to help men to identify the Christ who is already there? The report stressed the need for fresh understanding of the nature of work in an industrial and increasingly technological society, a new consideration of the resources of power and raw materials, the nature and use of money, the greater concentration of power as the result of the growth of large-scale organizations and the multiplication of capital resources, and the evaluation of the aims and organization of industry. The following year the Social and Industrial

[13] *The Church and Industry.*

Council published the report of a group under the chairmanship of Sir John Wolfenden, on *The Task of the Church in Relation to Industry*, which covered much of the same ground as the BCC report and, although it did not enter into the theological discussion of that document, the justification for industrial mission was stated in starker terms. It refused to restrict the concern of the Church for what it called 'industrial evangelism', and insisted that 'the organisation and goals of industrial society itself (and therefore of industrial institutions) should be the proper consideration of Christians, for men are shaped by their environment and by what happens in their society, and can be damaged and stunted, or on the other hand, increased in human stature, by their material environment'.[14] The report urged dioceses to take industrial mission seriously and recommended the establishment of a central body to co-ordinate, encourage, and extend industrial mission on an ecumenical basis. The result was that in 1959 an Industrial Committee was established to take the place of the Social and Industrial Council and to undertake on a small scale many of the objectives set out in the report.

## 4. The Church and the Countryside

In the majority of dioceses the work of the Church lies largely in country parishes and the post-war years did not leave rural English unscathed. Indeed, in some ways, the changes that occurred after 1945 were as radical as the upheavals in city and urban areas. Successive governments gave encouragement to agriculture in the determination that the inter-war agricultural depression should never re-occur. In many places business and professional men began to sink capital into agricultural projects and farming came to be recognized as an industry. Farm workers were better housed and better paid but, at the same time, mechanization began to reduce the number of farm workers, with the result that the close-knit nature of some village communities began to disintegrate as young people moved to the towns or spent their working and leisure hours there. With the closure of many village schools as a result of the 1944 Education Act, and the advent of the school bus, children

[14] Op. cit., p. 10.

ceased to be parochially orientated. At the same time, industries began to move to rural areas, providing jobs for the residents but also producing the influx of a work force for which housing and shopping facilities had to be provided, with the result that a village community would be absorbed into a new township. The landscape might be disfigured, a way of life might disappear, but new life was also brought to hamlets and villages which otherwise might have petrified. Except in remote areas, the village ceased to be the self-contained, inward-looking unit that it once had been, as many of the inhabitants found their livelihood and entertainment in the towns. With increased mobility, the tempo of country life changed and no longer could the countryman be stigmatized as backward. The breakup of the community spirit was augmented by the influx of townspeople who bought or rented cottages ·as weekend and holiday residences and who took little part in village activities. Faced with these great changes it was no easy task to build up a sense of community either in social or ecclesiastical terms.[15]

It might be thought that the disintegration of the fast-closed boundaries of the village communities might have facilitated the reorganization of rural parishes into groups. In fact, their innate conservatism led country churchpeople to cling to the conception that every village should have its own resident parson, little realizing that this was an ideal of recent origin, for prior to the middle of the nineteenth century pluralism and non-residence of the clergy was more the rule than the exception. The difference between that and pastoral reorganization in the twentieth century is that, whereas in the past the system was haphazard and the spiritual and pastoral needs of parishioners were rarely considered, today 'pluralism' is carefully regulated and the pastoral need of the parishes is of primary importance. Three factors contributed to pastoral reorganization in rural areas. First, there was the shortage of clergy; secondly, there was insufficient money to pay the stipend of a clergyman for every parish; thirdly, some parishes were too small to provide a full-time job for a priest, and if a man feels that he is not fully used he soon becomes frustrated and unhappy. Where pastoral reorganization was sensibly planned and where the laity

[15] Cf. Frank West, *The Country Parish Today and Tomorrow*, 1960.

were co-operative, it was found that an active clergyman with two or three villages, with a combined population of say three or four thousand, could still remain a familiar figure and be known by all his parishioners.

One of the earliest experiments in pastoral reorganization in a rural area began in 1949 in the Lincolnshire Wolds, where fifteen ecclesiastical parishes with twelve churches were grouped together in what came to be known as the South Ormsby Group, with a rector and two curates in place of six incumbents who formerly ministered to the parishes. It is significant that the people themselves requested the bishop to initiate the Group, which had to be constituted in stages as vacancies occurred. No church was closed and indeed most of them were restored after the Group came into existence. It was possible for everyone to attend the Sunday services without undue inconvenience because a parish bus transported parishioners to the churches in turn. The parishioners became fused into a wider family instead of remaining small and ineffective units. The laity had a greater part to play in church life for a good deal of the day-to-day management of church affairs devolved upon them. The first rector, the Revd. A. C. Smith, summed up the advantages of the grouping.

> The new system saves both manpower and money...
> The clergy, instead of being isolated and spiritually
> lonely, find a new and inspiring fellowship of wor-
> ship and work. This in turn is passed on to the
> people...The people are as well, and in some cases
> better, cared for pastorally; and since more and more
> devolves on the laity, the newly-found sense of
> responsibility brings about a more dedicated lay
> apostolate.[16]

The diocese of Norwich was another area which experimented with group and team ministries in the countryside between 1959 and 1971, under the leadership of its bishop, Dr Launcelot Fleming.[17] In 1961 he initiated the Hilborough Group of ten parishes, under Hugh Blackburne and in 1944 the Hempnall

---

[16] 'An Experiment in Lincolnshire', in *Theology*, February 1960, pp. 63ff. Cf. also A. C. Smith, *The South Ormsby Experiment*, 1960.

[17] Donald Lindsay, *Friends for Life: A Portrait of Launcelot Fleming*, 1981, p. 184.

Group of eight parishes, with Peter Bradshaw as the rector. By 1971, when Bishop Fleming retired, there were seventeen group and team ministries comprising more than 160 parishes in town and countryside.[18]

## 5. Canon Law Revision and the Reform of the Church Courts

An extraordinary feature of the Church of England in the post-war years was the fact that, faced as it was with its mission to the nation and its own immense administrative problems, its representative bodies spent such an inordinate amount of time on the revision of the canon law of the Church. The process began in Convocation in 1947 and was not completed until twenty years later and engendered a spate of legislation that exceeded anything known in previous ecclesiastical history. For many years it had been considered anomalous that the clergy should be subject to a legal code which had remained virtually unaltered for 300 years. Many of the 1603 canons were obsolete, many bore the marks of the controversies of the seventeenth century, and they failed to give direction on matters where guidance was most needed. The result was that most of the clergy ignored them.

In May 1947 the Convocations embarked upon the long process of revision. In his presidential address Archbishop Fisher declared that 'the reform of Canon Law is, I believe the first and most essential step in the whole process of Church reform... Because we have no body of Canons to turn to, the Church has lost its sense of obedience to its own spiritual ordinances. With no law of its own it has lost the sense of being law-abiding.' The proposed reform 'would restore, as nothing else can, essential habits of good order and good conscience within the Church'. These claims may be considered to assort oddly with the earlier part of his address in which he had referred to the grave problems facing the nation—re-equipping industry, providing homes, restoring trade, contributing to the peace of the world—and had added: 'To meet this trial the nation needs everything it possesses of political wisdom, spiritual integrity and economic efficiency...The first duty of the Church is to help its own members in these things...The second duty is to help all whom it can

[18] Cf. Anthony Russell (Ed), *Groups and Teams in the Countryside*, 1975.

reach to see what God is demanding of them in the setting of their citizenship.'[19] It is doubtful whether many people were able to see how the revision of canon law would contribute significantly to this task. Archbishop Fisher, however, had no doubt about the importance of the revision and he was probably never happier than when he was spending long hours in drafting canons in exact phraseology. He was to say later that the revision of canon law was 'the most absorbing and all-embracing topic of my archiepiscopate'.[20] Not everyone could agree with him as they saw some of the best minds in the Church of England occupied for twenty years on a task whose relevance in face of the far more crucial developments in Church and State was dubious to say the least. Dean Matthews of St. Paul's compared the bishops 'to a man who occupied himself in rearranging the furniture when the house was on fire'. They and the clergy 'worked hard on Canon Law when the future of the Church became day by day more precarious'.[21] Canon Edward Carpenter of Westminster Abbey doubted whether law-making of this kind was an exercise to which the Church of England ought at this time to be so earnestly committed, because it 'diverts interest and concern from more immediately important and urgent problems which the Church ought to be tackling... Lawful authority will not help the Church to be born anew in the society in which it lives.'[22] In 1956 the Editor of *Crockford's* maintained that the revision would effect little or nothing and he judged that 'to frame laws governing too many activities of the clergy and too many aspects of Church life and practice is rather a symptom of moral and spiritual weakness than of vigorous life'.[23]

Strictly speaking the making of canon law was a matter for the Convocations and was of no conern to the Church Assembly, but in this revision the Convocations consulted the House of Laity of the Church Assembly for two reasons. The first was the conviction, expressed by Archbishop Fisher, that 'to the utmost degree possible the making of canons is a work of the whole

[19] *The Chronicle of Convocation*, May 1947.
[20] William Purcell, *Fisher of Lambeth*, p. 206.
[21] *Memories and Meanings*, 1969, p. 307.
[22] 'Canons and Character', in *Theology*, October 1960, pp. 397ff.
[23] Preface to *Crockford's Clerical Directory*, 75th Issue, 1954.

Church done by representative members of the bishops, clergy and laity of the Church of England'. Secondly, no canon could possess legal authority if it ran counter to the law of the land and, as some of the canons would require a change in the law and as this could only be done by a Measure in the Church Assembly, it was wise to involve in the process of revision the House of Laity of the body which would be required to pass the necessary Measures. This greatly lengthened and complicated the process as canons were shuttled between five legislative houses in an attempt to secure agreement.

The marathon process of revision came to an end in 1969, but at an early stage in the process it had become apparent that, not only ought the law to be reformed, but it was necessary to provide a system of courts which would command ready obedience in enforcing the law. The existing system of Church courts suffered from two weaknesses. Alongside the traditional provincial and diocesan courts the practice had evolved of providing new kinds of courts and procedure for new offences and this had produced a veritable jungle of courts. It was estimated that in 1956 there was a total of four courts and five quasi-courts for each diocese and six courts for each province. Secondly, the courts had become unacceptable in many quarters in their jurisdiction over doctrine. The final court of appeal in ecclesiastical cases was the Judicial Committee of the Privy Council and the majority of clergy and many of the laity were united in opposition to a procedure whereby questions of the Church's doctrine and worship were ultimately decided, not by the Church, but by a court of laymen appointed by the State. Moreover, dissatisfaction with this final court had undermined confidence in the whole system, for the Judicial Committee recognized itself as bound by its previous decisions and therefore the other, admittedly spiritual, courts, both diocesan and provincial, were bound to follow the judgements which had been given in the past by the Judicial Committee, for otherwise the judgement was certain to be reversed. The result was that the authority of the Judicial Committee in spiritual questions was so widely and so strongly disliked that no such questions were ever brought before it. In 1954 a committee established by the archbishops proposed a drastic reduction in the number of ecclesiastical courts. Its crucial recommendation, however, was that in clergy discipline a clear distinction should be made between 'conduct cases', concerned with morals, unbecoming conduct, and neglect of duty, and 'reserved cases', concerned with doctrine and ritual. Conduct cases should be tried before the diocesan court, with appeal to the provincial court. Reserved cases should be heard by a new court, called the Court of Ecclesiastical Causes Reserved, to be composed of bishops and three lay members of the Church of England who held or had held high judicial office. In neither of these two classes of cases was the Judicial Committee to be involved.[24] The proposals found general acceptance and, with the major amendment that the Judicial Committee should remain the final court of appeal in conduct cases and some minor amendments, were embodied in the Ecclesiastical Jurisdiction Measure 1963. Unfortunately, complicated and cumbersome machinery was dismantled only to be replaced by procedures which were hardly less so.[25]

## 6. Evangelism

While the Church's official bodies were occupied with these matters, the Church was facing loss of membership and, despite popular attachment to the Church, was less at the heart of national life than once it was. This had not happened overnight —indeed, there was a slight increase in Church attendance at the end of the war—but was due to cumulative pressures which had been experienced for many years. The effect of Darwin on popular thought, the misunderstanding of the results of biblical criticism and the comparative study of religion had caused a breakdown in traditional belief. The democratic fashion that everybody's opinion was of equal weight in religious questions prompted suspicion of authority. Reaction to the widespread suffering in two world wars, faith in the power of social engineering, science, and technology to improve life, a break-up of old communities and the displacement of masses of people into new urban settings, all contributed to a weakening of the hold of religion on the nation. Thus, the conclusion drawn from a Mass Observation survey in 1947 was that 'religion...has in the minds of the great majority, become simply irrelevant to the

---

[24] *The Ecclesiastical Courts: Principles of Reconstruction*, 1954.
[25] Cf. E. Garth Moore, *An Introduction to English Canon Law*, 1967, pp. 137ff.

question of living. It seems to have no connection with life and
no relation to the real day-to-day problems of modern society.'
The Church was preoccupied with problems of reorganization
and finance, with canon law, and with other problems concerning its own life. In spite of the number of devoted priests, the
growth of industrial mission, and the heroic ministry witnessed
in many housing estates, a sense of mission and the spirit of
evangelism appeared to be lukewarm.

The year before he died, Archbishop Temple with the Archbishop of York appointed a commission on evangelism under
the chairmanship of Dr Christopher Chavasse, Bishop of
Rochester.[26] It was one of the largest commissions in the history
of the Church Assembly and its report, *Towards the Conversion
of England,* published in 1945, became a 'best seller', the first
edition being sold out overnight. The chairman and Dr Henry
Wilson, Bishop of Chelmsford, both traditional Evangelicals
were the driving force behind the Commission and its report,
which was a comprehensive document, as much concerned with
the need to strengthen the spiritual life of the Church itself as
with reaching the unconverted, for 'we cannot separate the
evangelisation of those without from the rekindling of devotion
within'. The Commission defined the aim of evangelism as 'so
to present Jesus Christ in the power of the Holy Spirit, that men
shall come to put their trust in God through Him, to accept
Him as their Saviour and serve Him as their King in the fellowship of His Church'. They analysed the spiritual and psychological needs of the age, which they regarded as full of opportunities for the Church, and they deplored the influence of
humanism, secular education and the scientific approach to life.
One feels that the Commission lacked any real appreciation of
the benefits of science and technology and did not see them as
in any way an expression of the human spirit co-operating with
God's creative gifts. It appeared to have little sense of the
Church being prepared to 'listen to the world' and to appreciate
the world's own particular insights. A realistic appraisal of the
frustrations and spiritual deadness of many of the clergy led the
Commission to call for the provision of opportunities for their
spiritual renewal. The 'Apostolate of the Church', however, is
that of the laity as well as of the clergy, for it is the laity who,

[26] Cf. Selwyn Gummer, *The Chavasse Twins,* 1963, Chapter 12.

through their contacts with the world, can most clearly influence society and for this they require training. It advocated the full use by the Church of modern agencies of propaganda, including the cinema, drama, television, the press, literature, and a Church Information and Publishing Centre. Here the Commission exaggerated the potentiality of the media and appeared unaware of its limitations and its inability to do much more than remove prejudice and to prepare the way for more definite teaching and commitment. It dealt in some detail with the question of advertising and envisaged a Five Year Plan in this field. It was surely naïve, however, to believe that the Church would ever consider the expenditure of a million pounds over five years on advertising. The final section of the report dealt with methods whereby the Church could become a more effective instrument for evangelism—schools of preaching for the clergy, a new short Catechism, diocesan groups for study, Christian cells, the better ordering of liturgical worship and the provision of 'popular services'. Its most important proposal was that the archbishops should establish a permanent Council on Evangelism. The report was full of confidence and displayed no doubts about the contents of the Gospel. It had great faith in the evangelistic power of education, believing that once the Gospel was taught and understood it had its own evangelistic momentum. It paid little attention to the social implications of the Gospel, preferring to place all its emphasis on personal commitment and displaying some reluctance to appreciate that Christian penetration into the structures of society could rightly be understood as evangelism.

The reaction to the report was not universally enthusiastic. The Church Assembly refused to accept the most important recommendation of the Commission to set up a Council on Evangelism, asserting its inability to provide the money for such a venture and maintaining that the responsibility for follow-up rested with the dioceses. Archbishop Fisher is on record as saying that he refused to set up the Commission 'because there did not seem to be any desire for one. Because everyone seemed to distrust schemes or organisations for the promotion of evangelism —and I share that distrust.' On the other hand, the report prompted diocesan, deanery and parochial missions in many parts of the country. Diocesan Missioners were appointed, a

large number of clergy and laity were given new encouragement, schools of evangelism for clergy and laity were held, and
the Village Evangelists, inspired by Bishop Walter Carey,
retired Bishop of Bloemfontein, and Brother Edward,[27] came
into being in 1948.[28]

Among the evangelistic enterprises of these years was the
great Mission to London in May 1949. Two years earlier Dr
William Wand, the Bishop of London, had held an episcopal
Visitation. In answer to his articles of enquiry a number of
clergymen had suggested a diocesan mission. Considerable
strides were being made to raise three-quarters of a million
pounds for reconstruction in the diocese, but it was felt that
material reconstruction without spiritual renewal was inadequate and therefore some of the money was used for the
Mission. The latter had three aims—to win the outsider, to stir
up new interest among those who had lapsed, and to show how
Christianity spoke not only to the individual but also to the
common life of the community. To 'sell' the idea to the diocese
a mass meeting was held in the Albert Hall in May 1948. Then
clergy were gathered in groups for retreats and refresher courses
on evangelism and spiritual direction. Prayer cells and study
groups were set up in parishes. The most notable feature of the
Mission was the big part played by the laity, who formed themselves into bands of visitors going from house to house visiting
every home in the parishes throughout the diocese. A hundred
and twenty centres were chosen where the mission was to be
preached and to these came over 150 missioners from every part
of the country. In order to fulfil the third aim of the Mission
three great centres—St. Paul's Cathedral, Westminster Abbey,
and Southwark Cathedral—were chosen for a series of addresses
on such topics as the modern state, world peace, work and
leisure, and family life. Bishop Cuthbert Bardsley, then Bishop

[27] Cf. Kenneth E. Packard, *Brother Edward: Priest and Evangelist*, 1955, pp.
145ff. Brother Edward was born Gordon Bulstrode. He was ordained in 1909, but after
his first curacy he became a 'free-lance' evangelist. He established an evangelistic
'double community' for men and women at Westcote in the Cotswolds, but it proved a
failure.

[28] I am grateful to Canon Leonard Chidzey, the Secretary of the Commission, for
allowing me to make use of a paper, '"Towards the Conversion of England": An
Appraisal Twenty-Seven Years On', written in 1972. Cf. also John Gunstone, 'Towards
the Conversion of England', in *Church Times*, 3 July 1970.

of Croydon, addressed 1,000 business men at a lunch-time meeting in the Guildhall and it was estimated that over three-quarters of a million attended the various services and meetings. The Mission certainly resulted in a larger number of regular communicants, a larger attendance at other services, and an increase in the number of Confirmation candidates. 'Here was a demonstration', wrote Roger Lloyd, 'staged in the battered capital city of the country, that churchpeople had faith in the Gospel, and in their mission to proclaim it, and that they did not intend to sit down tamely before the reproaches of paralysis.'[29] As in all missions, everything depended upon the 'follow-up' which fell to the parish priest, although the diocese organized a 'School of Religion', in which those who had been helped by the Mission could carry further their understanding of the faith. This took three years to prepare and was held in Lent 1952 and, in Dr Wand's judgement, 'proved remarkably successful'.[30]

Dr Billy Graham, the American Baptist evangelist, visited Great Britain in 1954 and his nationwide crusade captured the popular imagination and drew enormous crowds. Although it was organized on an interdenominational basis it received greatest support within the Church of England from the evangelicals, and it has been argued that if fewer church members had held back, debating the merits of this kind of evangelism, the sixties would have been very different for both Church and nation. By its very nature this must forever remain an open question, but it is true that during the campaign Christianity became headline news and Dr Graham caused many people to face the challenge of Christ and made parishes more aware of their responsibility to preach the Gospel. Moreover, he insisted that his evangelism must be linked with the Church and every enquirer without a Church allegiance was commended to a local church. As a result of the campaign some were brought to a new faith, many had their faith renewed, and a number found a vocation to the ordained ministry. As with all such demonstrations, however, the momentum could not be sustained and the final judgement must be that the effectivenesss of the cru-

[29] *The Church of England, 1900-1965*, p. 521.
[30] J. W. C. Wand, *Changeful Page*, pp. 190-5.

sade was felt more by those within the Church than by those outside.

Over the years a number of the recommendations of *Towards the Conversion of England* have been implemented. The Church's Enquiry Centre was set up in 1957, a revised Catechism was produced in 1962, the use of the laity by the Church is no longer a new thing, and the Church is much more 'media conscious'. In 1960 the College of Preachers was inaugurated, with the Revd D. W. Cleverley Ford, Vicar of Holy Trinity with All Saints, South Kensington, as its director, and for the next ten years residential courses were held for clergy to help them in their task of preaching. The College later widened its scope to include Readers and women workers and its influence extended beyond the Church of England as Roman Catholic priests and Free Church ministers participated in its courses. One bishop has described the College as 'the most constructive activity in the Church today'.[31]

We have referred to the refusal of the Church Assembly to implement the Commission's recommendation that a Council on Evangelism should be established. In the sixties a few people who were deeply concerned about evangelism, led by Cuthbert Bardsley, by then Bishop of Coventry, secured the archbishops' consent to establish an unofficial Council which was to depend for its finances on the voluntary giving of well-wishers. The Council was inaugurated in 1967 and consisted of twenty-five members drawn from industry, commerce, the professions, the religious communities, and the parochial ministry, under the chairmanship of Bishop Bardsley. It was not very effective until the appointment of the Revd John Poulton as full-time secretary in 1969. The Council's aim was to stimulate and guide evangelism in England and to act as a clearing house for news and ideas. It mounted surveys and projects, and made these available to the whole Church through its regular bulletin, *ACE*. The strength of the Council lay in the fact that its members were deeply concerned with evangelism and many of them very experienced in it; its weakness lay in its unofficial nature and its consequent lack of support from the Church's official bodies. It was formally disbanded at the end of 1978 and in its place a small indepen-

---

[31] Cf. *A Short History of the College of Preachers, 1960-70*, n.d.

dent body, called 'Tomorrow's Church Group', came into existence with a much more limited responsibility than the Council.

*Towards the Conversion of England* itself was soon forgotten. Perhaps the real reason for this was the tremendous social and theological revolution which took place during the following years and which began shortly after the report was published. The consequences were such that much of the report was soon 'dated'.

## 7. Broadcasting

The Commission on Evangelism expressed the view that 'today, religious broadcasting is, perhaps, the greatest power for indirect evangelism offered to the Church'. In 1948 Sir William Haley, Director-General of the BBC, declared that 'the BBC...bases its policy upon a positive attitude towards Christian values.... The whole preponderant weight of its programmes is directed to this end.'[32] In those days the BBC regarded making 'Britain a more Christian country' as an important task, to be discharged by avoiding anything which might appear to undermine Christian morality and by fostering the understanding of the Christian religion. This was supported by the Central Religious Advisory Council's (CRAC) belief that the BBC had the four-fold task of maintaining 'standards of truth, justice and honesty in private and public life', of explaining the Christian faith and its contemporary relevance, of leading non-churchgoers to see Christian commitment as involving active membership of a congregation, and of providing opportunities to challenge people to personal faith in Christ.[33] Two years later, however, the British Council of Churches called for 'free religious discussion' in face of 'the great debate of our time between the emergent unity of Christian opinion and the secular materialist view'.[34]

At that time there was a well-established diet of religious programmes, mostly services. On Sunday there were three services, together with Sunday Half-Hour and an Epilogue. There was a

---

[32] 'Moral Values in Broadcasting', quoted Asa E. Briggs, *A History of Broadcasting in the United Kingdom*, Vol. 4, *Sound and Vision*, 1979, p. 765.

[33] Cf. CRAC document, 'Review of the Aims and Achievements', 5 October 1948, quoted Asa Briggs, op. cit., pp. 765-6.

[34] *The Church and Broadcasting*, 1950, pp. 13ff.

daily service, a 'Lift up Your Hearts' programme and a weekly choral Evensong. There were religious broadcasts to schools, prayers in Children's Hour and, in the early years after the war, religious broadcasts to the Forces. Listener research in 1948 revealed that four million listeners tuned in to the People's Service and some seven million listened to Sunday Half-Hour.[35] In 1949 the broadcasting of Holy Communion was introduced experimentally, but not without sharp controversy. The practice soon ceased to be experimental and in 1950 Dr C. S. Woodward, Bishop of Gloucester, could say that 'the fear of irreverence has been completely overcome'.[36] A topic of discussion in the forties was the right of non-Christians to broadcast, and in 1946 CRAC was unable to agree to this step being taken. Nevertheless in 1947 the BBC sponsored a series of talks on 'What I Believe', followed by a second series on 'Belief and Unbelief'. These were high-powered intellectual pieces and therefore caused no popular reaction.

BBC television was inaugurated in 1946, but was somewhat neglected as a vehicle for religious broadcasting because many in the television service believed that religion did not make good television and because many Christians felt that it was impossible to communicate on television the sense of reverence and holiness, while some judged that short and crisp services on television would make viewers disappointed when they went to a service in Church. The British Council of Churches, however, declared that 'it cannot over-emphasise its conviction that the door must be entered'. The only religious service to be televised before 1948 was the consecration of the War Memorial Chapel at Biggin Hill airfield on 15 September 1946. There was a BBC television news feature of the Bishop of London's Visitation in 1947 and the Coventry Nativity Play was televised from the studio at Christmas that year. On the occasion of the wedding of Princess Elizabeth and the Duke of Edinburgh in 1947 no television cameras were allowed in Westminster Abbey. Gradually, however, the climate began to change, although by 1955 there were only twelve outside broadcast services on television each year. The successful broadcast of the Coronation in 1953, which incorporated Holy Communion, encouraged more Eucharistic

[35] Cf. Asa Briggs, op. cit., p. 770.     [36] Quoted Ibid., p. 771.

broadcasting, including High Mass in 1954 from Leeds Roman Catholic Cathedral.

In January 1955 Mrs Margaret Knight, lecturer in psychology at Aberdeen University, gave a series of talks on the Home Service from 'A Humanist Point of View', in the course of which she made some critical comments on conventional religious beliefs and set out her own approach to morality. Furore followed, with angry protests from a large number of people who rebuked the BBC for an attack on Christianity, for popularizing atheism, and for sowing the seeds of doubt in the minds of Christian believers.[37] The extreme reaction of the opposition has to be judged alongside a poll conducted by the *Evening Chronicle* in Manchester, which showed that 91 per cent were against Mrs Knight's opinions. On the other hand, there was a minority which echoed the words of the Revd Donald Soper, a leading Methodist, that 'Christians would do themselves harm if they assumed that the Christian faith was a hot-house plant which needed to be protected against all weathers'.[38] This was the pattern of conflict which was to be often repeated in the sixties.

[37] Asa Briggs, op. cit. p. 800ff.
[38] Quoted in Asa Briggs, op. cit., p. 802.

# 3

# THEOLOGY, WORSHIP, AND MORALS

Every day makes it more and more evident that the thorough study of the Bible, the investigation of what it teaches and what it does not teach, the determination of the degree of authority to be ascribed to the different books, if any degrees are to be admitted, must take the lead of all other studies.

Frederick Temple in *Essays and Reviews*, 1860

## 1. The Follies of Dr Barnes

DR E. W. BARNES, Bishop of Birmingham, was a controversial figure throughout his public life. He was Ramsay MacDonald's first episcopal appointment and the editor of *Crockford's Clerical Directory* later judged that 'he would have been better served and his abilities better used, if he had remained at Cambridge, or in his Westminster canonry'.[1] W. R. Matthews, who admired Barnes as a good Christian, believed that 'he had no theology in the accepted sense. He had no doctrine of the Incarnation or of the Atonement. "Men saw that Jesus Christ was a very good man, so they called him son of God" would sum up his teaching on the divinity of Christ not inadequately.'[2] Dr Barnes was not a biblical scholar but that did not deter him from publishing in 1947 *The Rise of Christianity* which, according to the author's foreword, was designed to seek 'with firm impartiality to reach the truth, so far as can be ascertained', and to give an account of the Christian faith 'so far as possible, without bias'. The tenor of the whole work was to discredit the authority of the books of the New Testament, to date them well in the second century and consequently to weaken confidence in their accuracy. He eliminated the miraculous and thus dismissed the virgin birth and the resurrection. He discredited the crucifixion

---

[1] Preface to *Crockford's Clerical Directory*, 76th Edition, 1955/56.
[2] *Memories and Meanings*, p. 310.

narrative and minimized the duration of Jesus's ministry. The narrative of Paul's early life was unreliable and his letters were a patchwork of miscellaneous documents and fragments. Yet throughout the book Dr Barnes expressed the highest appreciation of the character and teaching of Jesus. 'The central fact of Christianity', he wrote, 'is, and always has been, Jesus. Upon him, upon men's belief in the truth of his teaching and the divine beauty of his character, the Christian movement was, and continues to be, based.'[3]

Not surprisingly the book caused both distress and indignation, which was ministered to by a series of popular articles by Barnes in the *Sunday Pictorial*. That in itself would not have mattered had his conclusions been supported by sound scholarship, but they were not. Review after review condemned the book as making no serious contribution to critical studies. Scholarly replies to Dr Barnes were made by Sir Frederick Kenyon[4] and by Professor C. H. Dodd.[5] The criticisms were fourfold. First, the subjective element predominated to such an extent that facts were made to fit the theory rather than theory emerging from an honest appraisal of the facts. Secondly, Dr Barnes's work in no way represented the results of modern scholarship for he relied upon a school of criticism which had been in vogue some fifty years past and almost completely ignored more recent scholarship. Thirdly, the author exhibited a wholly unscholarly readiness to accept the flimsiest arguments against traditional belief and to ignore the weight of evidence on the other side. Finally, the tone of the book displayed an arrogant attitude towards those whose views differed from those of the author, particularly if they were members of his own Church who (in his own words) 'feel bound to reach conclusions prescribed by the Christian community to which they belong'—which was a gratuitous insult to a line of great Christian scholars. Dr Barnes appeared to be living in an unreal intellectual world and 'had it not been the kind of book that one would not expect a bishop to have written, he might have found difficulty in finding a publisher'.[6]

[3] Op. cit., p. 125.
[4] *The Bible and Modern Scholarship*, 1948, Chapter 3.
[5] *Christian Beginnings: A Reply to Dr Barnes' 'Rise of Christianity'*, 1947.
[6] Charles Smyth, *Cyril Foster Garbett*, 1959, p. 471.

Although the Archbishop of Canterbury remained silent about the book, the Archbishop of York considered something should be done about it. Dr Fisher wrote privately to Barnes and expressed his grave disquiet, telling Barnes that the holding of such opinions was incompatible with episcopal office. Although he assured Barnes that he did not intend to make a public statement about the book, he was under pressure and he asked E. G. Selwyn, Dean of Winchester, and Professor Leonard Hodgson, Regius Professor of Divinity at Oxford, to prepare for him a theological assessment of the work. In the light of their report and in view of a resolution to be put to the Lower House of the Convocation of York in October, Dr Fisher felt obliged to make a statement. This he did in his presidential address to the Convocation of Canterbury on 15 October, having warned Barnes only on the previous night so that the latter had not even brought a copy of the book to London with him.[7] In his address Dr Fisher acknowledged Barnes's intended honesty in writing the book and his profound devotion to the person of Our Lord. He then listed the faults and the inadequacies of the work and concluded by saying that it 'so diminishes...the content of the Christian faith as to make the residue which is left inconsistent with the scriptural doctrine and beliefs of the Church in which he holds office....If his views were mine, I would not feel that I could still hold episcopal office in the Church.'[8] Bishop Barnes asked leave to make a personal statement but, because standing orders did not permit any debate on a presidential address, his request was refused. Later, however, the bishop made a statement in the Upper House in which he said that, although he appreciated the Christian spirit in which the archbishop had spoken, nevertheless 'I believe the conclusions reached in my book to be true and I hold them to be entirely compatible with my position as a Bishop in the Church of England'.[9]

There the matter rested. With hindsight and now that the Church has become accustomed to the radical conclusions of some New Testament scholars we may feel less inclined to criticize Barnes's conclusions, while still condemning the unscholarly and subjective process by which he came to those conclusions.

[7] John Barnes, *Ahead of His Time: Bishop Barnes of Birmingham*, 1979, p. 409.
[8] *Canterbury Chronicle of Convocation*, October 1947, pp. 187ff.
[9] Ibid., pp. 173ff.

Later scholars have reached their position as the result of a most rigorous scholarship. One does not necessarily accept some of their more radical pronouncements, but one accepts their academic integrity. It is difficult to feel such respect for Dr Barnes.

## 2. Post-War Theology

It has not been characteristic of the Church of England to produce theological work of a constructive and systematic character comparable with that of continental theologians. Indeed much Anglican theology has been prompted by contemporary ecclesiastical and pastoral needs and questions, such as in our own day the search for unity, the place of the Eucharist in worship and the relationship between Baptism and Confirmation. Moreover, British theology has been accused in the past of being isolated from developments in continental and American theology. In the war and post-war period it became less insular and Barth, Bultmann, Brunner, Kittel, Tillich, Bonhoeffer, and Reinhold Neibuhr among continental Protestants and Yves Congar, Karl Rahner and Hans Küng among the Roman Catholics have all had considerable influence upon British theologians. The ecumenical nature of theological scholarship has been another feature of war and post-war Britain. Alongside Michael Ramsey, Alan Richardson, Leonard Hodgson, C. F. D. Moule and other Anglicans stand the names of C. H. Dodd (Congregationalist), Vincent Taylor (Methodist), Donald and John Baillie (Church of Scotland), and Kingsley Barrett (Methodist) and others. It has been in biblical and historical studies that denominational walls of partition have been broken down as all Churches have rediscovered the religious and doctrinal importance of the Bible, and the stream of books dealing with the Bible and its theology became a torrent in the immediate post-war years.

The greatest single stimulus to biblical studies in Anglican circles had been the work of Sir Edwyn Hoskyns[10] who died in 1937. His constant theme was that there was the closest possible connection between history and theology in the New Testament and, while he insisted on a rigorous use of critical methods, he

---

[10] For an appraisal of his life and work, cf. E. C. Hoskyns and Noel Davey, *Crucifixion - Resurrection*, edited with a Biographical Introduction, by Gordon S. Wakefield, 1981, pp. 27ff.

maintained that questions about the New Testament are all ultimately questions of theology and history. Out of this there emerged a school of 'biblical theology', whose special characteristic has been described by A. R. Vidler.

It arose from a suspicion...that theologians both ancient and modern had been prone to interpret the Bible in terms of their own thought-forms and to read into the Bible ideas which were derived from other and later sources....The biblical theologians maintained that the right course was to try, as far as possible, so to get inside the minds of the biblical writers as to be able to explain their meaning without importing into it later presuppositions or interests. Further, they maintained that, if you did this, and succeeded, so to speak, in hearing what the Word of God in the Bible had to say for itself, then you would also find that it had something startling and unexpected to say to us in our contemporary situation.[11]

The best known and most influential of Anglican biblical scholars was Alan Richardson, Professor of Christian Theology at Nottingham University and later to become Dean of York. He popularized biblical theology in a widely-read book, *Preface to Bible Study*, published in 1943, although two years earlier, in *Miracle Stories in the New Testament*, he had demonstrated how specific incidents in the Gospels can be fully understood only in terms of the great themes of the whole Bible. Perhaps his most important book was *An Introduction to the Theology of the New Testament*, published in 1958, the preface to which provides an excellent account of the aims of the biblical theologians. Other notable exponents of biblical theology were William Barclay, C. H. Dodd, R. H. Fuller, A. G. Herbert, A. M. Hunter and Vincent Taylor. Although Michael Ramsey's scholarship can be seen at its best in his balanced and judicious appraisal of the work of other Anglicans,[12] in three books he operated on the assumption of biblical theology that the New Testament yields its meaning to those who are prepared to ask both historical and theological questions.[13] In the *Resurrection of Christ* he complained that in the past the historical problems

[11] *20th Century Defenders of the Faith*, 1965, pp. 92-3.
[12] Cf., e.g., *Gore to Temple*, 1960, *F. D. Maurice and the Conflicts of Modern Theology*, 1951.
[13] *The Gospel and the Catholic Church*, 1936; *The Resurrection of Christ*, 1946; *The Glory of God and the Transfiguration of Christ*, 1949.

of the narrative of the Resurrection had been too often discussed 'in separation from the Gospel with which the history is bound up and from the theology which made the story of Easter worth the telling'.[14]

Biblical theology could claim three positive achievements. First, its exponents rediscovered for the Church the unity of the Bible and the principle that the primary commentary on particular texts was the theological themes running through the whole Bible. Secondly, they demonstrated that what others might have regarded as historical questions were in fact theological questions which could only be answered theologically; textual and critical studies are but the necessary tools for preparing the ground for the central task of interpreting the meaning of a text and that central task is a theological one. Thirdly, it followed that the Bible was more than a source book for historians; it has its own authority as the Word of God.

The biblical theologians, by seeking to emphasize and expound the theological meaning and significance of the books of the Bible, provided a necessary balance against theological scholarship which, in their view, gave undue stress to matters of text and introduction. In doing so, however, they became vulnerable on two fronts. First, their concentration on the themes of the Bible and their insistence that its contents could be interpreted only in terms of the theology and the world-view of the Bible itself tended to produce work which appeared remote from the thought-forms and the empirical questions of the contemporary world. Indeed, Alec Vidler has argued that 'an effect of the fashionable preoccupation with biblical theology was to make those who fell for it less and less able to communicate with ordinary people'.[15] Secondly, because of the central importance attached to interpreting the Bible in its own terms, it became a victim of the rising school of theology which claimed that the Biblical world-view must be demythologized if the Gospel was to say anything relevant to the contemporary world.

In the meantime the textual critics were hard at work and during the post-war years a vast number of commentaries, monographs, dictionaries, lexicons, texts, and translations appeared.

[14] Preface.    [15] *20th Century Defenders of the Faith*, p. 94.

It was the period when form criticism was at its height. No longer were the Gospels studied as biographical memoirs of. the life of Jesus in which facts could be gleaned apart from interpretation. Form critics sought the oral tradition of the years prior to the writing of the Gospels, which were to be studied in the context of the post-resurrection preaching and teaching of the early Church in which the tradition was handed down, so that 'fact' and 'intepretation' were so interwoven that the story of Jesus was unknowable apart from the preaching of the early Church. The discovery in 1947 of the Dead Sea Scrolls near the site of the Community of Qumran threw considerable light on the biblical documents, the origins of Christianity and the religious ethos of Our Lord's day. Old Testament scholars were encouraged by the fact that among the scrolls and other fragments almost every book of the Old Testament was represented and that these confirmed the accuracy of the documents which had hitherto been available.[16]

It may be significant that in the fifties a wave of biblical fundamentalism, particularly in the universities, caused concern to many churchmen. After the war interest in religion was generally high in the universities; college chapels were well attended and a number of theological lectures drew large undergraduate audiences. The chief phenomenon of these years, however, was the rapidly increasing influence and membership of the Inter-Varsity Fellowship composed of Evangelical or Christian Unions through which many undergraduates were brought to a faith in Christ, some of whom offered themselves for ordination.[17] One of the chief characteristics of the IVF was a conservative approach to the Scriptures as the inerrant Word of God, a call for immediate conversion and decision for Christ and a 'penal substitution' doctrine of the atonement. In 1955 the Christian Union in Cambridge invited Billy Graham, the American Baptist evangelist, to conduct a University Mission. In a letter to *The Times*[18] the Revd H. K. Luce of Durham contended that the invitation 'raises an issue which does not seem to have been squarely faced

---

[16] Cf. F. F. Bruce, *Second Thoughts on the Dead Sea Scrolls*, 1956, and G. Vermes, *The Dead Sea Scrolls: Qumran in Perspective*, 1977. The literature on the Dead Sea Scrolls is voluminous.

[17] Cf. J. Davis McCaughey, *Christian Obedience in the University*, 1958, pp. 174ff.

[18] 15 August 1955.

in this country. Universities exist for the advancement of learning: on what basis therefore can fundamentalism claim a hearing at Cambridge?' A considerable correspondence followed which was later published.[19] Two related, though distinct, issues were debated. The first concerned the wisdom of the type of evangelistic campaign associated with Dr Billy Graham; the second was the biblical conservatism of the evangelicals who invited him. Not all who worried about the latter opposed the former. John Stott, Vicar of All Souls, Langham Place, drew a distinction between 'the bigoted rejection of all biblical criticism' and 'the traditional, conservative view of the Scriptures'. Dr Michael Ramsey, Bishop of Durham, accepted the fact that the strength of 'fundamentalist evangelism' lay 'in its emphasis upon decision and personal conversion to Christ', but what caused him misgiving was 'the crudity of the doctrine presented, so that the act of decision and conversion may involve the stifling of the mind instead of its liberation into a new service of God and man'. In an article in *The Bishoprick* in February 1956, under the title 'The Menace of Fundamentalism', Dr Ramsey took the matter further and described the fundamentalism of Billy Graham as heretical and sectarian. The Bishop of Rochester, Dr Christopher Chavasse, preached on the subject to the Evangelical Islington Conference in January 1956, when he disclaimed the crudities of literal fundamentalism and gave a number of illustrations of the error of the theory.[20]

Much of Anglican theology centred on the nature of the ministry, the theological status of Confirmation in its relation to Baptism, and the theological investigation of Christian Liturgy. One of the crucial theological issues dividing the Churches and which consistently frustrated movements towards reunion was that of episcopacy. The debate was opened afresh by the publication in 1946 of *The Apostolic Ministry*, edited by Kenneth Kirk, Bishop of Oxford, with L. S. Thornton, Austin Farrer, Gregory Dix, and Trevor Jalland among the contributors. The authors came from the catholic wing of the Church of England and the general conclusion of the essayists was, in the words of

---

[19] *Fundamentalism: A Religious Problem*, 1955.
[20] The sermon was published in *Theology*, March 1956, and also as a pamphlet, *Fundamentalism*, 1958.

the editor, that 'the Episcopate is the divinely ordained ministerial instrument for securing to the Church of God its continuance and organic unity...as a God-given city of salvation'. The
episcopate was the *essential* ministry. The writers said little
about the Reformation and what was said revealed a failure to
understand some of its theological concepts. It was true that the
view of the ministry set forth by the writers was held within the
Church of England, but it was one which was not widely accepted before the middle of the nineteenth century. The book was
severely criticized in reviews and pamphlets and in the following
year a group of evangelicals, including S. L. Greenslade, F. W.
Dillistone and C. F. D Moule, published in book form[21] their
reviews which had originally appeared in *The Record*. They
agreed that the ministry was 'from above' but they maintained
that the orthodox Anglican view is that episcopacy is of the
*bene esse* (i.e. for the well-being), but not of the *esse* (i.e. of the
essence) of the Church. In the Albrecht Stumff Memorial
Lecture[22] at Queen's College, Birmingham, on 3 May 1949
G. W. H. Lampe spoke of that somewhat storm-battered craft,
*The Apostolic Ministry*, and argued that the first Christians
were not concerned 'to think primarily of a hierarchy and
secondly of a church whose catholicity was guaranteed thereby'.
In 1954 seven priests, former members of Westcott House,
Cambridge, who believed that the old *esse* v. *bene esse* debate
on episcopacy was a sterile one, attempted a new approach in a
book[23] edited by Kenneth Carey, Principal of Westcott House.
Episcopacy, they contended, was neither of the *esse*, or the
*bene esse* of the Church, but belongs to the *plene esse* or full-
ness of the Body into which 'the coming great Church can
grow'. The book was criticised for being more concerned with
demolishing the position of their opponents than with establishing its own and many saw the thesis of *plene esse* as little
more than a strengthened form of the *bene esse* position.

The preoccupation of the Church with the theology of Christian initiation illustrates again the close link in Anglicanism
between theology and practice. The traditional sequence of

---

[21] *The Ministry of the Church*, 1947.
[22] *Some Aspects of New Testament Ministry*, 1949.
[23] *The Historic Episcopate*.

Baptism, normally of infants, followed by Confirmation at the age of fourteen to sixteen, and then first Communion was being questioned on a number of grounds. Some were perturbed by the indiscriminate baptism of infants and the fact that only a small percentage of those baptized were later confirmed and that the majority of those confirmed drifted rapidly away from Church membership. A few parishes had adopted a policy of baptizing only the children of committed believers, which caused much controversy. The theological question being asked was whether the Anglican position was in accord with New Testament theology and practice, and the discussion turned on the proper relationship between Baptism and Confirmation. This was no new debate, for in the last quarter of the nineteenth century a controversy initiated by F. W. Pullen[24] and J. A. Mason[25] was one which endured into this century. Then there had been a lull in the debate and it was not renewed until in 1944 a joint committee of the two Convocations published a report,[26] the theological conclusion of which was that the gift of the Spirit is bestowed in Holy Baptism, but that in Confirmation there was a fresh outpouring, completing what the Spirit had initiated in Baptism. Confirmation could be regarded as the 'ordination of the laity' and need not precede first Communion. The report was sharply criticized by L. S. Thornton,[27] Bishop K. E. Kirk,[28] and Gregory Dix.[29] Thornton rejected the notion that Confirmation was the ordination of the laity and claimed that it conferred 'the seal of the Spirit'. Kirk maintained that, while Baptism conferred sacramental remission and regeneration, it was Confirmation that bestowed the Spirit. Gregory Dix followed the earlier High Church theologian, A. J. Mason, in asserting that Confirmation consisted of a sealing or Chrism, the outward sign of the sealing of the Spirit. This view came to be known as 'the Mason-Dix line'. Michael Ramsay[30] resisted any change in the existing practice, which 'seeks to produce in its own way the totality of the apostolic faith; and if it fails to do so

---

[24] *What is the Distinctive Grace of Confirmation?* 1880.
[25] *The Relation of Baptism to Confirmation*, 1883.
[26] *Confirmation Today.*
[27] *Confirmation: Its Place in the Baptismal Mystery*, 1953.
[28] *Oxford Diocesan Magazine*, November/December, 1944.
[29] *The Theology of Confirmation in Relation to Baptism*, 1946.
[30] 'Confirmation', in *Theology*, September 1945.

wholly, did the patristic way succeed in doing so wholly and does the Eastern way succeed?'

Reports from the deaneries, to which the Convocation report had been sent for study and comment, revealed that the majority of clergy desired no far-reaching change in the pattern of initiation, but in view of the theological uncertainty on the subject, the archbishops appointed a theological commission, which included among its members Gregory Dix, Michael Ramsay and A. J. Rawlinson. When it reported[31] in 1948 the Commission's main contention was that Christian initiation should not be viewed as a series of acts but as a process beginning with Baptism and ending with first Communion. Confirmation was primarily 'a sealing unto the day of redemption'. The concept of Confirmation as the 'ordination of the laity' was rejected and admission to Holy Communion before Confirmation was viewed with disfavour because this would obscure the initiatory aspect of Confirmation, 'which is essential to its meaning in the teaching of the early Church'. In 1949 the Convocations issued a second report,[32] taking into account the views of the dioceses on its first report, the thesis of the theological commission, and the resolutions of the 1948 Lambeth Conference. The report concerned itself mainly with the problem of baptismal reform but was unable to propose any agreed recommendations.

An event which had considerable influence on all subsequent debates on the subject, was the publication in 1951 of a study of the doctrine of Baptism and Confirmation in the New Testament and the Fathers by G. W. H. Lampe,[33] who was to take a leading part in the discussions over the ensuing twenty years. His thesis represented a refutation of the 'Mason-Dix line', for in his view the Holy Spirit was given, not in Confirmation, but in Baptism, Confirmation being a post-apostolic rite for strengthening those baptized in infancy. Whatever gifts Confirmation bestowed, all the blessings of initiation are conferred in Baptism. Lampe's conclusions, based on a careful analysis of New Testament and patristic evidence, clearly influenced the final report of Convocation, published in 1954,[34] which described

---

[31] *The Theology of Christian Initiation.*
[32] *Baptism Today.*
[33] *The Seal of The Spirit.*
[34] *Baptism and Confirmation Today.*

Lampe's book as 'a useful antithesis to the Mason-Dix thesis', and added that it considered 'that our Baptismal Service can claim justification in the New Testament for the doctrine that the Spirit is bestowed in Baptism…The Baptism rite embodies the fulness of the Gospel'. The report is noteworthy for the realism with which it faced the ambiguities and tensions in Anglican belief and practice which, in its view, represented the culmination of the process of the disintegration of the original Christian initiation rite. For the next fifteen years or so there was another lull in the controversy in official circles although the debate continued unabated at diocesan and parochial level.

Before turning to the third theological theme—the nature of the Liturgy—there is another topic which must be noted. In May 1952 there was a debate in the Convocation of Canterbury commending the modern revival of spiritual healing and this resulted in the archbishops appointing a commission to examine the problems and opportunities raised by this revival. For some years there had been a slow recognition by the medical profession that man was a psychosomatic unity and that sickness and health are seldom purely physical phenomena but involve both the mind and the soul as well. At the same time the Churches were recovering their own ministry of healing which for centuries had been neglected. For too long the Old Testament view that sickness was God's punishment for man's sin had prevailed; now Christians were realizing what ought to have remained obvious—that Jesus's approach to disease was one of hostility and that his ministry revealed that God's will for man is wholeness of body, mind and spirit, although suffering has its place within the redemptive purpose of God. In 1905 the interdenominational Guild of Health had been founded to study the interaction of the spiritual, mental, and physical factors in well-being. The Guild of St. Raphael, a distinctively Anglican group, had been inaugurated in 1915 to revive the spiritual means of healing, with particular emphasis on the rite of the laying-on of hands and the sacrament of Holy Unction. In 1944 William Temple had established the Churches Council of Healing, on which all the Churches, except the Roman Catholic Church, were officially represented and the object of which was to co-ordinate the work of the various groups concerned with this matter, to encourage the co-operation of doctors and clergy, and to bring the work of healing into closer relationship with the regular ministry of the Church. The British Medical Association in 1947 gave approval to the work and nominated three representatives to serve on the Council. In addition to these organizations a number of important books were published,[35] houses of healing established,[36] small local groups for studying health and healing were started and one or two individuals, who possessed particular gifts of healing, were being sought by the sick.

The Commission established by the archbishops in 1952 included churchmen, theologians, medical practitioners, and others involved in medical and spiritual healing, under the chairmanship of Dr Maurice Harland, Bishop of Durham. It invited the co-operation of the British Medical Association, which set up a special group to deal with the commission's enquiries. In 1958 it published its report,[37] which was distinguished for its detailed and judicious consideration of an emotive subject. It assessed the theological, medical, psychological, and pastoral aspects of spiritual healing. It discussed the evidence for such healing and some of the common misconceptions held about it. Finally, wise and guarded guidance was given to the clergy on their ministry to the sick, together with suggestions for promoting co-operation with the medical profession. The Church was charged with a commission to heal the sick, but *all* healing was from God and it was idle to claim that a particular healing was due entirely to non-physical causes. 'It is not possible to dogmatise about the causal connection between faith and recovery'; suffering has a place in the redemptive purpose of God; the doctrine that sickness is punishment for sin is cruel and false; God has given some people a special gift of the power to heal, but 'Christ has given to the Church and to

---

[35] E.g. Leslie Weatherhead, *Psychology, Religion and Healing*, 1951; A. Graham Ikin, *New Concepts of Healing*, 1955; Christopher Woodard, *A Doctor Heals by Faith*, 1955; Evelyn Frost, *Christian Healing*, 1940; J. V. Wilson, *Healing Through the Power of Christ*, 1949.

[36] E.g. The Crowhurst Home of Healing was founded by Howard J. Cobb in 1928 (cf. Howard J. Cobb, *Miracle of Crowhurst*, 1970); Burrswood (The Dorothy Kerin Trust) was founded in 1948 (cf. Monica Furlong, *Burrswood—Focus of Healing*, 1978).

[37] *The Church's Ministry of Healing.*

every parish priest through ordination the sacramental ministry for the strengthening of body and soul'; public services of healing, unless safeguarded, may give a wrong emphasis in worship and can sometimes be a danger to those who participate, particularly in the absence of subsequent pastoral care. An appendix discussed critically Christian Science and the activities of Spiritualists.

An interesting feature of the post-war years was the number of lay theologians who contributed to the Christian debate. Perhaps the most successful apologists in the Church of England were the laymen T. S. Eliot, C. S. Lewis, Dorothy L. Sayers and Charles Williams. T. S. Eliot, through his poetry and plays enunciated the essentially religious themes of self-knowledge, grace, martyrdom, and how to live the spiritual life in a materialist world. C. S. Lewis,[38] through his broadcast talks and his symbolic novels, provided a whole generation with a Christian apologetic and seems to have been the only Anglican layman whose sermons have been published.[39] Dorothy Sayers[40] combined a high degree of professional competence with fresh and penetrating insights into the meaning of the Christian faith in the modern world. Charles Williams, in a series of much-read novels, presented Christian virtues and theological concepts in a singularly effective manner and, in addition, wrote a perceptive and unusual history of the Christian Church.[41] These lay theologians addressed and reached a far wider audience than all but a few of the academic theologians and much of their effectiveness was due to their skill as writers and communicators. Moreover, with their lay background, their approach to theology was fresh, while their concerns and the language in which they expressed them were those of the laity who read them. They formed an impressive group and although much of what they wrote appears too dogmatic and over-confident today, it was brilliantly expressed and carried weight at a time when the professional theologians had ceased to communicate with the public. Many Christians had their faith confirmed and a number of agnostics were brought closer to faith through reading their

[38] Cf. Roger L. Green and Walter Hooper, *C. S. Lewis*, 1974.
[39] *Transposition and Other Addresses*, 1949.
[40] Cf. James Brabazon, *Dorothy L. Sayers*, 1982.
[41] *The Descent of the Dove*, 1939.

works and for some years they were the most quoted writers in sermons and discussion groups. Nor must we forget the scientists who helped many ordinary Christians not only to reconcile their faith with the scientific method and outlook but also revealed to them the fact that fundamentally the scientist and the Christian were both engaged in complementary activities. Among these were the Methodist, C. A. Coulson, Rouse Ball Professor of Mathematics in the University of Cambridge,[42] and Roger Pilkington.[43] Another Methodist layman Herbert Butterfield, Professor of Modern History at Cambridge, broadcast in 1949 a series of lectures on 'Christianity and History', which were greatly appreciated and, in their published form,[44] were widely read, the *Times Literary Supplement* describing them as 'the most important pronouncement on the nature of history since Acton's Inaugural'.

Finally, tribute must be paid to the wide influence of the monthly journal, *Theology*, which from 1939 to 1964 was under the creative editorship of Dr Alec Vidler.[45] All the contemporary theological and ecclesiastical issues found their way into its pages. Contributors included those of the eminence of C. F. Evans, Austin Farrer, G. W. H. Lampe, C. S. Lewis, D. M. MacKinnon, E. L. Mascall, Norman Sykes, Michael Ramsey, and Alan Richardson. *Theology* formed a bridge between the scholars and the many parish clergy who read it avidly. It also encouraged young theologians and historians, many of whom saw their first published work in the pages of *Theology*. It is significant, however, that fundamental matters, such as belief in God or in Christ were seldom discussed in its pages, as though these theological foundations were secure and might be taken for granted.[46] This could be a symbol of much of the theology of the forties and fifties. There was a self-confidence and security so that even those who did write about God, Christology, or the Church did so as though the basis of belief was unquestionably right. It is not surprising that the radical questions of the sixties caught many theologians unaware and unprepared.

[42] *Science and the Idea of God*, 1958; *Science and Christian Belief*, 1953.
[43] *World Without End*, 1960.
[44] *Christianity and History*, 1949. Cf. also *History and Human Relations*, 1951; *Christianity in European History*, 1951; *Writings on Christianity and History*, 1979.
[45] Cf. Alex Vidler, *Scenes from a Clerical Life*, 1977, pp. 111ff.
[46] Cf. David Edwards, '*Theology* under Dr Vidler', in *Theology*, January 1965.

## 3. Liturgical Renewal

'The present century has seen an extraordinary recovery and renewal by the Christian Church of its worship and the understanding of that worship as central to its life and work. The name usually given to the means whereby this recovery and renewal has been brought about is the Liturgical Movement.'[47] The movement was a remarkable example of the convergence of theological concern and pastoral insight. Theologically, the origins of the movement are to be found in the Roman Catholic Church in France in the nineteenth century, but by the end of the Second World War it had spread widely in the Low Countries, Germany and England. The result was the production of a huge literature on Christian worship and the acknowledgment that liturgical theology is an important department of theological studies. In England the outstanding contributors to liturgical scholarship have been F. E. Brightman, W. H. Frere, Edmund Bishop, E. C. Ratcliff, A. G. Hebert and Gregory Dix. In 1935 A. G. Hebert published *Liturgy and Society* which demonstrated how the Eucharist was the centre of power from which the social order might be redeemed. Another work, by a lay theologian, which had considerable influence was Evelyn Underhill's *Worship*, published in 1936. The last year of the war, however, saw the appearance of a study which was to have a profound affect upon the course of liturgical reform. This was Gregory Dix's *The Shape of the Liturgy*, the product of fourteen years' study and a work of profound scholarship. It transformed Anglican liturgiology almost overnight from a remote and academic branch of scholarship into a study whose immediate relevance became evident to multitudes of parish priests.[48] Central to his thesis was the four-fold pattern of what Jesus did when he instituted the Eucharist and which was reproduced in the rites of the early Church. Jesus took bread and wine; he gave thanks over them; he broke the bread; he shared the bread and wine with the disciples. This four-fold pattern, which had been lost in the medieval rites and had not been recovered in the

[47] H. Ellsworth Chandlee, 'The Liturgical Movement', in *A Dictionary of Liturgy and Worship*, ed. J. G. Davies, 1972.
[48] E. L. Mascall, 'Anglican Dogmatic Theology, 1939–60', in *Theology*, January 1960, pp. 1ff.

Book of Common Prayer, was to form the basis of all future Prayer Book revision.

In 1937 A. G. Hebert had edited a series of essays on *The Parish Communion*, which brought together the insights of liturgical and theological scholarship and the movement in the parishes to make the Holy Communion the central act of worship. The theologians and liturgists had demonstrated that in the early Church the central act of worship was the eucharist, that this was a corporate act of the whole Body of Christ in a particular place, which involved the active participation of the faithful in a common action in which all shared in the saving work of Christ in and for the world. The Parish Communion movement in this country sought to make the theological concept a practical reality and the object of the movement could be summed up in the phrase 'The Lord's own service on the Lord's day for all the Lord's people'. If this was indeed to become a reality the service should be central, take place at a time when the most people could be present, and be fully corporate. The pioneer of the movement was Henry de Candole, who became Bishop of Knaresborough in 1949. Throughout his ministry he devoted time and energy to the liturgical revival in the Church of England. The result was that by the end of the war a growing number of Churches had introduced the Holy Communion as the main Sunday service and an increasing number of clergy were eager to understand more fully the significance of the liturgical movement. Out of this concern and interest was born, in 1949, the Parish and People Movement.[49] It emerged from a conference at Queen's College, Birmingham, to which eighty-two people had been invited. The four-page manifesto of the movement[50] showed that its concern was not merely with the ordering of worship nor with antiquarian studies of the origins and development of Christian worship, but with the whole mission of the Church. 'The formation of Parish and People', wrote Henry de Candole, 'gave the liturgical movement in the Church of England a spearhead—a voice of leadership and corporate expression, and a possible instrument for action.'[51]

---

[49] Cf. P. J. Jagger, *History of the Parish and People Movement*, 1978; P. J. Jagger, *Bishop Henry de Candole: His Life and Times, 1895-1971*, 1975.

[50] *Parish and People: What is it all about?* 1948.

[51] Quoted, P. J. Jagger, *Henry de Candole*, p. 155.

There had been some notable adaptations of the Prayer Book order of Holy Communion. We have already referred to the centrality given to the Parish communion at Halton and Darnell.[52] Joost de Blank at St. John the Baptist, Greenhill, Harrow, where he was vicar from 1948 to 1952, introduced the westward position at a nave altar, an offertory procession, and an Old Testament reading.[53] Another example was the 'Clare College Liturgy', produced in 1954 by J. A. T. Robinson and C. F. D. Moule. This was not a new liturgy, but the Prayer Book Order of Holy Communion was made more meaningful by the production of a carefully prepared manual with the words of the service on the right hand page and a commentary on the left-hand page. This manual, together with the accompanying ceremonial brought out certain integral parts of the Eucharist which had fallen into the background. The relevance of the liturgy to life was given expression by the use of a common loaf and a bottle of wine from the college cellar. The corporate nature of the rite was shown by wide participation by members of the congregation in readings, in intercession, and in the offering of the bread and wine. The westward facing position for the celebrant[54] was adopted because it cut across party divisions and because it focussed attention 'on a priest in the middle, as the Christ comes to stand among his people as the breaker of bread, and to direct their eyes upwards as they lift up their hearts to him as their ascended Lord'.[55] Finally, the rite emphasized the importance of the ministry of the Word as an essential partner to the ministry of the Sacrament. Here were all the new insights of the liturgical movement; here were the new features which were subsequently to find their place in liturgical revision.

In 1935 the chief service on Sunday in the majority of parish churches had been Mattins or a Sung Eucharist, often with no communion, at 10.30 a.m. or 11 a.m. Twenty-five years later in an increasing number of parishes divine service at 10.30 a.m. or

---

[52] Cf. above, pp. 34ff.

[53] Joost de Blank, *The Parish in Action*, 1954, pp. 124ff.

[54] In view of this and future practice in the Church, it is interesting to note that in 1954 the House of Bishops of the Canterbury Convocation issued a statement saying that further experience of the use of the 'westward position' was needed 'before it can become anything but a rare and exceptional use'. *Chronicle of Convocation*, October 1954.

[55] J. A. T. Robinson, *Liturgy Coming to Life*, 1960, p. 23.

11 a.m. no longer existed and in its place there was a Eucharist at 9 a.m. or 9.30 a.m., with a large congregation, a general communion, music, and a sermon. The form of service was the 1662 Holy Communion, sometimes with additions from the 1928 book. The days of modern versions lay ahead; liturgical experiment had hardly begun. What was happening, however, was of profound significance, for the Church of England was becoming 'a eucharistic Church' in a new way. In theory it always had been, but now in practice the Eucharist was beginning to take its central place in Sunday worship and congregations were beginning to see the Eucharist as the focus of their spiritual life, as the expression of their corporate fellowship as the Body of Christ, and as the point from which flowed the mission of the Church. This revival led to a new interest in liturgy and it is not surprising that many became dissatisfied with the Service of Holy Communion in the Book of Common Prayer as a vehicle for corporate worship in the twentieth century. It was felt that the Prayer Book must be made more relevant to modern needs and situations, for that book pre-dated democratic government and a world-wide Anglican Communion, while many of the needs of modern industrial and scientific society naturally found no place in it. Secondly, the 1662 service lacked flexibility and variety to meet the needs of different congregations and different occasions. Thirdly, the language of the book, some of which was archaic, was felt to be unsuitable and remote for use in worship in the modern age. Fourthly, the 1662 book sprang from the midst of the religious controversies of the sixteenth and seventeenth centuries with the result that certain doctrines were over-emphasized while others found little or no expression. Like the medieval Mass, the Prayer Book service focussed on the Passion and Cross of Christ and, unlike the early liturgies, failed to set the Passion in the context of creation, resurrection, and the work of the Holy Spirit.

The outcome of the growing liturgical restiveness was that in 1955 the archbishops established a Liturgical Commission, under the chairmanship of Bishop Colin Dunlop, Dean of Lincoln. There were twenty members drawn from different fields of scholarship and representing historical, theological, and liturgical knowledge and pastoral skill and experience in constructing services. In the early days the output of the Commission was

somewhat meagre, largely because the number of matters
referred to it by the archbishops was limited, but in 1958 it produced a draft service of Baptism and Confirmation, which went
behind the Reformation and medieval service books to the Bible
and to the rites of the early Church. However, the reaction of
the Church was unfavourable. The Commission was also asked
to do some preparatory work for the 1958 Lambeth Conference.[56]

In such ways the ground was laid for that process of liturgical
revision which was to occupy so much of the time of the official
bodies of the Church of England in the sixties and seventies.
Some saw this concentration as a sign of an unhealthy introver-
sion. On the other hand, if the primary purpose of the Church
is the corporate worship of God, then the most appropriate
expression of that worship must be a central concern. It may not
be without significance that the period in which the Church was
preoccupied with liturgical revision coincided with a greater
awareness of the need for social and racial justice at home and
overseas. This ought not to be surprising in view of the fact that
at the heart of the liturgical movement lay the conviction that
liturgy and life are inseparable.

## 4. Ethical Concerns

A number of ethical questions affecting the life of the individual
and the nation came before the Church of England during the
fifteen years following the end of the war. By far the most important was the issue of peace and war and the ethics of atomic armaments and this has already been discussed.[57] Christians also
became concerned about the increase in gambling and the evil
consequences that often followed. It was the era of the football
pools, which had secured a firm place in the life of millions. In
1947 the racecourse totalizer amounted to some £21 million,
which represented an increase of £6 million compared with that

[56] *Prayer Book Revision in the Church of England*, 1957. This was one of three
liturgical documents prepared for the Conference, the other two being a report prepared
by the Church of India, Burma, and Ceylon on *Principles of Prayer Book Revision*,
1957, and a report by a small committee of members of the Church of England on
*The Commemoration of Saints and Heroes of the Faith in the Anglican Communion*,
1957. These three documents were a quite outstanding summary of past progress and
future aspirations in the field of liturgical revision both in England and throughout the
Anglican Communion.

[57] Cf. above, pp. 25f.

of 1946 and £14 million compared with 1945. There was a similar increase in gambling on dog racing so that in 1945 there was a tote turnover of over £137 million. At the same time the number of funfares with games of chance proliferated. At the request of the Church Assembly the Social and Industrial Council published a report in 1950[58] on the ethics of betting and gambling. This closely reasoned document revealed that the commission responsible for the report was not prepared to assert that gambling was always and in all circumstances a sinful action. This conclusion laid the commission open to misinterpretation and criticism and the Press gave the impression that it was more indulgent to gambling than in fact it was. The commission, however, distinguished between 'the major interests and activities of life' and 'those necessary but minor interests and activities which may be included under the heading of amusement and recreation'. In the former sphere gambling was illegitimate, but in the latter it was legitimate. Therefore, gambling is not 'wrong in itself'. The main criticism of the commission was that it had done inadequate justice to the 'rigorist' point of view held by many Christians or to the extent to which many members of the Church had a real fear about gambling in the current acquisitive climate. Indeed, the Church Assembly formally declared that the report was not 'fully representative of the mind and conscience of the Church of England as a whole'.[59] Six years later Archbishop Fisher spoke in the House of Lords[60] against the Small Lotteries Bill and in the course of his speech attacked the issuing by the government of Premium Bonds as a means of attracting savings.

The Government's duty is by every means in their power to restore the true coinage without which we cannot continue as a great people. It has chosen instead...a rather second-rate expedient which may attract savings, but which adds nothing to the spiritual capital of the nation, and which enunciates on a large scale this undignified and unedifying adulteration of public duty by motives of private gain.

In the forties and fifties human sterilization came more and more to the notice of doctors and welfare officers and increasing

---

[58] *Gambling: an Ethical Discussion.*
[59] *Church Assembly Report of Proceedings*, Autumn 1950.
[60] *Hansard: House of Lords*, 26 April 1956.

references were made to it in the popular Press. A group of theologians was invited by the Moral Welfare Council to consider the facts and the principles involved and it came to three conclusions.[61] Therapeutic sterilization was legitimate if it was the only means of curing disease; eugenic sterilization, whether compulsory or voluntary, was illegitimate; and in no case was it legitimate for the State to use sterilization as a punishment for crime. In 1962 the matter was considered again against the background of the rapid world population explosion, particularly in the developing countries. The conclusion this time was more radical, for the new group reporting on the subject[62] recognized circumstances in which sterilization without medical necessity may be morally justifiable. 'Faced as we are with a situation in which a responsible government [i.e. India] is pursuing ...a policy of persuasion for voluntary sterilisation, and asked by Christian doctors and nurses involved in the carrying out of this policy for help in deciding for themselves how far they can co-operate, we are bound to conclude that we find no grounds on which to reply in terms of an absolute negative.' The basis for this judgement was that the life of an individual could not be treated in isolation from the society of which he was a member and this included the need to share adequately the meagre resources of the land. Unless action as dramatic as sterilization was taken other efforts to relieve poverty and hunger could be of no avail in the face of rapidly increasing population.

By 1945 artificial insemination of human beings, which hitherto had been practised on only a very small scale in England, had been brought to public attention and in that year Archbishop Fisher appointed a committee of experts to examine the evidence. Their report,[63] published three years later, was aimed, not at the general public, but at those who in their several professions had to consider the implications of the practice. The committee reached four conclusions. When artificial insemination could properly be regarded as the sequel to normal intercourse between husband and wife, it could be justified; when this was not possible, artificial insemination by

---

[61] *Human Sterilisation: Some Principles of Christian Ethics,* 1951.

[62] *Sterilisation: An Ethical Enquiry.* This was the report of a committee invited by the Board of Social Responsibility to consider the matter.

[63] *Artificial Human Insemination,* 1948.

the husband (AIH) could be justified; artificial insemination by a donor (AID) involved a breach of marriage, defrauded the child who was born, and deceived society, and was therefore not justified; the evils involved in AID were so great that consideration should be given to making the practice a criminal offence. This document formed the basis of the evidence given by the Archbishop of Canterbury[64] before a Departmental Committee set up by the Government in 1958.

A number of fundamental ethical questions arose out of the conclusions of the *Report on Homosexual Offences and Prostitution*, usually known as the Wolfenden Report, and published by the Government in 1957. The committee responsible for the report had before it the evidence that since the war there had been a rapid increase in the number of homosexual offences known to the police.[65] In 1952 increased police activity against known homosexuals began to produce a public reaction. The Moral Welfare Council, prompted by its lecturer, Dr Sherwin Bailey, conducted a full investigation of the problem and in December 1953 the Executive Committee of the Council sent a resolution to the Home Secretary asking him to initiate an official enquiry into the whole subject. When the Wolfenden Committee began work the Church of England, through the Moral Welfare Council, gave evidence,[66] the major responsibility for this falling on Dr Bailey, whose major work, *Homosexuality and the Western Christian Tradition*[67] was submitted to the Committee as a piece of private evidence.

The Wolfenden Committee recommended that homosexual behaviour between consenting adults in private should no longer be a criminal offence, it declined to make prostitution illegal, and it based these conclusions on the principle that the criminal law should not be regarded as synonymous with, or a substitute for, personal morality. 'Unless a deliberate attempt is to be made by society...to equate the sphere of crime with that of sin, there must remain a realm of private morality and

---

[64] *Artificial Insemination by Donor; two Contributions towards a Christian Judgment*, 1959, contains the Archbishop's evidence.
[65] The number rose from 622 in 1931 to 6,644 in 1955 - Cf. Peter Coleman, *The Christian Attitude to Homosexuality*, 1980, p. 161.
[66] *Sexual Offences and Social Punishment*, compiled and edited by D. S. Bailey 1956.
[67] 1955.

immorality which is, in brief and crude terms, not the law's business.'[68] This principle had wider implications than the question of sexual behaviour because it raised the whole issue of the purpose and the scope of the criminal law. It stimulated considerable public discussion which was highlighted by the Maccabean Lecture in Jurisprudence[69] given in 1959 by Lord Devlin in which he disputed the view that there was a realm of morality which lay outside the law. Lord Devlin was answered by H. A. L. Hart, in the Harry Camp Lectures[70] at Stamford University in 1962. In a pamphlet[71] written by Quentin Edwards, a barrister, published by the Moral Welfare Council in 1959, it was pointed out that in English law certain actions may be unlawful without being crimes. For example, fornication, adultery, and prostitution may not be crimes, but may still be unlawful because they concern more than one person and their consequences can be the subject of redress in the civil courts. More important is the fact that they are contrary to the code of right conduct and duty in behaviour generally and currently acceptable in society. The writer clearly took the view enunciated by Lord Devlin that the moral judgement of society is that which is accepted by 'the man on the Clapham omnibus' or 'the man in the jury box'.[72]

A particular example of the relationship between law and morals was suicide. Was suicide or attempted suicide, which Christians had always regarded as morally wrong, to remain an offence punishable by law? In view of the growing opinion among doctors, magistrates, and others that criminal proceedings were inappropriate against those who attempted suicide, the Archbishop of Canterbury invited the Board of Social Responsibility to examine the question and in 1959 the committee appointed for this purpose reported[73] that, although it

[68] Paragraph 61.
[69] Published, with other lectures on the same theme, in *The Re-enforcement of Morals*, 1965.
[70] *Law, Liberty and Morality*, 1963. The debate was analysed in the Edward Cadbury Lectures in 1966 by Basil Mitchell, later published as *Law, Morality and Religion in a Secular Society*, 1967.
[71] *What is Unlawful?*
[72] Op. cit., pp. 14f. It took ten years for Parliament to reach a decision that the recommendations of the Wolfenden Report could be implemented by Statute—the Sexual Offences Act, 1967.
[73] *Ought Suicide to be a Crime?*

must resist the dichotomy between sin and crime on the ground that if a law excludes certain behaviour then such behaviour inevitably assumes respectability, it must nevertheless affirm that suicide should be regarded as a tragedy and not as a crime and that it, together with attempted suicide, should be removed from the criminal law. The basis of this judgement was that any person who commits suicide or attempts the act must be in a state of mental distress or unhappiness which requires not punishment, but mental treatment or at least sympathy and understanding. A subsequent Government White Paper acknowledged that this report had influenced the framing of the Suicide Act of 1960, which removed suicide from the criminal law, although any person who 'aids, abets, councils or procures' the suicide of another person is liable to criminal proceedings.

This post-war ethical activity indicated an acute awareness by the Church of problems involved in developments in medicine and technology. The basic conviction was that Christian moral principles were not a static body of law but had to be interpreted and restated in situations which were new, while at the same time guarding against the abrogation of the traditional moral principles. The discussion showed that the State was willing to listen to the Church, to seek its views on moral issues as these impinged on the law of the land, and to allow it to influence its own conclusions.

# 4

# CHURCH RELATIONS

He that is not a son of Peace is not a son of God. All
other sins destroy the Church consequently; but
Division and Separation demolish it directly...Many
Doctrinal differences must be tolerated in a Church:
And why? but for Unitie and Peace? Therefore Dis-
union and Separation is utterly intolerable.
Richard Baxter, *The Saints' Everlasting Rest*, 1650

## 1. Dr Fisher's Cambridge Sermon and its Results

ON 3 November 1946 the Archbishop of Canterbury mounted
the pulpit in the University Church in Cambridge to preach a
sermon[1] which proved to be momentous because it initiated a
process which was to bring together the Churches in Britain in
an unprecedented search for unity. Since the Lambeth Conference's famous 'Appeal to All Christian People' in 1920 the pace
had been slow, although results had not been negligible. On
numerous occasions the Churches had been able to join together
in the fields of social action and international order and in 1942
the British Council of Churches (BCC) had been inaugurated.
This was a body representative of the Church of England, the
Church of Wales, the Church of Ireland, the Free Churches, the
Salvation Army, the Society of Friends, and five interdenominational organizations.

The Archbishop's Cambridge Sermon gave a much needed
impetus to the ecumenical movement. He described the divisions of Christendom as 'a scandal and rock of offence to be
overcome' and, although he did not believe that the English
Churches were ready for constitutional reunion, he suggested a
way forward. This was that 'while the folds remain distinct,
there should be a movement towards a free and unfettered
exchange of life in worship and sacrament between them as
there is already of prayer and thought and Christian fellowship

---

[1] Geoffrey Fisher, *A Step Forward in Church Relations*, 1946.

—in short, that they should grow towards that full communion with one another, which already in their separation they have with Christ'. In particular, since the Free Churches had often acknowledged that any future united Church would be episcopal, could they not now 'take episcopacy into their system' and explore its nature and value? Without sacrificing any principle and without making any new constitutional arrangements, they would thus come to possess a ministry 'mutually acknowledged by all as possessing not only the inward call of the Spirit but also the authority which each Church in conscience requires'.

The proposal that the Free Churches should 'take episcopacy into their system' was a new and hopeful concept and the Free Churches agreed to send representatives to a Joint Conference with representatives of the Church of England to assess the implications of the Cambridge Sermon. At about the same time a report[2] was published which was the result of an invitation issued by the Archbishop in November 1945 (before the Cambridge Sermon) to a group of Anglicans of the catholic school of theology to examine the causes of deadlock which occurred in discussions between catholics and protestants and to consider whether any synthesis between the divergent views was possible. The report set in the foreground the 'wholeness' of the Gospel and the Church, within which certain inevitable tensions were held together in the unity of the Church. The schisms which eventually occurred fragmented the unity and distorted the truth. All parts of divided Christendom must seek to recover the wholeness of catholicity, and unity would not be achieved by attempting to patch together the fragments of truth to which each tradition bore witness, but by a common rediscovery of the norm of faith and order in its totality. The Church of England, which itself held together catholic and protestant insights, was particularly well placed to take a lead in this search for catholicity. Two years later the Archbishop issued a similar invitation, with the same terms of reference, to a group of Anglicans of the evangelical school of thought and also to some leaders of the Free Churches. The latter were the first to report,[3] but unfortunately the report was dominated by a quite proper concern to

[2] Catholicity: A Study in the Conflict of Christian Traditions in the West, 1947.
[3] The Catholicity of Protestantism, ed. R. Newton Flew and Ruper E. Davies, 1950.

correct the descriptions of protestantism in the earlier report. Nevertheless, it presented a clear account of what protestants had contended for and it emphasized that 'belief in the one Holy, Catholic and Apostolic Church is integral to the faith of protestantism'. In the group's view the subject which most required further investigation was the nature of authority and the work of the Holy Spirit in the Church. It stressed that no Church must be asked to repudiate the reality of its ministries and sacraments and that no Free Church would find it possible to accept reordination of its ministers. Finally, differing views on the historic episcopate should be tolerated in any Church 'which attempts to comprehend both the Catholic and the Protestant traditions'.

The report[4] from the group representing the evangelical section of the Church of England made an eirenic attempt to account for the contrasts between 'catholic' and 'protestant' theology and asserted the protestant claim to be truly catholic. 'Protestantism is testimony on behalf of the catholic faith against uncatholic perversions of it.' In any united Church 'there will be great variety of belief and practice, vigorous controversy and much allowed which one side or the other will think wrong and erroneous'. Any reunion scheme must safeguard six fundamental truths—'justification by faith alone, the objective character of the sacraments as means of grace, the final authority of the Bible and the relative nature of the Church's tradition,...the spiritual nature of the Church summed up by the definition of its visible aspect in terms of the vehicle of the gospel, and the visible historical nature of the Church summed up in the acceptance of the historic episcopal ministry'.

In 1950 the Joint Conference of the Free Churches and the Church of England published *Church Relations in England*, in which the conclusion was reached that 'negotiations for the establishment of intercommunion would have to be conducted in a parallel series between the Church of England on the one hand and the individual Free Churches on the other'. For such negotiations to be successful six conditions would require fulfilment. The negotiating Churches must be satisfied of each other's loyalty to the apostolic faith; a Free Church would 'take

---

[4] *The Fulness of Christ: The Church's Growth into Catholicity*, 1950.

episcopacy into its system' by the acceptance of an episcopate consecrated through bishops in the historic succession and by adopting episcopal ordination for the future, provided that both negotiating Churches accorded to each other the same liberty of interpretation of the nature of episcopacy and priest-hood as already obtained in the Church of England; the Church of England would agree to mutual intercommunion of baptized and communicant members; the Church of England would hope that the rite of Confirmation, episcopally administered, would come to be the norm in the Free Church; the Free Church which became episcopal would maintain the relations of fellow-ship and intercommunion which it already enjoyed with non-episcopal churches; and both Churches would agree that the continued existence of two parallel Churches in the same area was but a temporary stage of the road to full unity. 'The Confer-ence is satisfied that only upon such terms as these could the Archbishop's proposals be implemented.' The Report left it to individual Churches 'to decide whether, as a result of our work, they shall enter upon the stage of definite negotiations'. We have set out in some detail the views expressed by these different groups because they constitute the basis of conversations between the Churches which occupied the next thirty years and reveal some of the rocks upon which many hopes were shattered.

The only Free Church which was ready at that time to make a positive response to the Archbishop's sermon was the Methodist Church, which differed from the other Free Churches because the separation between Methodism and Anglicanism did not occur at a particular time and over a particular doctrine, but was gradual and almost accidental. Moreover, Methodism, un-like the other Free Churches, never formulated a sharp doctrinal position of its own in opposition to that of the Church of England. The Methodist Church entered into correspondence with the Church of England and received an assurance that any discussion between the two Churches would be regarded as taking place *within* the Body of Christ, while the office and function of a priest in the Church of God would be safeguarded in the ordinal and in the practice of the Methodist Church if it took episcopacy into its system. On the basis of these assurances and the conditions stated in *Church Relations in England* the two Churches initiated in 1955 official 'Conversations' with the object of establishing intercommunion. The leader of the Methodists was Dr Harold Roberts, Principal of Richmond College, and the Anglican representatives were led first by Dr Bell, Bishop of Chichester, and after his death in 1958, by Dr H. J. Carpenter, Bishop of Oxford. An *Interim Report* was published in 1958 which set out the common ground between the two Churches. The most important conclusion, however, was the rejection of the concept of partial communion between the two churches. Instead, the group looked forward to *full* communion from the outset, following the unification of both ministries. It then declared that 'we have been led with impressive unanimity to the conviction that nothing short of organic unity...should be our final goal'. As a stage on the way to that goal the two Churches, once the unification of ministries had been secured, would become parallel entities in full communion with each other. Here lay the genesis of the two-stage scheme which was to be the characteristic feature of the next stage of the negotiations. The Commission made no positive recommendations but commended its report for discussion in the two Churches. Both Churches accepted the report and organic unity thus became the official goal.

Among the representatives of the Free Churches who took part in the conversations which produced *Church Relations in England* was one from the Presbyterian Church of England. Over a period of years before the Archbishop's Cambridge Sermon conversations had been taking place, first between the Church of England and the Church of Scotland and then between those two churches and the Scottish Episcopal Church and the Presbyterian Church of England, although the talks had languished since the nineteen-thirties. After the Cambridge Sermon conversations were reopened between the Church of England and the Church of Scotland, with 'observers' from the Episcopal Church of Scotland and the Presbyterian Church of England. The report[5] published in 1951 acknowledged the formidable barriers between the two Churches arising from past history, from long-continued separation and from conscientious

---

[5] *Relations between the Church of England and the Church of Scotland: A Joint Report.*

convictions about the form of the Church's ministry and government. As a step towards the long-term goal of unity it looked to
the establishment of closer relationships between the two
Churches by permission being granted to the ministers of the
two Churches to preach in each other's buildings and for communicant members of the Church of Scotland to receive Holy
Communion in Anglican Churches. The Convocations of
Canterbury and York noted 'with satisfaction' the recommendations of the report and requested the archbishops to promote
a resumed series of conversations in which the Episcopal Church
of Scotland and the Presbyterian Church of England should be
officially represented. The new group, largely composed—so far
as the Church of Scotland was concerned—of academics, made
definite and unanimous proposals in 1958.[6] As the basis for
intercommunion, it proposed the adoption of 'bishops-in-
presbytery' in the Church of Scotland and of a more corporate
and conciliar practice of episcopacy in the Church of England.
It also proposed that the Church of England should accept a
form of lay eldership with a permanent place in the government
and pastoral oversight of the Church. Such changes would
'represent a recovery of elements in that wholeness of the
church to which both the Episcopal and Presbyterian Churches
are deeply committed'. The proposals provoked a storm of
opposition in Scotland, fuelled by Lord Beaverbrook, the son of
a Canadian presbyterian manse and proprietor of the *Scottish
Daily Express,* which suggested that the whole concept was a
secret ecclesiastical plot to enslave the Scots to the English. It is
true that the members of the Commission may have been in-
sensitive to the long memories among the Scots of the tragic
attempts to introduce episcopacy in that Church in the past nor
did they appear to recognize the link between Scottish national-
ism and the preservation of the Church of Scotland's own
polity.[7] In 1959 the General Assembly of the Church of Scotland resolved that what had come to be called 'the Bishops'
Report' implied 'a denial of the catholicity of the Church of
Scotland and of the validity and regularity of its ministry within
the Church Catholic'. At the same time it was prepared to

[6] *Relations between Anglican and Presbyterian Churches.*
[7] Cf. Ian Henderson, *Power Without Glory,* 1967.

continue talks to clarify central issues and a large commission of a hundred and fifty, representing the four Churches, was appointed. It produced a report[8] clarifying some of the key issues, but the only positive recommendation it could make was to propose conversations in each country between Anglicans and Presbyterians in the hope that the result might be a united Church in England and a united Church in Scotland. In the event, however, the only result was a 'slow grinding to a halt',[9] although specific unity negotiations were initiated between the Church of Scotland and the Episcopal Church of Scotland.

The growing understanding between the non-Roman Catholic Churches in England and their willingness to enter into conversations in a search for unity was in sharp contrast to the intransigence of the Church of Rome, which permitted no discussions on theological matters and no sharing of prayer or worship. It is true that during the war there was published in *The Times*[10] a joint letter over the signature of the two Anglican archbishops, the Cardinal Archbishop of Westminster and the Moderator of the Free Church Council, setting out five peace points advocated by the Pope in the previous year. The publication of the letter was important in Anglican-Roman Catholic relations because the ability to take common action on matters of social concern was a first essential step towards mutual understanding. Yet it was but 'a flash in the pan', for Rome continued to forbid common acts of worship and even the public recitation of the Lord's Prayer together. In a letter to *The Times* in November 1949 Dr Haigh, Bishop of Winchester, referred to the doubts in the minds of the Roman Catholic organizers of a joint meeting at Bournemouth about his giving the blessing at the end of the proceedings, to which the Roman Catholic coadjutor Bishop of Brentwood replied by saying that the Roman Catholic 'attitude is the logical outcome of their belief that, so far as they are concerned, and from their point of view, the Bishop of Winchester is a layman'.[11] Yet in that same year the Holy Office

[8] *The Anglican-Presbyterian Conversations*, 1966.

[9] Rupert E. Davies, *The Church in Our Times*, 1979, p. 59.

[10] 21 December 1940.

[11] *The Times*, 15 November 1949. The whole correspondence was published later that year as a pamphlet, *Catholicism Today*.

Rodogma factory'[14] was a negation of biblical and historical scholarship. A further blow was the publication in the same year of Encyclical, *Humani Generis*, condemning many ideas which appeared to be gaining ground among Roman Catholic scholars, the most serious of which was the principle that, although fundamental truth is unchanging, its formulation could and should change from age to age. Any who attempted to deny the identification of the Mystical Body of Christ and the Roman Catholic Church were condemned. The growing feeling among Anglicans that the future of Anglican-Roman Catholic relations was hopeless was reinforced the following year when the fifteenth centenary of the Council of Chalcedon was celebrated and Rome issued the Encyclical, *Sempiternus Dei*, which included the words: 'Is it not holy and salutary and according to the will of God that all at long last return to the one fold of Christ?' Bernard Pawley has commented that 'a dark night of ecumenical estrangement seemed indeed to have set in, and hopes were again extinguished. But as so often in the history of the Church the majority were mistaken and a new age was about to dawn'.[15] In the course of the ten years from 1958 to 1968 an immense change took place in Anglican-Roman Catholic Relations and within the Roman Catholic Church itself. Angelo Giuseppe Roncalli, at the age of seventy, was elected Pope in 1958 as John XXIII. That election changed the whole scene.

The British Council of Churches had been inaugurated in 1942 as a fellowship of Churches in the British Isles 'which confess the Lord Jesus as God and Saviour'. The Council possessed departments for education, faith and order, international affairs, social responsibility, and youth, together with a committee on evangelism. It was probably best known through its Inter-Church Aid and Refugee Service, later to be called Christian Aid, which raised large sums each year, interested a great number of Church members, and aroused much local enthusiasm. The BCC was an instrument for enabling the Churches to act together on matters of national importance and public interest. It sponsored the annual Week of Prayer for Christian Unity which is held from 18 to 25 January. In the early post-war

[14] *The Pot and the Knife*, 1979, p. 12.     [15] *Rome and Canterbury*, 1974, p. 314.

issued an Instruction *On the Ecumenical Mov*
carefully guarded permission was given to Ro
engage in theological dialogue with other Chris
part in mixed gatherings which had as their p
counsel together concerning joint action in the
fundamental principles of Christianity and the
'to deal with the rebuilding of social order and
tions'. Moreover, the Instruction allowed such m
opened or closed with the common recitation o
Prayer. In spite of this, Archbishop Garbett noted
four years later a problem raised in connection with
United Peace meeting in Hull, in which he declined t
if the Roman Catholics refused to allow him to use
Prayer. 'It is humbug', he wrote, 'to call the nations
ship when we Christians cannot even say the Lord
together.' It was agreed that the Lord's Prayer *would*
with the result that no Roman Catholic priest appeared
platform and no tickets for the meeting were sold in
Catholic churches.[12]

It has to be remembered that two years before the end
war Pope Pius XII had issued the Encyclical, *Mystici Corp*
*Christi*, which reaffirmed that the Church of Christ and
Roman Catholic Church are identical, and that in 194
Instruction from the Holy Office had gone so far as to
bishops to be 'on their guard against those who under false
texts stress the points on which we agree rather than thos
which we disagree'. The year 1950 saw the dogmatic defin
of the Assumption of the Blessed Virgin Mary, who—dec
the definition—'having fulfilled the course of her earthly
was taken up in body and soul to heavenly glory'. There
scriptural, historical, or scientific evidence for such an event
it can be described only as a pious opinion based on a leg
but belief in that legend was now to become a dogma nece
to salvation. This was a blow to a Church like the Churc
England which has always taught that nothing is necessa
salvation unless it is to be found in, or can be proved by,
Scripture.[13] To most non-Roman Catholics what John Drury
described as 'one of the last achievements of the great

---

[12] Charles Smyth, op. cit., p. 381.     [13] *Articles of Religion*, Articles VI and

years it made representations to the Government on the religious and social problems of new housing areas, on federation in Central Africa, on the terms of reference of the Royal Commission on marriage and divorce, and on a number of other issues. It was responsible for a large Conference on Christian Youth in 1951 where a thousand delegates took part, and in the same year it was the channel through which the Churches took part in the Festival of Britain. Local Councils of Churches began to be established in many areas and in 1950 there were 119 such local councils, which had increased to 300 in 1960 and to 700 in 1969. They did much to bring together members of local Churches for common witness and common action, which in turn led to a growth in mutual understanding, out of which was born an intense desire at local level for greater unity.

Outside these shores the Church of England was in full communion with the Old Catholics[16] and its relations with the Orthodox Churches and the Churches of Sweden and Finland were close but fell short of full communion. In 1920 the Oecumenical Patriarch had accepted that the Anglican Church had preserved the apostolic succession and a true doctrine of orders, and he declared that her orders possessed 'the same validity as those of the Roman, Old Catholic and Armenian Churches'. Subsequently, the patriarchs of Alexandria, Jerusalem, and Romania and the Churches of Cyprus and Greece accepted them. This has not been followed through in practice and Anglican clergy who join the Orthodox Churches in question are reordained. It cannot be used as a basis for intercommunion between Anglicans and Orthodox because of the prior Orthodox insistence that orders cannot be considered in isolation from doctrine.[17] There had been official visits of Anglican bishops and archbishops to Orthodox Churches and a steady dialogue between the Churches. Besides official negotiations, conferences, and visits, there were useful developments on the informal and personal level through the work of the Anglican and Eastern Association and the Fellowship of St. Alban and St. Sergius, which published the informative periodical, *Sobornost*.

[16] Cf. C. B. Moss, *The Old Catholic Movement*, 1964.
[17] Cf. Timothy Ware, *The Orthodox Church*, 1963, Chapter 16.

In 1954 the Church of England recognized the true succession of the Swedish episcopate and recommended that duly qualified members of the Church of Sweden should be able to receive Holy Communion in the Church of England and that Swedish clergy should be permitted to preach in Anglican Churches, to celebrate Holy Communion according to their own rite, and to assist at the Anglican rite when in Anglican Churches. A new situation arose in 1958 when the Church of Sweden began to ordain women but in 1961 the former permission was reaffirmed, although women priests were excluded. In the past there had been occasions when Anglican bishops had participated in Swedish consecrations, but after 1959, when Bishop Hunter of Sheffield co-consecrated the Bishop of Linköping, no invitations to participate were accepted lest such action should appear to endorse the ordination of women.[18] The position of the Church of England with regard to the Church of Finland has since 1935 been similar to that with Sweden, although it was not until 1951 that the first Anglican bishop[19] took part in a Finnish consecration.

## 2. The Anglican Communion

The Anglican Communion has been defined as 'a fellowship, within the One Holy Catholic and Apostolic Church, of those duly constituted Dioceses, Provinces, or Regional Churches in communion with the see of Canterbury' and on taking office one of the main preoccupations of Archbishop Fisher was the heavy preparations for the 1948 Lambeth Conference, which except during the Second World War had met at roughly ten-year intervals since its inauguration in 1867. Before the Conference the Archbishop visited the United States to attend the General Convention of the American Episcopal Church and thus helped to develop closer relationships with the American Church, the largest of the Churches in the Anglican Com-

---

[18] After the Church of England had affirmed in 1975 that there were 'no fundamental objections' to the ordination of women (cf. below p. 256) participation in Swedish consecrations were resumed and in 1976 the Bishop of Coventry co-consecrated the Bishop of Karlstadt. In 1979 Bishop Bengt Sundkler took part in the consecration of the Bishop of Manchester.

[19] The Right Revd G. Ingle, Bishop of Fulham.

munion. Three hundred and twenty-six bishops attended the 1948 Conference, much of the success of which was due to the superb administrative ability of the episcopal secretary, Bishop Mervyn Haigh of Winchester, and to the brilliant chairmanship of Archbishop Fisher. The result was that a great spirit of unity pervaded the whole Conference, in great contrast to the disunity of the world outside. Three important practical proposals emerged from the Conference. The first was the recommendation to set up an Advisory Council on Missionary Strategy. The second was the immediate establishment of a Central College for the Anglican Communion, if possible at St. Augustine's College at Canterbury, as a place where members of the overseas Anglican Communion could stay to meet, pray, and study with others. The College opened in 1952, with Canon Kenneth Sansbury as the first warden. Thirdly, the Conference welcomed the suggestion that an Anglican Congress should be held, if possible in 1953. Another outcome of the Conference was the creation of the Anglican Cycle of Prayer, the purpose of which was to unite Anglicans throughout the world in prayer day by day.

The bishops of the Church of South India were not allowed to attend the Conference. The Church of South India had been inaugurated in 1947 and the problems it raised were of constant concern in the post-war years both to the Church of England and to the Anglican Communion as a whole. The three Churches which came together to form the Church of South India were the Anglican Church, the Methodist Church, and the South India United Church, composed largely of Presbyterians and Congregationalists. Episcopacy was accepted as part of the basis for union and, although existing non-episcopally ordained ministers would not be episcopally ordained, after union all ordinations would be episcopal. This inevitably produced an interim period—thirty years—during which the uniting Churches would grow together, although there would be certain anomalies within the Church and in its relations with other bodies. On the whole encouragement had been given to the Churches in South India, but Anglo-Catholics were opposed to the creation of a Church without complete episcopal government in the apostolic succession and universal episcopal consecration and ordination. The Lambeth Conference of 1930 had noted that the United Church would not be a province of the Anglican Communion and, although it would have inter-communion with the Churches of the Anglican Communion, for a time that would be limited by the rules of those Churches. When at the beginning of 1947 it became clear that the inaugu-ration of the new Church would take place before the end of the year various bodies in England had to determine their attitudes towards it. One of these was the Society for the Propagation of the Gospel, which reached the conclusion that its charter pre-cluded it from allocating grants to dioceses not in communion with the Church of England. Individual workers in South India would receive the equivalent of one year's salary and thereafter the Society's responsibility for them would cease. It was agreed, however, that a special fund should be opened to which SPG subscribers might contribute to the support of those workers who joined the Church of South India.

On 27 September 1947 the Church of South India was solemnly inaugurated in St. George's Cathedral, Madras, al-though 30,000 Anglicans in the diocese of Dornakal refused to enter the union. It was a momentous event as 'for the first time since the sixteenth century the great divide between episcopal and non-episcopal Churches springing from the Reformation had been bridged'.[20] So began what the editor of *Crockford's* declared to be ' a very dangerous experiment which ought to be tried'.[21] The 1948 Lambeth Conference gave thanks for the measure of unity thus achieved but, although the majority was ready to recognize the ministers of the new Church at once, a substantial minority held that it was too soon to pass any judge-ment upon the status of those ministers and that they could not, therefore, recommend their acceptance into the Anglican Communion. What was of significance was the resolution of the Conference that in future schemes for union the unification of ministers either at the inauguration of the union or as soon as possible afterwards was likely to be a prerequisite of success. In 1950 the Convocations of Canterbury and York proclaimed an Act of Convocation declaring that the question of the Church of South India should be reconsidered at the end of five years and

[20] Barry Till, *The Churches Search for Unity*, 1972, p. 291.
[21] Preface to *Crockford's Clerical Directory*, 72nd Issue, 1948.

that in the meantime clergy of that church might preach or officiate in Anglican Churches in this country only under certain strictly controlled circumstances. Five years later the Convocations agreed that the Church of England should accept all ministers consecrated or ordained at or after the inauguration as true ministers of the Church of Christ, although full communion was not likely for another twenty years when all ministers would be episcopally ordained.

In the post-war years the spirit of national autonomy and equality sweeping through the nations of the world, which transformed relationships between the nations of the British Commonwealth and the mother country, affected the Anglican Communion. Indeed, it is significant that independence was granted to the Churches before political autonomy was achieved so that in those nations there was a self-governing Anglican Church which could often give an element of cohesiveness to the new nation. In 1950 the new and independent provinces of West Africa, of Central Africa, and of East Africa were inaugurated and the following decade saw the establishment of the Province of Uganda, Rwanda, and Burundi, the Province of the Episcopal Church of Brazil, and the division of the Province of East Africa into the Provinces of Kenya and Tanzania. The establishment of autonomous provinces came in course of time to change profoundly the ethos and relationships of successive Lambeth Conferences. Hitherto these had been predominantly Western orientated, but as the African and Asian Churches acquired confidence and as they attempted to tackle the religious, political, and social problems in their own countries they gained status and influence which widened the horizons of the Lambeth bishops and thus provided a balance to the Western way of thinking.

The 1958 Lambeth Conference recommended the establishment of an Anglican Consultative Council, consisting of the Archbishop of Canterbury as Chairman, the primates and presiding bishops of the national or provincial Churches and representatives of dioceses under the direction jurisdiction of the Archbishop of Canterbury. Its purpose would be to continue the work of the Conference between sessions and to be advisory to the Archbishop and the other bishops. No action was taken until after the 1968 Conference when a Consultative Council of

different composition was established. What did happen, how-
ever, was the appointment of a full-time Anglican Executive
Officer. The archbishop invited the Bishop of Johannesburg, Dr
Ambrose Reeves, to be the first occupant of the post, but he
declined[22] and Stephen Bayne, Bishop of Olympia in the
United States, was appointed.

### 3. The World Council of Churches

Archbishop Fisher went straight from the 1948 Lambeth Conference to Amsterdam for the inauguration of the World
Council of Churches. Ever since the great World Missionary
Conference at Edinburgh in 1910 the Church of England had
taken a full share in the world-wide ecumenical movement and
gave to it two of its most outstanding leaders in William Temple
and George Bell. The Council was inaugurated on the following
basis: 'The World Council of Churches is a fellowship of Churches which accept our Lord Jesus Christ as God and Saviour.'
Archbishop Fisher was in the chair at the historic moment of the
inauguration on 23 August 1948 at Amsterdam, at which were
gathered 351 delegates from 147 Churches, the only notable
absentees being the Roman Catholic Church and the Russian
Orthodox Church. 'Almost every grade and denomination was
to be found', wrote Bishop Bell, 'and more striking, laymen
and women and ministers of every colour and race. It was a
truly international and inter-racial gathering, ecumenical in the
largest sense.'[23] Dr Fisher's reaction to the ceremony was charac-
teristically detached—'Some chairmen would at that time have
been emotional in their prayers, their thanksgiving, their loud
*Te Deum*. Being myself a very restrained person, I had to say
something, and said a few words of unpremeditated prayer: but
it was all on a very quiet and deep, and unostentatious, note.'[24]
For Bishop Bell on the other hand it was a 'thrilling moment,
for here at last the hopes and prayers of years were to be fulfilled'.[25]

In 1952 the third World Conference on Faith and Order was

[22] J. S. Peart-Binns, *Ambrose Reeves*, 1973, pp. 149f.
[23] *The Kingdom of Christ*, 1954, p. 50.
[24] William Purcell, *Fisher of Lambeth*, p. 189.
[25] Op. cit., p. 50.

held at Lund in Sweden and it marked a change in direction by transferring concern from the differences dividing the Churches to the factors which united them. The Conference's *Word to the Churches* enunciated what came to be known as 'the Lund Principle': 'Should not our Churches ask themselves...whether they should not act together in all matters, except those in which deep differences of conviction compel them to act separately?' It was a representative of the Church of England, Oliver Tomkins,[26] who first propounded the principle.[27] The second Assembly of the World Council at Evanston, Illinois, in 1954 had as its theme, largely at Bishop Bell's instigation, 'Christ: The Hope of the World', which was a relevant topic at a time of great concern about Soviet totalitarianism, the Cold War, and the atomic bomb. The Assembly revealed a division between those who saw the Church's task primarily as a spiritual one to prepare people for the Second Coming of Christ and those who believed that the Church's vocation was to address itself to the problems of society in the name of Christ. Another important feature of the Assembly was the growing leadership of the Churches in Asia and Africa. 'They are rising to adult status', wrote Michael Ramsey,[28] 'they are the leaders and we the learners'. Dr Ramsey also drew attention to another feature of the Assembly—'the primacy and poignancy of the question of Race for the Christian conscience'.[29] Thus there emerged what was to become a major and continuing topic for the World Council in the years to come. The third Assembly at New Delhi in 1961 was notable for the emphasis placed on local unity so that unity may be visible as well as theological. A statement spoke of 'the unity which is both God's will and his gift to the Church...being made visible as *all in each place*...are brought into one fully committed fellowship'.[30] The most important event at New Delhi, however, was the reception into the World Council of the Orthodox Churches of Russia, Bulgaria, Romania and Poland. It was also the first Assembly to which the Roman Catholic Church sent official observers.

[26] Then secretary of the Faith and Order Department in Geneva; Bishop of Bristol, 1959-75.

[27] Rupert E. Davies, op. cit., p. 62.

[28] 'Evaston', in *Durham Essays and Addresses*, 1956, p. 83.

[29] Ibid.

[30] Author's italics.

By 1959 the Church of England had changed comparatively little since the end of the war. It is true that moderate alterations had been made in the parochial system and that heroic efforts had been made to cope with the needs of new housing areas, the repair of war damage, the demands of the Education Act and the financial problems of the clergy, but in many ways it was a Church sailing on an even keel, content with the old tried ways and the conventional orthodoxies. There was an atmosphere of complacency and an apparent unawareness of trends already present which were to burst to the surface in the sixties. For the majority of churchmen Christian theology was an assured package of unalterable truth and Christian ethics unchallengeable. Services in most parish churches were much as they had been for a century. Bishops, deans, and archdeacons dressed, as they had done for centuries, in apron and gaiters— an apt symbol of an old order which was soon to change as the Church in the sixties was to encounter challenges from all sides. The response to the coming crisis would result in restatements of the Christian faith, the expressions of new views of morality, the radical revision of Church services, a demand for a thorough reorganization of the parochial system and a great debate on the nature of ministry. The sad thing was that although the seeds of these changes were already present, they were largely unperceived. This was particularly true in the realm of morality. The abandonment of moral commitment and the decline in moral authority were already occurring and were beginning to emerge particularly in cultural forms in the theatre, the cinema, books, and broadcasting. Shortly before his death in 1956 Dr Spencer Leeson, Bishop of Peterborough, noted that 'the more I look at the moral state of this country as a whole, the more conscious I feel of a kind of creeping paralysis that is affecting not only the official teaching of moral philosophy...but also the normal standards of value and contested assumptions on which people usually rely'.[31]

---

[31] Quoted, *Spencer Leeson: A Memoir*, by Some of his Friends, 1958, p. 131.

PART II

# THE SIXTIES

# 5

# THE BEWILDERMENT OF
# THE SIXTIES

It was the best of times, it was the worst of times, it
was the age of wisdom, it was the age of foolishness,
it was the epoch of belief, it was the epoch of in-
credulity, it was the season of light, it was the season
of darkness, it was the spring of hope, it was the
winter of despair, we had everything before us, we
had nothing before us, we were all going direct to
heaven, we were all going direct the other way.
                Charles Dickens, *A Tale of Two Cities*, 1859

THE INVASION of Suez by the British in 1956 and the subsequent
withdrawal marked a watershed for Britain. Throughout most of
the world the action was regarded as aggressive. 'Whatever the
purpose of the expedition, judged by its results it was a diplomatic blunder of the highest order.'[1] It was also ironic that at
the very moment that the British forces were attacking Suez
Russian tanks were moving into Bulgaria. The consequences of
Suez for the British people were two-fold. First, it divided the
nation and this division was evident in the reaction of churchmen to the crisis. Speaking in the House of Lords on 31 October,
the Archbishop of Canterbury urged that there was a strong case
for saying that the British action was contrary to the spirit and
letter of the United Nations Charter. 'It has produced a total
political cleavage in Britain', he said, 'and something worse: a
perplexed and alarmed feeling among people who have nothing
to do with politics.' The Archbishop engaged in a ruthless five
minutes cross-examination of the Lord Chancellor, who had
claimed that Egypt was the attacking power.[2] On the other
hand, the Bishop of Exeter told his Diocesan Conference that
Sir Anthony Eden's action revealed 'superb moral courage' and

[1] David Thomson, *England in the Twentieth Century*, 1978, p. 255.
[2] *Hansard* (*House of Lords*), 1 November 1956, pp. 1293-1297; 1352-1354.

that he had led the country 'into an action which is morally courageous and right', and the Bishop of Durham claimed in a sermon that there is 'no doubt that the action taken was of the highest order of courage'. The division of opinion within the nation, however, went deeper than reaction to this particular event. It brought to the surface the growing split in society between established figures, and the avant-garde which had lost patience with what it regarded as the self-confidence, complacency, and superiority of the 'establishment', which had led the country into this situation. The second result of the crisis was that it demonstrated to the British people for the first time that their country had ceased to be a major world power and that the consequence of this meant a radical reappraisement of her relationship with other nations. Psychologically, this weakened the self-confidence and complacency of a section of the nation which, as a result, adopted a defensive and almost fearful attitude towards the avant-garde.

These traumatic events coincided with an increase in wealth for the majority of people on a scale never previously known. Income per head of the population almost doubled between 1952 and 1960 and those who before had been obliged to be thrifty now found within their means consumer goods and domestic appliances they had never dreamed of possessing. Between 1956 and 1960 the country's hire purchase debt rose faster than at any other time before or since. The possession of cars, washing machines, refrigerators, and television sets became the rule rather than the exception in working-class homes and large sums of money were spent on alcohol, tobacco, entertainment, and holidays. Young people used their new-found wealth to purchase long-playing records and transistor radios and 'created for themselves a phantasy world of juke-box delights confined within the realities of late-night cafes... Cultural bulldozers were at work.'[3] Materialism, never far below the surface, came to be regarded as an appropriate way of life. It is not altogether surprising that some young people, while enjoying the benefits of an affluent society, sought to 'drop out', to 'do their own thing', to establish their own 'communes'. The reaction is seen also in the rise of the cult of the psychedelic,

[3] David Thomson, op. cit., p. 272.

of the 'drug scene', of the theatre of cruelty and of the absurd. It was manifested in music, in dress, and in sexual experimentation.

Affluence bestowed independence and confidence which many used, paradoxically, to rail against a society which had produced these very qualities, for the sixties were also an age of disillusionment and protest, typified by John Osborne's play, *Look Back in Anger*, first performed in 1956. The weekly television programmes *Beyond the Fringe* and *That Was the Week that Was*, which eventually attracted an audience of over twelve million, spared from its satire none of the British institutions and 'establishment' figures. There was, however, a dark and more sinister side to this voice of protest. 1958 was the year of the first race riots at Nottingham and at Notting Hill. In the same year the crime rate, particularly for crimes of violence, rose alarmingly; 2,105,631 indictable crimes were known to the police in 1975, compared with 513,339 in 1952, and between 1967 and 1974 the prison population nearly doubled. Nowhere was the voice of protest more strident than among the student bodies, a minority of whom openly claimed to be challenging the very basis of society as it existed in Britain. Here is another paradox. 'There ain't any big, brave causes left', Jimmy Porter had said in *Look Back in Anger*, yet the sixties was a decade of causes and this can be regarded as the positive side of the protest movement. Race, the bomb, Cuba, Biafra, Vietnam, Oxfam, War on Want, Christian Action, Save the Children, Voluntary Service Overseas—all these attracted many young people, while great disasters such as floods, earthquakes, and famine evoked money, service, and self-sacrifice. The plight of the Third World lay consistently on the hearts of young people.

One of the most important phenomena of the sixties was the questioning by many, and the abandonment by some, of traditional values. English society was no longer prepared to accept the Christian framework of a transcendental order or a moral universe of absolute values. Sexual ethics in particular underwent a rapid and drastic change as did also the concept of what constituted 'public decency' with regard to literature, the stage, the cinema, and television. If one event symbolized the change in this field and the polarization which the change produced, it was the 'Profumo Affair'.[4] In 1963 Mr John Profumo resigned as Secretary of State for War because of his association with a group of characters whose sexual activities made astonishing reading and because of his confession of having lied to Parliament. Public reaction, not least among Christians, often exhibited a somewhat unattractive self-righteousness. One does not minimize the seriousness of the moral issues involved by recognizing the language of hysteria and the absence of a sense of proportion. The fact that when Christine Keiler, one of the key figures in the affair, sold her story to the *News of the World* no less than an extra quarter of a million copies were sold might well cast doubt on the sincerity of much of the moralism. The height of hysterical absurdity was reached when an enraged churchman wrote to the *Church Times* putting the blame for the corruption of morals revealed in the Profumo affair on the publication of *Honest to God* and the writings of other Cambridge and South Bank divines.[5] The affair polarized opinion and for the rest of the decade that polarization was to be the background to moral judgements on the changing values and on the notion of acceptable behaviour. 'Permissiveness' for many people began to take the place of the Christian ethic. That is to say that the sixties saw not only a change in behaviour but also a change in the criteria by which behaviour was to be judged. Legislation such as the Obscene Publications Act 1959, the Abortion Act 1967, the Sexual Offences Act 1967, the Theatres Act 1968, and the Divorce Reform Act 1969 contributed to this shift from traditional moral foundations and was regarded by many as granting legal sanction to 'permissiveness'. The notorious prosecution of Penguin Books for the publication of *Lady Chatterley's Lover* in 1960 made the book a best-seller, rivalled only by the sale of the *New English Bible,* published in the same year, and it was followed by such works as William Burroughs' *The Naked Lunch* (1964), Philip Roth's *Portnoy's Complaint* (1969) and H. Selby's *Last Exit from Brooklyn* (1968). On stage and screen the display of nudity, simulated sex, and the use of expressions and 'four-letter words' to shock followed the abolition or modification of

---

[4] Cf. *Lord Denning's Report,* 1963.
[5] Mr. George Goyder, in *Church Times,* 14 January 1963.

censorship. All these trends led many to describe Britain in the sixties as a money-grubbing, sordid, and decadent society. There can be no doubt that there was much unhappiness and disintegration which always accompany rootlessness, the breakdown of authority, and the fevered search for transitory goals and satisfactions. Yet the concern of so many people, especially. the young, for the poor, the underprivileged, and the persecuted both at home and overseas, the search in strange places for spiritual values, the contribution which was made to scientific knowledge and technological achievement, did not betoken an entirely demoralized and decadent society.

As would be expected, the bewilderment of the nation was reflected in the response of Christians to the changes in the sixties. Churchmen shared the general affluence, but they were rightly critical of the materialistic values of so many of their fellow-countrymen. Writers and preachers, while acknowledging the fuller quality of life which affluence could produce, denounced the pursuit of material goods when this was an end in itself or was a means to unworthy goals. On the other hand, there were those who reacted from this negative and denunciatory attitude to the good things of life by seeking to affirm that all good things are the gifts of God and that a proper enjoyment of them was the authentic response of a Christian. It is significant that it was in the sixties that Christian stewardship of time, money, and talents became the official policy of the Church of England and the Central Board of Finance began its campaign for the teaching and acceptance of its principles. Nor was the Church indifferent to the plight of the hungry multitudes in the Third World. Parishes were called upon to inform themselves as fully as possible about the problems of hunger and population growth and to support fully the Freedom from Hunger Campaign which was launched in 1960 by the Food and Agricultural Organisation of the United Nations.

The Church was equally concerned about the increase of violence and drug addiction among young people. Amidst much blanket condemnation there was a growing willingness to seek the causes of these phenomena and to show personal concern for those involved. A significant piece of work was undertaken at St. Anne's, Soho, under the leadership of the Revd Kenneth Leech, who had considerable knowledge and understanding of the drug scene[6] and who saw in 'the counter-culture' a search for spirituality.[7] At the Isle of Wight pop festival in 1970, attended by 250,000 young people, the local rural dean organized an ecumenical team to move among the crowds and to minister to them. In the sixties the Bishop of Birmingham (the Right Revd Leonard Wilson) appointed the Revd David Collyer as his 'Chaplain to the Unattached', to work among the young people in the city who were 'unclubbable' and for whom the Church and the existing youth service seemed to have no relevance or common ground. Collyer saw 'a need for caring ministry in the discotheques, folk music gatherings, the beat clubs, the bowling alleys, the pubs, dance halls and pop concerts—a neglected need as great as that in any other area of pastoral work'.[8] He developed an astonishing ministry to the Rockers and later to the Hell's Angels. He became in a real sense 'one of them', although he never disguised the fact that he was a priest, walking the streets, visiting the night clubs to which young people were attached, on more than one occasion risking death or maiming. He established a club, known as Double Zero, which at one time had a membership of between three and four thousand, and a number of the members began to participate in community work, visiting teams, discussion groups, and religious services. His unconventional ministry earned him opposition in both church and city, but throughout he had the unswerving support of his two Bishops—Leonard Wilson and his successor, Laurence Brown. David Collyer later launched the 'Invest in Birmingham' scheme, the object of which was to place working among the unattached on a wider basis in an attempt to tackle the problem of young people on the streets, not piecemeal, but on a long term basis. 'Conquest by friendship' was the phrase which ruled his life[9] and who can tell what the effect of this friendship may have had on the vast number of young people whom he met?

It was changes in the attitude to sexual morality which evoked from churchmen the loudest volume of criticism and succeeded

---

[6] Cf. Kenneth Leech, *Keep the Faith Baby,* 1973 and *A Practical Guide to the Drug Scene,* 1974.

[7] Kenneth Leech, *Youthquake,* 1973.

[8] David Collyer, *Double Zero,* 1973.

[9] Ibid., p. 210.

most clearly in polarizing attitudes within the Church. Some saw the challenge to traditional ethical concepts as a healthy reaction to what they believed to have been a represssive outlook stemming from a distorted view that all ethical issues were amenable to textbook solutions and judgements. In their view Jesus had set forth ethical principles which had to be interpreted and applied in particular situations and judgement had to take into account the situation as well as the principles. They recognized, too, that in a pluralist society, in which Christians could no longer claim a monopoly, it was unreasonable to expect the State to enforce a morality which only a section of society was prepared to accept. They acknowledged the dangers inherent in the new liberalization of sexual attitudes, but they saw in the trend a recognition of the joy in sex and its vital place in building up relationships which was more in accord with a true Christian view of sexuality than the guilt-ridden and repressive attitude of the Church during most of its history. Other churchmen, however, were deeply disturbed. Such attitudes, they felt, were destructive because they led to a view of sex which was mechanical, biological, and hedonistic, divorced from the love, compassion, and deep personal relationship with which it must be always associated. It dehumanized, debased, and deformed the most fundamental of human actions. Moreover—they affirmed —the new sexual freedom was symptomatic of an impending moral landslide, for morality is all of a piece, a rope with many strands, and to loosen part was to endanger the whole. Secular institutions, therefore, had a duty to guard and enforce this over-arching and given pattern of moral behaviour. Christians who believed otherwise were compromising with the ungodly spirit of the age.

In this period, when authority was being questioned, accepted institutions scorned and traditional restraints and standards cast aside, the Churches were seen by many to be irrelevant survivals from a pre-technological age, and of little social, political, cultural, or moral significance. Their theological and moral teaching seemed anachronistic in the world of emancipated modern man. The Church shared with parents and the government the stigma of being instruments for the suppression of what is natural, joyful, and free. They were institutions which looked back; many of the people of the nation wanted to forget the past and look to a future seen in terms of more possessions, an ever-increasing standard of living, and a life free from restraints. With such a vision of the future, the Gospel message of discipline, sacrifice, and sin cut little ice. Inevitably all this tended to produce a failure of nerve and a lack of confidence within the Church itself, particularly among the ordained ministry, and it was aggravated by the decline in organized religion which was a consequence of uncertainty and confusion among Christians themselves. Between 1960 and 1970 there was a 19 per cent decline in regular church attendance and, whereas 636 men were ordained in 1963, this fell to 373 in 1973. Even more significant was the drop in the number of those recommended for training, which in the same ten years fell by 58.9 per cent. Yet in 1964 a report[10] prepared for Social Survey (Gallup Poll) Ltd revealed that 34 per cent of those interested put 'the priest, vicar or minister' as the person with the greatest influence for good in the community, the second on the list being the doctor with 32 per cent. In theory, therefore, the ordained ministry was still held in esteem, but what comfort was that if in practice he and his ministrations were ignored? All this gave rise to a radical movement within the Church calling for a reappraisement of its theology and ethical teaching, for a reorganization of its structures, for new styles of ministry, for a greater involvement of the Church in the world, for the breaking down of walls of partition between the sacred and the secular and for the removal of the dead hand of traditionalism. Now began the long debates on the nature and purpose of the Church and the nature and purpose of the ordained ministry. The last question was crucial for the morale of many clergymen who were passing through 'a crisis of identity'. Some of them felt they were servicing a Church which was irrelevant, proclaiming a message which was outmoded, leaders of an institution which had ceased to attract and to serve people, whose membership was declining and whose working plant was archaic, expensive, and time-consuming. People turned elsewhere for pastoral guidance, to the psychiatrist, to the social worker, to Alcoholics Anonymous, to the Samaritans, all of which were specialized agencies which dealt with areas in which formerly

[10] *ITV and Religion.*

the clergyman was involved. The result was that many a clergy-man felt that he was 'more often than not an odd man out, involved in great personal tension over what he should or should not do, puzzled over his status and above all isolated and removed from the general life of society'.[11] This led some of them to 'opt out' of the parochial ministry and to exercise 'their Christian idealism in the (better-paid) professions such as the social services, teaching or the BBC'.[12] A notable example was the Revd Nicolas Stacey who in 1969 resigned his benefice of Woolwich. On his appointment he had found the Church with an average congregation of fifty. In the eight years he was rector it doubled and he created a social centre at the Church, opened a discotheque in the crypt and housed the offices of the local Council's social services. He created an ecumenical team minis-try and founded a housing association. But he left the parish on his own initiative as a self-confessed failure and worked first for Oxfam and then for the social services. He felt that he and his team had failed to bring the Gospel to the community and the community to Christ and yet, through his involvement with the community, he had demonstrated that the Church cared.[13] Dr Leslie Paul has asked whether eight years was long enough to tackle such a vast job when so much was against him, set as he was 'in the great secular suburban desert of south-east London, a commuter land with a population of about 1,000,000…cultur-ally a wasteland, one vast subtopia'.[14]

In the chapters that follow many of these issues will be explored in greater detail. What is not always realized, how-ever, is that, behind the changes, the questionings, and the radicalism, lay a fundamental desire to shed what was regarded as the dead hand of the past. No progress is indeed possible for those who are chained to the past; 'as it was in the beginning, is now, and ever shall be' is stultifying, repressive, and a counsel of despair, depriving men of the dynamic necessary for creative and fulfilled life. It is, however, one thing to escape from the

[11] John Bowden, *Voices in the Wilderness,* 1977, p. 67. Written in 1977, it is a more realistic description of the feelings of many clergymen in the sixties.
[12] David Edwards, *Leaders of the Church of England,* 1978, p. 374. For a detailed analysis of the change in the clergyman's role and its effects on morale, cf. Anthony Russell, *The Clerical Profession,* 1980, Chapters 17 to 19.
[13] Cf. Nicolas Stacey, *Who Cares?* 1971.
[14] Leslie Paul, *A Church by Daylight,* 1973, p. 176.

dead weight of history; it is quite another to attempt to destroy the past in the supposed interest of the future. During the sixties the continual spoliation of the countryside and the destruction of many buildings of architectural and historical importance was visible evidence of a contempt for the past and a desire to destroy it—an attempt at self-inflicted amnesia. Yet a people without a past is like a man who has lost his memory— impoverished, sad, and an object of pity. Religion is one of the means whereby man is kept in touch with history and it provides him with occasions whereby he can re-establish his relation with the past and bring past, present, and future together within the context of eternity. It is a cause of thankfulness that the people of this country failed—as they were perhaps bound to fail—to kill the past, with the result that the seventies saw a revival of interest and involvement in past history and in the roots of our civilization.

# 6

# THEOLOGICAL AND MORAL RADICALISM

Away then with that cowardly language which some of us are apt to indulge in when we speak of one period as more dangerous than another; when we wish we were not born into the age of revolutions, or complain that the time of quiet belief is past, and that henceforth every man must ask himself whether he has any ground to stand upon or whether all beneath him is hollow. We are falling into the temptation when we thus lament over it. We are practically confessing that the Evil Spirit is the Lord of all; that times and seasons are in his hands. Let us clear our minds from every taint of that blasphemy. God has brought us into this time; He and not ourselves or some dark demon. If we are not fit to cope with that which He has prepared for us, we should have been utterly unfit for any condition that we imagine for ourselves. In this time we are to live and wrestle, and in no other.... If easy belief is impossible, it is that we may learn what belief is, and in whom it is to be placed.

F. D. Maurice, *Sermons on the Lord's Prayer*, 1848

## 1. Dr Ramsey becomes Archbishop

IN JANUARY 1961 the resignation of Geoffrey Fisher as Archbishop of Canterbury was announced. 'I am convinced that day by day my wisdom increases', he modestly told Convocation, 'and I am also satisfied that my stock of patience diminishes and that is why I feel the time has come.'[1] He later declared that he had led 'the Church as far as I could along a very difficult road in order that it might recover a proper sense of co-operative authority. I thought that now we had got to a point when the

---

[1] *Chronicle of Convocation*, January 1961, p. 2.

brow of the hill had been topped, and that I could without injury to the cause leave the task to others to complete.'[2] After his resignation he went to live at Trent Rectory in Dorset where he acted as 'unpaid curate' to the incumbent and proceeded to misuse his retirement. 'Few figures prominent in public life can have made themselves such an embarrassment to their successors.'[3]

Most churchmen regarded Dr Michael Ramsey's appointment to Canterbury as inevitable.[4] He possessed none of the administrative gifts of his predecessor, but he was above all 'a man of God' and a theologian, having held the chair of divinity at Durham University from 1940 to 1950 before becoming Regius Professor of Divinity at Cambridge. Michael Ramsey's scholarship was never an arid intellectuality for he was always concerned to show the relevance of theology for the modern world. He possessed the ability to assess new ideas, to sift them, and to help people to see old truths from new angles. He came from the catholic tradition of the Church of England and possessed deep theological convictions about the nature of the Church, its ministry, and its sacraments, but his wide outlook and deep charity enabled him to appreciate and work with those with different theological convictions. Basically, however, 'Michael is a simple man, who loves his Lord and wants others to do so too'[5] and amid the upheavals of the sixties he never allowed the Church of England to forget the priority of the spiritual element in its work. The rare combination of learning, depth, and wisdom with simplicity, humility, and love, sometimes disguised both the shrewdness of his mind and the depth and strength of his utterances. Acute shyness, a somewhat artificial mode of speaking and the absence of small talk, coupled with his patriarchal appearance and a number of mild eccentricities, gave to some an appearance of remoteness from the modern world. He never became a popular figure and appealed more to the clergy than to the laity. Shy and hesitant though he may have been, in speaking of theology and spirituality he displayed the note of

[2] Quoted William Purcell, *Fisher of Lambeth*, p. 291.
[3] Preface to *Crockford's Clerical Directory*, 85th Issue, 1975, p. xii.
[4] Although there is evidence that the Bishop of London, Dr Stopford, was a candidate favoured by some. Cf. Harold Evans, *Downing Street Diary*, 1981, p. 134.
[5] Eric Treacy, quoted in John Peart-Binns, *Eric Treacy*, 1980, p. 192.

authority of one who had grasped the fundamentals. So often in the history of the Church God raises to leadership the right man for the times. No one could have led the Church through its administrative reorganization in the post-war years better than Geoffrey Fisher. Amid the theological upheavals and the spiritual questionings of the sixties, Michael Ramsey displayed the theological and spiritual gifts required for leadership in such a period, and time was to show that it was his steadfastness of faith which was to undergird the Church of England during the years of his primacy.

Dr Donald Coggan, Bishop of Bradford, succeeded to the Archbishopric of York and thus an evangelical balanced the churchmanship of his fellow primate. Like Dr Ramsey he was a scholar and a man of deep personal spirituality, but his pastoral gifts were greater and he possessed more of 'the common touch'. If such comparisons are valid, he was the layman's archbishop whereas Ramsey was the clergyman's archbishop. 'Both the archbishops of the Church of England', wrote the editor of *Crockford's*, 'are men whose training is primarily that of a theologian—but who also show real understanding of the present situation of the church and real care for the right and effective understanding of its pastoral and evangelistic work'.[6]

Dr Ramsey was enthroned in Canterbury Cathedral on 27 June 1961. In his sermon[7] he spoke of three matters which were of concern to him as he embarked on his primacy. First, the Church of England 'must reach out in the quest for unity, for Christ is longing that there will go with him not separated bands of followers, but, as one band, all those whose heart God has touched'. Secondly, in England the link between Church and State is of service to the community, 'but in that service and in rendering to God the things that are God's we ask for a greater freedom in ordering and in the urgent revising of our forms of worship'. Thirdly, the Church must be involved in the community and to this end 'we shall strive to penetrate the world of industry, of science, of art and literature, of sight and sound, and in this penetration we must approach as listeners as well as teachers'. Then came the characteristic note of spirituality, for undergirding all endeavours was the need for 'a

---

[6] Preface to 79th Issue, 1962.       [7] *Whose Hearts God has Touched*, 1961.

constant detachment, a will to go apart and wait upon God, in silence, lest by our very busyness we should rob ourselves and rob others of the realisation of God's presence'.

## 2. The Debate about God

'In the midst of a post-war society absorbed in making money and seeking pleasure', wrote David Edwards, 'the Established Church found its organization in disarray and its message uncertain, and the process of dechristianization seemed to be taking another great leap forward into a world where the death of God would be finally acknowledged.'[8] The first rumblings were heard in 1962 when a group of Cambridge theologians published a volume of essays under the title, *Soundings: Essays Concerning Christian Understanding*, edited by Alec Vidler, Dean of King's College, Cambridge. These were the result of the private discussion of a group of members of the divinity faculty[9] who were concerned about the neglect of the fundamental questions concerning Christian belief. They expressed very plainly some of the problems inherent in Christian doctrine, New Testament studies, Christian ethics, the philosophy of religion, and the relation between religion and science, but they recognized that the time was not ripe for 'major works of theological construction or reconstruction....It is a time for making soundings, not charts or maps'.[10] Their work represented an attempt to rouse Anglican theology from its dogmatic slumbers to face the important and difficult intellectual problems that hitherto the Church had neglected.

It is doubtful whether the slumbers of many were unduly disturbed by this symposium, but the following year Churchmen were startled into full wakefulness by the publication of *Honest to God* by John Robinson, Bishop of Woolwich. This was partly due to unplanned circumstances. The editor of the *Observer* invited Bishop Robinson to write an article to replace one that

---

[8] David Edwards, *Leaders of the Church of England, 1828-1978*, 1971 Ed., p. 343.

[9] They included Howard Root, Dean of Emmanuel College, John Habgood, Vice-Principal of Westcott House and later to be Bishop of Durham, Harry Williams, Dean of Trinity College, Hugh Montefiore, Dean of Gonville and Caius College and later to be Bishop of Birmingham, Geoffrey Lampe, Ely Professor of Divinity, and Alec Vidler himself.

[10] P. ix.

had not been sent in. The result was that there appeared a front-page article with the startling title, 'Our Image of God must Go'. This was on the Sunday before the book's publication and it created immense public interest, particularly as its author was a bishop and the book was a cheap paperback.

John Robinson had already attained a certain notoriety for his support of the publication of *Lady Chatterley's Lover* and for his appearance at the trial, where he expressed his view that Lawrence was trying to portray the sex relation as a form of holy communion. He was later rebuked by Archbishop Fisher for thinking that he could take part in the trial without being 'a stumbling-block and a cause of offence to many ordinary Christians'. Prior to this the bishop had been known chiefly as a New Testament scholar and a protagonist of liturgical reform. *Honest to God*, written very quickly by a bishop recovering from a slipped disc, was in some ways a moving book for it was permeated by a passionate sincerity and a deep concern for those who were unable to accept the traditional Christian position. Having been dean of a Cambridge college and a suffragan bishop in a diocese where the Church had been losing ground rapidly, Robinson was in a unique position to know and understand many of the questions addressed to the Church by the 'outsider'. He saw himself as fulfilling the function of a bishop in a missionary situation. The book was not the production of a frustrated and thwarted man, but of an honest and inquiring mind, with no intent to shock or hurt. A certain naïvety and a failure to understand the ways of the world and the power of publicity may have prevented him from seeing all the consequences of his action.

The book was not written in a popular style and was a difficult and often confused piece of theological and philosophical writing. Indeed the author himself has been reported as remarking, 'I do not fully understand myself all that I am trying to say'. Drawing much of his inspiration from the German theologians, Paul Tillich and Dietrich Bonhoeffer, his main thesis was that we now live in the period of man's 'coming of age', by which he meant that man had reached an intellectual and psychological maturity in which religion and its attempts to keep men in leading-strings are dismissed as childish. The old images of God are no longer adequate and pictures of God as 'up there' or 'out there' are unhelpful. Instead, making use of depth psychology, Robinson argued that we should think of God in terms of 'depth', as 'the ground of our being'. We live in a world in which we no longer have to turn to God as an explanation of what happens or as a means of meeting our needs. Man never meets God as it were directly, for God 'is to be found only in, with and under the conditional relationships of this life'. The traditional view of the coming of Jesus—the notion of a God 'who visits the earth in the person of his son'—is a notion incredible to man 'come of age'. What the New Testament really tells us is that if we look at the man Jesus we see God. 'Here was more than a man: here was a window into God at work.' Jesus is united with 'the ground of his being' because he was utterly concerned with other people. He was 'the man for others'. The purpose of worship is not withdrawal from the world to be with God, but to make men more sensitive to 'the depth in the common', to 'the beyond in the midst', 'to the Christ in the hungry, the needy, the homeless and the prisoners'. Morals ought not to subordinate individual relationships to some external moral sanction or code, for 'compassion for persons overrides all law'.

This was indeed a strange amalgam. Much that Robinson affirmed as new about God as the ground of our being was in fact commonplace in the teaching of many spiritual writers from the earliest times. His emphasis on 'the Christ for others' and the finding of God in personal relationships was orthodox theology. But many of his statements bore little resemblance to the traditional Christian gospel. Nevertheless, he was in fact passing on to the public what some theologians had been teaching for some time. The book aroused an immense amount of interest in religion among many people and took theology right out of its old academic remoteness. Indeed Bernard Levin has commented that 'he had started a theological discussion, in a profoundly untheological time, on a scale that had certainly not been seen since the Tractarians'.[11] In its first year 350,000 copies were sold and in the years following, in many different countries and many different languages, the total came to well over a million. There is no doubt that it led many clergy and lay people to think

---

[11] *The Pendulum Years*, 1970, p. 108.

out and discuss what they meant by the traditional statements of religious belief. To others the fact that such questions *were* debatable brought a sense of relief and liberation. Such an un-radical and distinguished evangelical as Max Warren, Canon of Westminster, having read the manuscript of the book, warmly encouraged John Robinson to publish it.[12]

That, however, was not the typical reaction. What enlightened and heartened a number of Christians shocked many others who greeted the book with cries of dismay, some of them hysterical and savage. A leading daily newspaper commented: 'The faith-ful are dismayed. The indifferent maintain their indifference. The unbelievers mock, or seize the opportunity to extend and to re-inforce unbelief.' The *Church Times* complained that 'it is not every day that a bishop goes on public record as apparently denying almost every Christian doctrine of the Church in which he holds office'.[13] There were those who deplored the under-mining of the faith of those they called 'the simple believers' and who did not realize that the truly faithful, however simple, cannot be made less faithful by honest discussion. Indeed, the hysterical reaction of many was distressing because it indicated 'a deep insecurity unworthy of a Christian's attitude to truth'.[14] The controversy tended to polarize both clergy and laity into radicals and conservatives, cutting across the traditional division between catholics and evangelicals.

The Archbishop of Canterbury was urged to take action. One Scottish lady declared that 'if the Archbishop of Canterbury doesn't unfrock him, I and the women of England will'.[15] It was fortunate for the Church of England that it had Michael Ramsey as its archbishop at this crucial time. His predecessor, in a per-sonal letter from his rural retreat in Dorset was to complain in 1967 of the lack of a 'firm lead of the right sort from Church House or Lambeth'. What sort of lead Fisher himself would have given is indicated when, in the same letter, he maintained that 'more than 50% of the unsettlement is due to publicists of one kind and another crying their own wares or decrying the wares of others ad nauseam', and referred to 'the old danger of

[12] F. W. Dillistone, *Into All the World: A Biography of Max Warren*, 1980, p. 155.
[13] 'Summary of the News', 22 March 1963.
[14] Frank Wright, *The Pastoral Nature of the Ministry*, 1980, p. 43.
[15] Quoted, Bernard Levin, op. cit., p. 107.

schemers covering up their real motives and purposes and so deceiving the faithful'.[16] Michael Ramsey's way was much more constructive, although he later admitted that initially he was unsympathetic. In 1981 he gave Dr Mervyn Stockwood, Bishop of Southwark, his considered opinion in retrospect. 'My initial reaction', he wrote 'was very harsh and very unsympathetic and "over-reacting". Very soon, within a few months, I came to see the matter differently and with, I think, more understanding, and I blame myself for my initial attitude.'[17] In his presidential address to the Convocation of Canterbury in May 1963 the Archbishop began by saying that the questions discussed in the book were real questions and should not be debated in an obscurantist spirit. He confessed, however, that he had been 'specially grieved at the method chosen by the bishop for presenting his ideas to the public', and he doubted whether 'any argument could show that the doctrine which so far emerges [from the book] is the same as the doctrine of the Church'.[18] That Dr Ramsey took the book seriously is shown by the fact that he had already published a booklet, *Image Old and New*,[19] which was followed in 1964 by a second pamphlet, *Beyond Religion*. Both works displayed considerable sympathy with Robinson's theological intentions and with the categories he employed.

We need to see if there are some who are helped by thinking not about God above us in heaven...but about the deep-down meaning of human life in terms of love....As a Church we need to be grappling with the questions and trials of belief in the modern world....We state and commend the faith only in so far as we go out and put ourselves with loving sympathy inside the doubts of the doubting, the questions of the questioners, and the loneliness of those who have lost their way.[20]

*Honest to God* was not the only piece of radical theology to be published in 1963. In the Lent term of that year four open lectures were given by members of the University of Cambridge which were published under the title, *Objections to Christian*

[16] Letter from Fisher to Eric Treacy, Bishop of Wakefield, January 1967, quoted John Peart-Binns, op. cit., p. 169.

[17] Quoted, Mervyn Stockwood, *Chanctonbury Ring*, 1982, pp. 150-1.

[18] *Chronicle of Convocation*, May 1963.

[19] 1963.

[20] *Image Old and New*, p. 14.

*Belief*.[21] These lectures, which dealt in turn with the moral, psychological, historical, and intellectual objections to traditional belief, attracted gatherings of over a thousand undergraduates and for several weeks the published work was a top-selling book and was translated into several languages. The same year the American theologian Paul Van Buren published *The Secular Meaning of the Gospel,* which rejected theism on the logical positivist's premiss that statements about God, who is beyond empirical experience, are meaningless. Jesus Christ, however, still had great meaning for the world, not in religious or theistic terms, but as the perfect expression of freedom, for in him alone there is seen perfect freedom—freedom from tradition, from fear, from the pressures of society, from self. Herein lay his authority, and Easter was the moment when the followers of Jesus awoke to the fact of his freedom and were liberated so as to share in it among themselves and with others. The book provoked a strong reply from E. L. Mascall in *The Secularization of Christianity,*[22] which also contained a critical assessment of *Honest to God.* In 1965 *The Secular City*, by another American, Harvey Cox, was published, describing modern technological culture not as a contradiction of biblical truth but as its genuine fulfilment. The doctrine of creation liberates man from superstition and Jesus is the bestower of freedom to all men in every situation and is the personification of the Kingdom of God. Man's fulfilment is now to be found in the secular city; the Church, in its capacity as servant of the city, must be a community which is in the process of liberation from 'compulsive patterns of behaviour based on mistaken images of the world'. Misleading metaphysics and irrelevant otherworldliness must be discarded so that men may meet God in the only place where he can be found—'in the human relationships and duties of secular life'.[23]

The ultimate in theological radicalism found expression also from American theologians. Unlike the works of Van Buren and

---

[21] By D. M. Mackinnon, H. A. Williams, A. R. Vidler, J. S. Besant, with an introduction by A. R. Vidler.

[22] 1965.

[23] It ought to be added that Harvey Cox, like some of his fellow leaders of the secular style of theology, later changed his mind and placed a much higher value on religion. Cf. Harvey Cox, *Feast of Fools*, 1969.

Harvey Cox, those written by the 'death of God' theologians, T. J. J. Altizer and William Hamilton, were not read so widely or received with such approbation in Britain. Altizer contended that God died when Jesus came, there being no further need for him. Since then he has been wholly immersed in history, becoming progressively incarnate in the universal body of humanity.[24] William Hamilton, unlike Altizer, saw the twentieth century, not the first century, as the period of the death of God. It is a modern phenomenon and there is no point in waiting for God, for God will never come. Man must create his own meaning and for this Christ can still provide the key.[25]

Dr Ramsey had the ability to analyse seriously radical theological concepts with sympathy and understanding, to interpret them to the public and to subject them to judicious and sometimes devastating criticism. We have referred to the two booklets he wrote in response to *Honest to God*. In 1966 he devoted his Holland Lectures to a study of the other-worldly and this-worldly aspects of Christianity.[26] He discussed the problems of language and imagery in describing the world above and beyond the temporal and—as against the radicals—asserted the Church's commitment to a primacy of worship and prayer. On the other hand, Christians 'by love and charity within the temporal order' show their heavenly citizenship and 'to contract out from that love and duty is not to enhance the heavenly citizenship but to belie it'. In 1969 he wrote *God, Christ and the World*, in which he examined the theology of Van Buren, Harvey Cox, Rudolf Bultmann and the 'death of God' theologians and concluded that the traditional supernatural character of Christianity can only be asserted if we are ready to learn from the contemporary conflicts, the chief lesson being that transcendence must be realized in the midst of secular life and not apart from it.

The response to the theological radicalism of the sixties revealed something of the intellectual poverty of many of the clergy. Those who had maintained their theological studies took

---

[24] Cf. *The Gospel of Christian Atheism*, 1966.

[25] Cf. *The New Essence of Christianity*, 1966. Cf. also William Hamilton and T. J. J. Altizer, *Radical Theology and the Death of God*, 1966 and T. Ogletree, *The Death of God Controversy*, 1966.

[26] *Sacred and Secular*, 1967.

the spate of radical publications in their stride for they were aware that these were bringing to the surface questions which had been asked over a long period. The response also showed the complacency with which Christians had accepted uncritically the theological statements of the faith. Consequently, for many the new ferment could be seen only as a threat, an undermining of faith, and as the first signs of the disintegration of the Church. On the other hand, it compelled other Christians to ask questions which otherwise they might never have asked, to re-examine and re-think issues which they had accepted uncritically, with the result that their basic faith was strengthened and they were enabled to distinguish between essential and inessential articles of belief. Certainly the Church of England was never to be the same again.

In the midst of the theological ferment there emerged a new voice. Teilhard de Chardin was a Roman Catholic priest who was also a scientist. On palaeontology and other scientific subjects the Papacy allowed him freedom to publish what he wished, but his theological writings were banned until his death in 1955. From 1959 onwards a stream of books by Teilhard poured from the press, beginning with *The Phenomenon of Man*[27] and a veritable 'cult' gathered round his name. He expounded the divine process of creation and salvation as evolutionary. The early stages of what he described as man's progress into the 'noosphere' consisted of the emergence of man and the development within him of rationality and self-consciousness. Within the 'noosphere' all things and persons will be gathered up into Christ and God will be all in all. His work has been helpful to many because it points towards the unity of all things and all people in Christ, looking beyond our present differences of culture and theology.

In 1967 the Archbishops' Commission on Christian Doctrine was established for the purpose of considering and advising upon doctrinal questions submitted to it by the archbishops. It was not the kind of body to reach immediate agreement on many matters. The diversity of the membership of the Commission was great, for it contained two evangelicals, two catholics,

---

[27] For a list of his nineteen works published between 1959 and 1970, cf. Vernon Sproxton, *Teilhard de Chardin*, 1971, p. 120.

two radicals, three professional philosophers, five professors of theology, and only one member who was also a parish priest. Ian Ramsey, Bishop of Durham, was chairman. One of the subjects to which Archbishop Ramsey suggested that the Commission might give its attention was the apparent lack of theological cohesion in the Church, but it made no progress in this field. He also proposed that the Commission should consider the difficulties experienced over the place and authority of the Thirty-Nine Articles of Religion, and in due course it completed this task.[28] Apart from this, the other issues which came before it were hardly momentous, however important they may have been for the life of the Church. They dealt with the question whether it was theologically necessary for extra bread and wine required at the Eucharist to be consecrated by a spoken formula, with certain aspects of the Eucharist,[29] with the nature of prayer,[30] and with prayers for the departed.[31]

### 3. 'The Journey Inwards'

It was inevitable that the theological climate of the sixties should challenge traditional notions of spirituality. Writing seven years after the close of the decade Kenneth Leech could affirm that the publication of *Honest to God* 'represented the lowest point of collapse of the spiritual tradition, the climax of a process by which Christian people, including bishops, lost touch with and grew ignorant of their tradition and their spiritual history'.[32] Yet, paradoxically, the decade also saw the birth of a revival of spirituality in unexpected places, while radical criticism and healthy scepticism had a purifying effect upon the tradition it challenged.

There were three reasons why the validity of prayer in its traditional form was challenged. The first derived from certain characteristics of the modern age. So many of the powers once ascribed to God were now in the hands of man who had achieved a considerable mastery over his environment. As a result, the popular concept of intercession as a specific request for the inter-

---

[28] *Ascription and Assent to the 39 Articles*, 1968; cf. below p. 235.
[29] *Thinking about the Eucharist*, 1972.
[30] *Our Understanding of Prayer*, 1971.
[31] *Prayer and the Departed*, 1971.
[32] *Soul Friend: A Study of Spirituality*, 1977, p. 139.

vention in the human situation by an absentee God was unacceptable. For others the technological age, with its increasing
ability to satisfy man's material requirements, removed the
sense of need and dependence upon a power other than that
possessed by man himself. The second reason was a consequence
of the current debate about God. For some, prayer was regarded
as a form of escapism leading men to look to a mythological God
'up there', thus distracting them from their primary task of
responsibility for the world and of discovering God 'in the
human situation'. There was much talk of 'holy worldliness',
while some denied the very existence of 'religious experience',
preferring to speak only of human experience interpreted by
a Christian perspective. Whereas traditional spirituality gave
primacy to the First Commandment, from which inspiration for
the Second will flow, the new spirituality began with the Second
and sometimes evaded the First. John Robinson had affirmed
that prayer is to be defined 'in terms of penetration through the
world to God rather than of withdrawal from the world to God'.
He wrote of 'prayer in the midst of life', of 'seeing the diary in
depth and preparing on the telephone to meet our God', of the
test of prayer being how far it made a person sensitive to 'the
beyond in our midst'.[33] It is significant that the spiritual diary[34]
of a former Secretary General of the United Nations, Dag Hammarskjöld, was widely recommended. Hammarskjöld saw Christ
and his cross as the symbol of the Christian reaching out to the
world and many seized with approval upon his statement that
'in our era, the road to holiness necessarily passes through the
world of action'.[35] What was not realized was that Hammarskjöld had been fascinated by the mystery of God and that it was
the writings of the great medieval mystics which had led him to
return to the beliefs of his youth. It is interesting that the only
book he had with him on his visit to the Congo, which ended
fatally, was *The Imitation of Christ*.[36]

In 1967 Douglas Rhymes, a Canon of Southwark, published
*Prayer in the Secular City*, in which he attempted to relate John

[33] *Honest to God*, pp. 97, 86, 101, 90.
[34] *Markings*, 1964.
[35] Ibid., p. 108.
[36] For further information, cf. Henry Van Dusen, *Dag Hammarskjöld*, 1967, and
Gustaf Aulen, *Dag Hammarskjöld's White Book*, 1969.

Robinson's theology to the prayer life of modern man. It was a work of considerable merit and insight which, not only helped many at the time of its publication, but also had an enduring value. Another work which revived prayer for many people was Michael Quoist's *Prayers of Life*. These prayers were the product of a Roman Catholic group which met at Le Havre in the early fifties and the work was published in this country in 1963. The prayers were theologically orthodox and they used the traditional techniques of meditation, but—unlike the classical tradition, where the material lay in the world in which Jesus lived—the novelty of their approach was that they began wherever a man happens to be—spending money, on the subway or in the stadium, looking at a pornographic magazine or suffering from an empty stomach. Quoist thus helped many to see the ordinary incidents of the contemporary world as 'signs' pointing beyond themselves to God. It was because these prayers related the gospel so relevantly to actual situations in the contemporary world that they gained their tremendous vogue.

The third reason for questioning traditional spirituality was the limitations which it seemed to place on the concept of prayer. Too often spirituality appeared to be a special kind of activity for special places at special times. It was linked with a formalism and schemetization which was foreign to the spontaneity and directness in spirituality which was being sought in the sixties. Not surprisingly, 'little books' on the spiritual life, which had nourished the spirituality of earlier generations, were despised for forcing people into methods which took no account of individual temperament and which appeared to apply external rules rather than to meet inner needs. There emerged a trend towards simplicity, by-passing structures and schemes. For example, the traditional progress of the spiritual life from the purgative, through the illuminative, to the intuitive came to be regarded not so much as a successive progress in a journey as expressions of different paths for different people. Dom John Chapman's dictum to 'pray as you can, and don't try to pray as you can't'[37] was much heard. Again, many saw meditative prayer as taking a subordinate place to contemplative prayer,

---

[37] *The Spiritual Letters of Dom John Chapman*, ed. Dom Roger Hudleston, 1938, p. 25.

partly because the former raised distracting intellectual questions about the material meditated upon, whereas contemplation is non-mental absorbed attention upon the object. Moreover, the accepted view that contemplation was an advanced stage of prayer was disproved by experience. The result was that at the end of the sixties the writings of Anthony Bloom[38] and Monica Furlong[39] began to introduce many to contemplative prayer. The writings of the Christian mystics appeared in paperback and, in particular, many discovered Julian of Norwich, the fourteenth-century mystic, and found in her *Revelations of Divine Love* a naturalness of approach to God in contemplation which matched their own longing.

The clergy were not immune from the general disenchantment with traditional spirituality. Middle-aged clergymen, trained to observe a rule of life, including the recitation of the Divine Office of Morning and Evening Prayer, private prayer, and regular intercession, found the practice of a life-time challenged. Some, who were honest, found relief in the admission that what they had been doing for so long had acquired a formality which was spiritually deadening. Others were worried and puzzled. Among the younger clergy there was reluctance to apply rules or schemes to their prayer life and there was evidence that many priests gave up saying the Daily Office and limited their private devotion to intercession for the affairs of the day, although for most of them the Eucharist remained an anchor. Indeed, the Offices were in danger of being completely displaced by the Eucharist as the only expression of corporate piety and as the one spiritual centre which prevented the disintegration of spiritual life. The work on the Divine Office produced by the Liturgical Commission was greatly welcomed with its wider range of material, its smaller amount of psalmody and scripture reading and its provision of a much shorter alternative Office.

While Christians were criticizing traditional spirituality on the ground of its remoteness from the world in the modern age, there was evidence elsewhere of a renewed interest in spiritual issues in reaction to the feeling that the materialism of the modern world diminished man's humanity. This was found

[38] E.g. *Living Prayer*, 1966, *School for Prayer*, 1970.
[39] *Contemplating Now*, 1971, *Travelling In*, 1973.

particularly among certain sections of young people. The emergence of 'the hippies', who attempted to 'drop out' of society and to seek, often through drugs, a mental state of calm and sensual perception, was one example. Others turned to Eastern mysticism, the psychedelic and the occult. Kenneth Leech has written: 'The particular form of the "traditional wisdom of mankind" which was being rediscovered and re-experienced in the 1960s was eastern rather than western, Hindu rather than Christian, non-rational rather than rational, occult rather than prophetic, and emotional rather than intellectual.'[40] Usually it was a spirituality devoid of God and without morality. For many young people individual morality appeared to be less important than social justice and they failed to trace the connection between personal ethical transgression and the evils of society, and in their spiritual practices the search was more for a state of mind than for communion with God. Whatever critique Christians might apply, however, it had to be recognized that a considerable number of young people were searching for spiritual experience in revolt from the bankruptcy of the materialism of western society, were concerned for peace, justice, and freedom, and found in their own groups and communes the loving and tolerant relationships which they were unable to discover elsewhere. The paradox was that so many were seeking a transcendental dimension for human life precisely at the time when the Church was questioning the validity of the transcendental. Nevertheless, the Church was not unscathed by the youth concerns of the sixties and the following decade witnessed the upsurge of the Jesus movement and the charismatic movement, in both of which young people were greatly involved and which were characterized by that unconventionality and spontaneity which had hitherto been conspicuous by their absence from institutional religion and which many during the sixties sought but seldom found.

The religious orders in the Church of England were not insulated from the contemporary debate and heart-searching on the nature of spirituality, the relation between the sacred and the secular, and the reform of the liturgy. Some religious came to the conclusion that the spirituality of monasticism was no longer an authentic vocation; some saw that their vocation lay instead

[40] *Soul Friend: A Study in Spirituality*, 1977, p. 10.

in teaching or social work; some chose the more conventional life of marriage and family; some were disillusioned by the passing of a liturgy which had been maintained since long before their profession. The result was that in the sixties many monks and nuns sought release from their vows and a return to secular life. The period passed and the seventies saw a halt to the exodus and a greater degree of stability. The number of vocations increased, but there were two differences. First, women appeared to be called by God in greater numbers than men and it was the enclosed women's orders which attracted novices. Secondly, men chose to be friars rather than monks. This all had a profound effect upon the older established orders, which were faced with a crisis of membership and finance, with the result that some houses were closed, members migrated from smaller houses, and there emerged a greater diversification of ministry within the orders. Most religious houses revised their liturgy in such a way that quality mattered more than quantity. Constitutions were revised to exclude some of the petty regulations of the past and there were simplifications of time-tables and modes of dress. The Communities became more open to visitors and more knowledgeable about the life of the world. It was significant how many of them became centres which attracted considerable numbers of lay people seeking quietness and tranquillity.

## 4. Ethical Concerns

In *Honest to God* John Robinson had asserted that 'nothing of itself could be labelled as wrong'. Our moral decisions must be guided by the actual relationships between the persons concerned at a particular time in a particular situation, and 'compassion for *persons* overrides all law'. 'The only intrinsic evil is lack of love.'[41] John Robinson's 'new morality' was given systematic statement by Joseph Fletcher, whose *Situational Ethics* was published in this country in 1966. In this work and in earlier articles Fletcher emphasized that the Christian ethic is not a scheme of codified conduct but a purposive attempt to relate love to particular relational situations. John Robinson developed his views in a series of lectures delivered in Liverpool Cathedral

[41] Pp. 116-18.

in 1963, under the title, *Christian Morals Today*,[42] in which he maintained that 'in Christian ethics the only pure statement is the command to love: every other injunction depends on it and is an explication or application of it'. Moreover, 'I believe that an ethic will have authority for most of our generation only as it is empirical and starts firmly from the data of actual personal relationships as they now are.'[43] For Joseph Fletcher, John Robinson, and their followers this view of morality was far more searching, demanding, and responsible than a 'code morality'. The controversy which centred upon 'situational ethics' tended to polarize into those who would see all moral issues in terms of rule and law and those who affirmed that all rules and laws must be tempered and modified by particular human situations. The strength of the 'new morality' lay in its concern to do 'the loving thing' and to temper the harshness of legalism by sensitive interpretation 'in the situation'. Its weakness lay in a false optimism of human nature which assumed that individuals were rational enough to distinguish between emotional response to a situation and an intelligent appraisal of the ethical implications of that situation.

The sixties certainly saw much debate about the fundamental nature of ethical action, although the focus was largely on sexual morality. Nevertheless, there were other important discussions, not least on the ethical implications of the advances in medicine, covering such issues as brain surgery, heart transplants, sterilization, the 'test-tube baby', abortion, and euthanasia. The ethics of scientific research and the social responsibilities of scientists and technologists for the use to which their discoveries were put was another source of moral discussion. A leading figure in the Christian debate between religion on the one hand and medicine and science on the other was Ian Ramsey, formerly Nolloth Professor of the Philosophy of Religion in the University of Oxford, who became Bishop of Durham in 1966.[44] This diminutive figure was a man of immense moral and intellectual stature who had a unique appeal and became the most influential figure on the episcopal bench. Alongside academic brilliance

---

[42] Published in 1964; reprinted in *Christian Freedom in a Permissive Society*, 1970, pp. 7ff.

[43] Pp. 16, 37.

[44] Cf. David Edwards, *Ian Ramsey*, 1973.

he had a gift for understanding working people, who sensed that he was a man who cared. Possessing some of the characteristics of William Temple, it was widely expected that he would succeed Michael Ramsey as Archbishop of Canterbury.

Ian Ramsey saw his vocation as a builder of bridges between theology and modern problems, between religion and science, between Christianity and philosophy, and he was deeply interested in the relationship between Christian ethics and the moral issues raised by medicine, industry, and politics. 'The theologian justifies himself', he wrote, 'only in terms of the issues and problems which the world raises'.[45] Again, 'the time is ripe for inter-professional, inter-disciplinary study' to produce 'balanced decisions and a technology of fulfilment and release'.[46] He played a leading part in the creation of the Institute of Religion and Medicine in 1964, bringing together clergy, doctors, and others in the study of health and healing both medically and theologically. He became chairman in 1971. His search for reconciliation between religion and science is seen in a series of lectures he gave in 1966 and which were later published,[47] while other works[48] illustrate his role as a builder of bridges. His most influential publication was *Religious Language*,[49] which was an attempt to show that the contemporary philosophical interest in language could illuminate the problems of theology and to defend the objectivity of that to which the Christian responded.

Ian Ramsey was not destined to have the opportunity of being considered for the archbishopric. He died in 1972 and it was generally acknowledged that he killed himself with overwork. David Edwards's view was that some of those responsible for the appointment to Canterbury would have hesitated because of his theological and political liberalism.[50] If he had gone to Canterbury would he have made a good archbishop? In spite of his undoubted greatness, our knowledge now of the over-worked life which led to his death must cause us to doubt this, and it was Trevor Beeson's judgement that 'in retrospect it can be seen

[45] Quoted Edwards, op. cit., p. 65.        [46] Quoted, ibid., p. 72.
[47] *Religion and Science: Conflict and Synthesis*, 1966.
[48] He edited a number of symposia, including *Biology and Personality*, 1965, *Ethics and Contemporary Philosophy*, 1966, and *Science and Personality*, 1966.
[49] 1957.        [50] Op. cit., pp. 12-13.

that even had Ian Ramsey gone to Canterbury a man of his temperament who could never decline an invitation would have been unable to survive the constant pressures of the office'.[51]

## 5. Religion in Schools

The theological and ethical climate of the sixties had a considerable effect on the theory and practice of education. Teachers found themselves teaching children who were influenced by the cynicism and the materialistic assumptions of contemporary society, and those concerned with religious education were themselves uncertain and confused by the new theologians and moralists. At the same time Harold Loukes was advocating, in place of the Bible-centred approach to religious teaching, 'the problem-centred approach', which meant the discussion of a wide range of personal, political, and moral problems in the light of Christian insight and experience.[52] R. J. Goldman propounded the thesis that up to about the mental age of thirteen children think in a concrete way and are not capable of abstract thought. Religion ought therefore to be taught to young children through a series of 'life themes', starting from the child's experience and leading up to a Bible story. It is impossible, he affirmed, to teach the Bible as such to children under eleven.[53] Goldman's ideas encouraged a considerable amount of experimental work in schools and the whole question of religious teaching came under discussion. The official government position remained positive and the Crowther, the Newsom, and the Plowden Reports[54] all stressed the importance of religious instruction, although the Plowden Report included a minority memorandum opposing the religious education of young people mainly on the ground of the inherent unsuitability of the material. The humanist organizations, however, were actively hostile and the emergence in Britain of a pluralist society pressed the question even further. The situation was made more serious by the expectation that a new education bill would come before Parliament in 1970. It was against this background that the Church of England Board of Education and the National Society set up in 1967 a Commission on Religious Education, under the

[51] Quoted, David Edwards, op. cit., p. 13.      [52] Cf. *Teenage Religion*, 1961.
[53] Cf. *Readiness for Religion*, 1965.                  [54] 1959, 1963, 1967.

chairmanship of the Bishop of Durham, Dr Ian Ramsey, representative of teachers in schools, colleges of education, and universities, together with educational administrators and advisers. Its report, *The Fourth R*, was published in 1970 and received considerable publicity. It called for three changes. First, it asked for the repeal of the provisions of the 1944 Act in relation to religious instruction and school worship and the abandonment of the machinery for making agreed syllabuses, which was described as 'a relic of the ecclesiastical era in religious education'. There should be some statutory obligation but it should allow schools a wide measure of flexibility. Secondly, the term 'religious instruction' should be replaced by 'religious education', which 'should form part of the general education received by all school pupils', acknowledged on educational grounds and not by making it alone of all subjects legally compulsory. Thirdly, the Commission urged that the dual system should not be perpetuated for 'denominational advantage', but only to enable the Church 'to express its concern for the general education of the young people of the nation'. The key words in the report were 'flexibility' and 'openness' and the whole argument represented a retreat (though there were some who would have said an advance) from the definiteness of the 1944 Act. There was widespread acceptance of the report as a document which set out fairly the *educational* justification for teaching religion in schools and which demonstrated 'that the debate about religious education is essentially a serious educational question and not simply a tussle between some good people called Christians and some wicked people called atheists'.[55]

## 6. The Mirror of Television

The theological and moral debates were carried on, not only in academic circles and through the written word, but also on the television screen. 'Meeting Point', under the expert guidance of Oliver Hunkin, was intended to be 'a sorting-house for fundamental ideas in which the Christian was confronted by people of widely differing views', and in which 'the Christian was shown in the setting of, and up against, the pressures of the world'.[56]

[55] Alexander Wedderspoon, quoted David Edwards, *Ian Ramsey*, 1973, p. 93.
[56] Roy McKay, *Take Care of the Sense*, 1964, pp. 77-8.

A number of these programmes 'made news'. In January 1962
eight million viewers saw the Archbishop of York, Dr Donald
Coggan, talking to the pop star, Adam Faith, which was an
occurrence inconceivable twenty years before. They discussed
God, sex, and the teenager, but although the Archbishop was
friendly and reasonable he cut little ice. Shortly afterwards
Ludovic Kennedy interviewed Paul Ferris, the author of a controversial book on the Church of England,[57] and Dr Alec Vidler,
who had contributed an essay on 'The National Church' in
*Soundings*.[58] The programme was critical of the Church of
England, but neither unfairly nor destructively so.[59] It caused
considerable opposition from churchmen, led by the *Church
Times*, which complained that viewers were given the impression 'that the Church was an outmoded organisation in a hopeless muddle' and that Vidler 'gave no hint of understanding the
Church or its authority, its mission or its Lord. He did not
mention God.'[60] During the following week the Church Assembly listened to a somewhat hysterical speech from Mr George
Goyder, who described the programme as 'a deplorable broadcast'—he had not seen it, although he had read the script—and
declared that Vidler had replied to a question, whether fornication is all right, in such a way as to lead ordinary people to
think that it was. Vidler in fact had done no such thing. None
the less, Mr Goyder's speech, which gave the impression that
the purpose of the programme had been to attack Christian
morals, was received with loud acclaim, indicating that those
present had not seen the programme either. Mr Goyder had
second thoughts, however, and in a letter to the *Church Times*[61]
declared that Dr Vidler had not received fair treatment and
hoped that 'no-one will think for a moment that I believed Dr
Vidler capable of deliberately advocating easy morals'. He
blamed the balance of the programme and its manner of presentation as being responsible for creating a wrong impression.
Another 'Meeting Point'[62] dealt with 'Towards a Quaker View
of Sex',[63] which raised a number of controversial issues, two

---

[57] *The Church of England*, 1962.     [58] Cf. above, p. 110.
[59] Cf. McKay, op. cit., p. 101.         [60] *Church Times*, 9 November 1962.
[61] 21 December 1962.                    [62] February 1963.
[63] An essay by a group of the Society of Friends, 1963.

others[64] were based on *Objections to Christian Belief*,[65] and a third[66] dealt with *Honest to God*,[67] but none of these aroused the interest and bitter controversy generated by the Ferris-Vidler programme.

A programme on 'Panorama' in 1968, which set out to portray the Church of England, gave a distorted picture of a Church made up of the old and the reactionary versus the young and the radical. Another programme, produced in 1971, entitled 'The Church of England Today', was also a caricature. On the other hand, a programme in 1969 in the 'Twenty-Four Hours' series presented an accurate and informative picture, setting out as objectively as possible the issues at stake in the Anglican-Methodist unity proposals, while the comparison of parish life in rural Suffolk and in South London in the 'Philpott File' in 1972 was both fair and informative. 1969 saw the start of 'Stars on Sunday'. Although the Archbishop of Canterbury and Cardinal Heenan of Westminster were among those who took part, the programme offered ordinary people a range of sentimental music, only some of which was specifically religious, together with comforting songs and readings, in an escapist and nostalgic setting. It became the most successful religious programme in the history of broadcasting, with an audience of some thirteen million by 1972. Its theatrical nature, its fantasy world and its sentimentality were criticized by some Christians as presenting a distortion of the Christian faith. On the other hand, it was argued that the programme touched a chord which was often ignored by other religious programmes and that much biblical teaching came through.

Criticism of the BBC by the Churches extended beyond the specifically religious programmes to the way in which Church matters were handled in current affairs and documentaries, to the portrayal of violence and sex, and to the use of bad language in drama and variety programmes. In 1964 a Clean-Up TV Campaign was officially launched by Mrs Mary Whitehouse, a middle-aged housewife who was a committed Christian of evangelical persuasion, and the following year the National Viewers and Listeners Association was inaugurated under the same auspices. Mrs Whitehouse became a symbolic figure; she

---

[64] March/April 1963.
[66] April 1963.
[65] Cf. above, pp. 114f.
[67] Cf. above, pp. 110ff.

was a competent speaker, a good organizer, confident, optimistic, and totally committed to her cause.[68] Much criticism of radio
and television by churchmen stemmed from a lack of understanding of the nature of the medium. Such facts as that Britain
was becoming a pluralist society and the implications of this for
broadcasting, or that the relationship between artistic integrity
and freedom of expression on the one hand and restraint and
censorship on the other is an extremely difficult one—these
were not always understood. Moreover, not everyone accepted
the central fact that broadcasting existed to be a mirror to society
as well as a messenger to society. There was a reluctance to recognize that the Christian view could not be protected on radio and
TV, but ought to be subject to the same critical analysis and
discussion as any other topic. The nineteen-sixties was a period
of moral and theological ferment, of radical criticism of the
Church as an institution, and religious broadcasting mirrored
this. In 1975 Charles Curran, the Director General of the BBC,
was to affirm that 'it is not our job to adopt a particular morality
and then to try to persuade everybody else to follow it'.[69] This
was a radical departure from Sir William Haley's declaration in
1948 that the aim of broadcasting was to safeguard and foster
Christian values.[70] On the other hand, since Christianity is the
basis of established institutions in Britain, the BBC 'cannot
reflect the country without reflecting its Christian origins and
institutions'.[71]

[68] Cf. Mary Whitehouse, *A Most Dangerous Woman?* 1982.
[69] Quoted in *Broadcasting, Society and the Church*, Report of the Broadcasting Commission of the General Synod of the Church of England, 1973, p. 1.
[70] Cf. above, p. 50.
[71] Charles Curran, *The Seamless Robe*, 1979, pp. 91-2.

# 7

# PARISHES, PRIESTS, AND PEOPLE

What is the province of the laity? To hunt, to shoot, to entertain. These matters they understand, but to meddle with ecclesiastical matters they have no right at all.

George Talbot, nineteenth century

A true philosophy of the Church... will recognise that the right methods, the right ministries and orders of worship, are those which best serve its nature in the midst of contemporary conditions.

F. R. Barry, The Relevance of the Church, 1935

## 1. The Paul Report

IN JULY 1960 the Church Assembly accepted a motion moved by Lt. Col. H. E. Madge of Winchester asking the Central Advisory Council for the Ministry to consider, in the light of changing circumstances, the existing system of the payment and deployment of the clergy. The Council, believing that the totality of the problem could be best grasped by a single mind, invited Mr Leslie Paul, author, sociologist, and philosopher, a committed member of the Church of England and Director of Studies at Brasted Place College, to undertake an enquiry and to make recommendations. His report, *The Deployment and Payment of the Clergy*, usually known as 'the Paul Report', was published in January 1964.

This revealing document presented a generally discouraging picture. Considered socially, the Church of England was still an important national institution and a majority of the population still declared themselves to be members of the National Church and had recourse to it for 'rites of passage'. On the other hand, the decline in the number of Confirmation candidates, communicants, and regular worshippers indicated that, viewed religiously, the Church was in an unsatisfactory condition.

Based on extensive enquiries and relevant statistics, the Report was able to clarify what many had long believed to be the situation, namely that the Church was chronically short of manpower and that it was failing to use efficiently such clergy as it had. The distribution of manpower was haphazard so that half the benefices of the Church covered only ten per cent of the population while at the other end of the scale—the heavily populated end—less than one-tenth of the benefices covered about one-third of the population. The Church was still a rural-based Church which seemed only half-heartedly concerned with the great cities. Further signs of danger were that the total number of men ordained was not increasing in proportion to the growth of population, coupled with the rise in the average age of the clergy. There were insufficient men in the non-parochial ministry to meet the demands of a new society and the Church was short of youth chaplains and of chaplains in industry and the new universities. Private patronage and the parson's freehold made constructive and rational deployment impossible.

The workload of the clergy was unequally distributed. One-third of the clergy was under-employed and a quarter grossly overworked. One clergyman cited in the report had so little to do that he had accepted no less than fourteen posts outside his parochial work, while a town incumbent wrote that 'the parish will quite literally kill me one day and I am quite prepared for this'. The report quoted the incumbent of a parish of 24,000 who in one year, in addition to his other pastoral duties, officiated at 130 weddings, 160 funerals, and 250 baptisms. Only a quarter of the priests who replied to Mr Paul's questionnaire had a regular day off each week. The country clergy had their own debilitating problems, particularly the need to raise vast sums of money from small communities to repair historic church buildings. 'The amount contributed for all Church purposes last year', wrote one depressed incumbent, 'was £23. I have had five Confirmation candidates in 17 years. There is no P.C.C, no organist, no choir and no verger. There is no heating in winter.' This may have been an extreme case, but the report cited others which were almost as depressing. It may be that Leslie Paul failed to give sufficient weight to some of the clergy's own personal shortcomings, such as lack of faith, commitment, and energy. On the other hand overwork, indifference, isolation, poverty, large houses and gardens, non-payment of clerical expenses, the feeling of being ignored and irrelevant, and the constant fund raising, could dull faith and quicken despair in the hearts of many able and caring priests. Others, however, did splendid and faithful work in spite of the system under which they laboured. The report revealed the incredible salary inequalities among incumbents. In one diocese one incumbent's stipend was £400 and another's was £4,702. On the other hand, the *average* stipend, if a free house was added, compared favourably with that of graduate teachers, although the Church was failing to pay the heavy expenses incurred by its clergy. Looking at the whole picture, the report accused the Church of being a bad steward of its resources. It required more clergy but it had little right to ask for these until it had some efficient machinery to deploy them and pay them effectively and equitably.

The report made sixty-two recommendations aimed at using the whole force of the clergy to best advantage within a coherent plan, in the belief that this would re-vitalize the Church and improve clergy morale. The parson's freehold should be abolished and become a leasehold, the distinction between beneficed and unbeneficed clergy should come to an end, patronage should be replaced by regional appointment bodies, together with a central Clergy Staff Board, and there should be a new form of parochial unit—the 'major parish'—staffed by a college of clergy, all of incumbent status, to cope with the high density urban areas and the widely-scattered rural parishes. A national salary structure and a common stipends fund, together with the pooling of all endowment income, should be established. The stipends of the clergy should keep in step with those of the teaching profession and there should be increments for long service and salary loadings for posts of special responsibility. In other words, stipends should be related to the man rather than linked to a place. Clergy should retire on full pension at the age of sixty-five. Finally, the report stressed the need for the laity to exercise ministry and it recommended the formation of a parochial lay apostolate and street organizations based on house communions.

With its grim analysis and its radical proposals it is not surprising that the Paul Report was a source of great interest to the general public and that there was extensive coverage by the media. Within the Church itself conservatives were horror-struck, while for the radicals it represented the dawn of new hope. The latter believed that the Church now had before it a document setting out with unmistakable clarity the true nature of its disorders and presenting it with an opportunity for re-organization that it would ignore at its peril. They echoed the words of the editor of the *Church of England Newspaper*— 'January 17th will go down in the Church history books as the day when the Church of England took off its rose-coloured spec-tacles, surveyed its full-time ministry and paused shivering on the brink of the waters of rationalisation....In broad terms some such policy as that advocated by the Report must be adopted if the Church is to survive and be effective in the 1970s and 1980s.'[1]

On the other hand, many churchmen accused Leslie Paul of adopting a sociological, and therefore superficial, approach to the Church of England, which displayed a lack of understanding of the spirituality of the Church and regarded the ordained ministry as a professional career instead of a divine vocation. Suspicion was expressed of the report's generalizations about the loneliness and frustration of the clergy and Paul was accused of using emotive language about patronage and the freehold. He was told that he should not assume that the clergy were branch managers of a multiple store, for the responsibilities and duties of a clergyman in a particular parish could not be assessed on statistics alone. It may be true that Leslie Paul failed to appreci-ate that more priests per head of the population were necessary in rural parishes than in urban parishes, for geography and local traditions were important factors. Nevertheless, the question was whether, with the acute shortage of manpower, the differ-ence between town and country was too wide for the survival of the Church. There were four storm centres of criticism. The first was the proposed abolition of patronage and the new system of appointments, which was described by Guy Mayfield as 'des-tructive of the spirituality of the Church of England'. 'What', he asked, 'would the new type of clergyman, acceptable to ecclesiastical bureaucracy, be like?'[2] and the editor of the

---

[1] 17 January 1964.

[2] 'The Planners' Paradise', *Church Times*, 17 January 1964.

*Church Times* declared that a priest's vocation 'is not to be a pawn on a vast, impersonal, bureaucratic chessboard'.[3] Secondly, any modification of the freehold was seen as the first and decisive step in depriving the parish priest of his necessary independence, and its replacement by the status of contract would have far-reaching consequences for the whole ethos and character of the ministry. The third target was centralization because this would produce a bureaucracy run by ecclesiastical civil servants and would result in the emergence of clergy with a civil service mentality. Finally, there were those who claimed that the time and energy required to implement the proposed reforms would deflect the Church from its primary purpose of mission, evangelism, and pastoral care. A sad thread running through so much of the criticism was the implication that somehow it was less than godly to be businesslike and efficient and that Christian stewardship might be applicable to financial matters but not to the organization of the Church's ministry. Above all, there appeared to be a refusal to face the fact that the Church was fast reaching a crisis in manpower and that, therefore, any sincere concern for the mission of the Church in this land demanded considerable reform. Reform did not occur in the wake of the Paul Report and the Church took twenty years to implement, in a very modified form, what was then proposed. Who can tell what the course of the Church of England might have been if it had had the will and the vision possessed by some of those it dubbed radicals?

The radical churchmen of the sixties accepted the insights of the 'new theology' and the 'new morality' and the need for restructuring the Church's institutions. Going to the roots, they asked whether the foliage and the fruit were congruent with what they discovered about the roots. They called for a true theology and use of the laity, for a thorough overhaul of plant and organization, for a revision of the liturgy and for the concept of the Church as a servant Church concerned with the poor and underprivileged. Above all, the existing complacency of the Church must be punctured. Their organ of publicity was a small and well-written magazine called *Prism*, edited by Christopher Martin and Nicholas Mosley, which began publication in 1958

---

[3] *Church Times*, ibid.

and eventually reached a circulation of 5,000. It enabled a scattered number of individuals who were unhappy with the traditional stances and structures of the Church to become a more
coherent and better informed body of opinion. In 1965 *New
Christian*, sponsored by Timothy Beaumont, took its place. Its
launching was an act of faith, backed by the immense generosity
of the proprietor, but within a year it had some 10,000 readers.
It remained in circulation for five years, in the course of which
some of the best theological writers in Britain, together with
some of the leading radicals in Europe and North America, contributed articles.

In 1960 a group of radicals of high calibre attended a noteworthy conference at Keble College, Oxford, to consider the
value of group ministries within the Church of England.[4] Its
interests soon broadened so that in the years to come the 'Keble
Conference' helped to organize, canalize, and mobilize the
forces of reform. Thus alongside disillusionment, depression,
and a sense of failure, there grew up an air of expectation, hope,
and enthusiasm. The movement initiated by the Keble Group
acquired strength in 1963 when it was merged with the Parish
and People Movement.[5] This was no easy marriage because the
Keble Group was more radical and political than the generality
of the members of Parish and People and expressed a greater
urgency for the need to reform the Church of England. From
now on Parish and People had a wide range of concerns—the
liturgy, ministry ordained and lay, ecumenism, industrial mission, group and team ministries, the payment and deployment
of the clergy, and the constitutional reform of the Church. The
merger of these two bodies occurred just a month before the
Paul Report was due to be published. Shortly afterwards the
Revd Eric James, Vicar of St. George's, Camberwell, was appointed its full-time director. He travelled the country in the
hope of harnessing to the movement the spirit of reform which
he and his colleagues believed to be abroad in the Church. In
spite of his own enthusiasm, however, he was obliged to report
that the result of his peregrinations disclosed the fact that the
notion that there was a considerable radical movement in the
Church waiting to be mobilized was completely mistaken.

[4] P. J. Jagger, *A History of the Parish and People Movement*, 1978, p. 78.
[5] Ibid., Chapter 7.

When in 1966 he was asked the question, 'In view of your experience are you *hopeful*?' he had to reply: 'Humanly speaking I have little or no hope, if by your question you mean, "Does the Church of England look as though it will wake up?"'[6] Eric James resigned in order to devote himself to the inner-city areas of London.

## 2. The Morley Report

In February 1965 the Church Assembly took the first tentative steps to implement one of the recommendations of the Paul Report. It accepted the principle of the 'major parish' and legislation enabling the establishment of group and team ministries subsequently formed part of the Pastoral Measure 1968. The other major proposals in the Paul Report were committed for consideration to a commission on the deployment and payment of the clergy, under the chairmanship of Canon Fenton Morley, Vicar of Leeds. Its report, *Partners in Ministry*, was published in June 1967 and confirmed Leslie Paul's view that the way in which deployment and payment of the clergy was handled was inadequate and wasteful, was failing to meet contemporary needs and was distorting the image of the Church as a divinely constituted society. It proposed that the Church as a whole should assume responsibility for enabling a clergyman to exercise his ministry and to receive his stipend, so that he derived both status and security from being an ordained priest and 'on the strength' of a diocese, and not from the office he held. In each diocese a Ministry Commission should be established to make all appointments and a central Ministry Commission would make decisions on policy and secure co-ordination throughout the two provinces. The diocesan commissions would take over all patronage and the freehold would be replaced by a form of tenure for a term of years. The report was much concerned about the absence of any built-in provision of pastoral care for the clergy and it recommended that each diocese be divided into 'units of pastoral care' in which suffragan bishops or archdeacons

[6] Ibid., p. 116. In the later sixties ecumenical activities began to dominate Parish and People, with particular reference to the Anglican-Methodist Scheme. In this they worked closely with the Methodist Renewal Group. Out of this emerged, in 1970, a completely new movement called 'ONE for Christian Renewal'. Cf. ibid., pp. 129ff.

would be entrusted with special responsibility for the pastoral oversight of the clergy. Seventy should be the terminal age at which a clergyman should have the right to remain in office and receive a stipend. The second part of the report dealt with the payment of the clergy. A Central Payment Authority should be responsible for the payment of all stipends and it was proposed that the Church Commissioners should become that Authority. Greater flexibility would be achieved by the pooling of all endowment income and statutory fees, and all glebe should be vested in the Central Payment Authority. In such ways the commission believed that the Church of England would be enabled to use its resources to better advantage and 'generally, engage the ministry at the points of the greatest need at the moment when these needs manifest themselves and not after they have given way to others'.

The reaction was the same mixture of enthusiasm and disapproval which marked the reception of the Paul Report. The most effective opposition came from Dr Gerald Ellison, Bishop of Chester, who regarded the proposals as radically altering the character of the Church of England. He published a pamphlet, *Progress in Ministry,*[7] attacking the concept of a Central Ministry Commission, upholding the merits of the freehold and the patronage system and criticizing the pooling of endowments. In his view sufficient rationalization was proceeding already and what the Morley Commission was proposing was alien to the history and ethos of the Church of England. Reform there must be, but there were better and more gradual ways of advance than the radical steps recommended by the commission. After a long debate in the Church Assembly the dioceses were asked for their reaction to the proposals and as a result it became clear that there was insufficient support from the Church for the comprehensive changes envisaged by the Morley Commission to justify their wholesale adoption. There was general agreement that greater uniformity in remuneration was necessary, there was deep division on the wisdom of abolishing freehold and patronage, and there was little support for diocesan and central Ministry Commissions. On the other hand, there was clear evidence of a desire for moderate reform of patronage. The Church

[7] 1968.

Assembly, therefore, asked a committee to produce a scheme modifying the patronage system in order to procure co-operation between patron, diocese and parish.

During discussions on the Morley proposals reference was often made to the Pastoral Measure, which was before the Church Assembly from 1964 to 1968 and was one of the longest and most complex Measures ever to emanate from that body. Its purpose was to make better provision for the cure of souls through the reorganization of parishes and ministries. It amended the law relating to pluralities and the union of parishes and benefices, it enabled parishes to be created without a parish church, and it provided for the setting up of team and group ministries and for the alteration of ecclesiastical boundaries. It also dealt with the preservation and disposal of redundant churches. The latter represented a significant piece of new co-operation with the State because, if a redundant church was of notable historical or architectural importance, it was to be vested in a Redundant Churches Fund, to which the State agreed to contribute £200,000, to match £200,000 from the Church. This was to operate for a five-year period, but the grants have been renewed at each subsequent quinquennium. During the first five years after the Measure became law the pace was slow but the number of pastoral schemes grew to 300 a year, while the number of churches declared redundant built up to a peak of 106 in 1973-4. There can be no doubt that operations under the Measure have produced tensions—between the diocese, which can see the total picture, and parishes, which are concerned with preserving their own identity and retaining their own clergyman; between the Church Commissioners, who have to prepare pastoral reorganization schemes, and dioceses and parishes; between those whose concerns are essentially pastoral and those who represent antiquarian, architectural, and conservationist opinion. Procedures under the Measure were complex and the time required to complete a scheme could be long, but in a Church which contains so many legitimate interests and which accepts the principle of full consultation, this would appear to be inevitable. In the context of these factors, the judgement that the Measure 'established a just balance'[8] is a fair one.

[8] *Report of the Working Party on the Pastoral Measure 1968*, 1975, p. 4.

### 3. The Ministry of the Laity

The Paul Report was criticized for its failure to deal with some fundamental questions. What should be the form of the Church for the modern age and what is the right structure for the ordained ministry? In particular, what is the true distinction between ordained and lay ministry? Although these questions did not form part of Leslie Paul's brief, he did affirm that 'the whole of my recommendations would prove worthless if an increase in the ordained ministry led simply to a retreat of the laity from responsibility and joint ministry'. We thus come to two key questions which issued in prolonged debate during the sixties and seventies. The first was the place of the laity in the Church and the second, which is fundamental to the first, was the nature of ministry, ordained and lay. The year before the Paul Report was published the Keble Group, believing that any scheme for pastoral reform and any reconsideration of the task of ministry, 'which did not enlist the laity as equal partners was wrong in theory and useless in practice', held a conference, the papers presented at which were published as *The Layman's Church*.[9] They represent a distillation of the very wide discussion of this topic which, under the leadership of people like J. H. Oldham, Kenneth Grubb, Kathleen Bliss, and Ralph Morton, was to result in a new understanding of the place of the laity in the Church. This debate was inevitable for four reasons. First, the laity had begun to share in making decisions which had formerly been restricted to the bishops and clergy. This began with the revision of canon law, when the approval of the House of Laity of the Church Assembly was sought for each of the new canons.[10] Then the laity became involved in liturgical revision, and finally the establishment in 1970 of synodical government was to produce a partnership of bishops, clergy, and laity in the government of the Church.[11] Secondly, there was greater involvement of the laity at parochial level as laymen and women began to take a share in liturgical and pastoral activities which had formerly been regarded as the preserves of the

[9] 1963, edited by the Bishop of Woolwich. Other works on this theme which were published at this time were Kathleen Bliss, *We the People*, 1963, Stephen Neill and Hans Rudi Weber, *The Layman in Christian History*, 1963, Mark Gibbs and T. R. Morton, *God's Frozen People*, 1964.
[10] Cf. above, p. 42f.        [11] Cf. below, pp. 147ff.

clergy. Thirdly, one of the consequences of the liturgical movement was the recovery of the theological truth that the celebrant
at the Eucharist was the whole People of God in a particular
place and that the priest was the president. This was given practical expression by increased participation by the laity in the
conduct of the rite. Fourthly, there was a proliferation of accredited lay ministries—readers, licensed lay workers, the
Church Army, Church social workers, parish elders, etc. How
did these lay ministries relate to the ordained ministry? Many
clergymen and laymen welcomed and encouraged this lay involvement, but there were still too many parishes where lay
initiative was discouraged or where the laity themselves were
content to remain passengers in an ark whose captain was the
authoritative incumbent. Gradually, however, a proper theological view of the nature of ministry began to emerge. The
Church is the People of God—the *laos*—and ministry is a function of the whole *laos*, both ordained and lay. The priesthood
and ministry of the ordained man is not different in kind from
that of every other Christian, but ordination conveys the authority of Christ and his Church to be the representative person of
the Church which ordains. The priest's task is to maximize the
participation in ministry of every member of the Church committed to his charge. 'To equip God's people for the work of his
service, to the building up of the Body of Christ', was the oft-
quoted text[12] describing the function of the ordained minister.
Perhaps the most succinct statement of the new emphasis was
that made by Hans Rudi Weber: 'The laity are not the helpers
of the clergy so that the clergy can do their job, but the clergy
are the helpers of the whole people of God, so that the laity can
be the Church.'[13]

There can be no doubt that one of the most profound changes
that has occurred in the Church of England since 1945 has been
the enhanced position of the laity in the ministry of the Church
in every sphere—governmental, administrative, pastoral, evangelistic, and liturgical. Alongside this has grown the conviction
that, with their enhanced status, there is need for systematic
training for the laity. A number of dioceses invested in such

---

[12] Ephesians 4:12, in *The New English Bible*.
[13] Quoted, Bishop of Woolwich, 'The Ministry and the Laity', in *The Layman's
Church*, 1963, p. 17.

training, but on the whole lamentably inadequate resources have been devoted to lay education and development. The growing volume of verbal support for the laity's role in the life of the Church has not been matched by figures in diocesan budgets. A notable piece of lay training was the establishment in 1970 of the Institute of Christian Studies at All Saints', Margaret Street, London, the purpose of which was defined as providing 'the necessary resources to begin the task of lay education in the Church of England'. Four years earlier St. George's House was established at Windsor Castle under the guidance of the Dean, the Rt. Revd Robin Woods, who received enthusiastic support from the Queen and the Duke of Edinburgh. It has remained a place where lay-people of influence and responsibility in every area of society—industry, commerce, the professions, politics, science, and the arts—come together to explore and to share their insights and anxieties.

The debate about ministry produced a formidable array of documents from the British Council of Churches[14] and the Church of England's Advisory Council for the Ministry,[15] the object of which was to stimulate discussion. A particular aspect of ministry to which the Advisory Council gave attention was the concept of a 'supporting ministry',[16] consisting of men ordained while continuing in full-time secular employment. The Lambeth Conference of 1958 had declared that no theological principle forbad a suitable man being ordained while continuing his lay occupation. In 1968 the Advisory Council for the Ministry published a report[17] discussing the theological and practical questions involved and making recommendations about the selection, training, and supervision of these men. In due course the concept of an auxiliary ministry was endorsed and the bishops issued regulations for their selection and training. Since then a steady number of men have been ordained while retaining their secular occupations. It has taken time for

[14] E.g. *The Shape of the Ministry*, 1967.

[15] E.g. *Ordained Ministry Today*, 1968, *Specialist Ministries*, 1971.

[16] No satisfactory title has been found for this group of ordained priests. 'Supporting Ministry' and 'Auxiliary Ministry' have been used and discarded. Currently the term 'Non-Stipendiary Ministry' is the official title but because it is descriptively a very limiting title it is still not wholly satisfactory.

[17] *A Supporting Ministry*. Cf. also, *The Place of Auxiliary Ministry, Ordained and Lay*, 1973.

people to realize that those in this ministry are as much priests as those in the full-time ordained ministry (there can be no such thing as a 'part-time priest'), and the view that the auxiliary ministry is a second-class ministry has been hard to kill. Non-stipendiary priests tend to fall into two groups. There are those who see their ministry orientated mainly towards the places where they work and there are those who see it orientated mainly towards the parish in which they live. It is disappointing that too many of them appear to be reluctant to grasp the theological implications of an ordained ministry in a frontier situation and to be over-concerned to model their ministry on that of the full-time priest. At the same time, while recognizing that this type of ministry must have its own intrinsic validity, its function must also be seen in the context of the pastoral needs of the Church. The shortage of clergy, the declining number of candidates for full-time ministry and the problems in an inflationary period of paying the full-time clergy adequately, mean that there could be a crucial role for the non-stipendiary clergy to play if the life of the Church is to be adequately maintained.[18]

## 4. The Crisis in the Theological Colleges

Inevitably the debate about ministry and the initiation of new patterns of ministry impinged upon the question of the training of the clergy. For many years the traditional training offered by the theological colleges had undergone little change and many clergy working in parishes in the sixties maintained that their training had ill-equipped them for their task. In 1968 there were twenty-five residential colleges, together with two colleges for pre-theological training. Each college was an autonomous body, differing in churchmanship, size, endowments, and educational facilities. Some were sited in or near universities, some were in close relationship with cathedrals. Some were

[18] By 1977 there were 131 men in the non-stipendiary ministry. In that year a report prepared by W. H. Saumarez Smith, *An Honorary Ministry*, reviewed this form of ministry—its distinctiveness, its training, and the problems experienced by men engaged in it. In 1971 ACCM published a report on *Specialist Ministries*, dealing with priests who had become industrial chaplains, hospital chaplains, chaplains to the armed services, to prisons and borstals, etc. In the same year an unpublished ACCM document, *Priests in Secular Employment*, looked at the situation of a small group of less than 200 who had left the full-time ordained ministry to work in secular occupations.

for graduates, some for non-graduates and some were mixed. Two—Rochester and Worcester—were specifically for the training of older men, most of whom were married with families. Two were affiliated to the religious communities at Mirfield and Kelham. The non-residential Southwark Ordination Course trained men for the ordained ministry while they continued in their secular occupations.

The problem facing the colleges was a financial one caused by the continuing decline in the number of ordination candidates. Between 1960 and 1968 the number of ordinands became about twenty per cent less than the number of residential places available. As the main source of income was the students, the drop in numbers meant that the cost per head had mounted. Since 1956 training grants had been made to theological students from central Church funds to cover about half the cost of training, the other half being borne almost entirely by local education authority grants. In recent years these grants had constituted the largest single item in the Church Assembly budget. In addition, capital grants to the colleges from the Church Assembly had totalled £713,128 between 1960 and 1968. Consequently, independent institutions though the colleges might be, their financial plight was of crucial concern to the whole Church which could not afford to continue subsidizing empty places. At the same time, the decline in the number of students, the increasing financial worries and the uncertainty about the future were demoralizing to the governing bodies, staff, and students of the colleges themselves. Finally, there were the searching and critical questions that were being asked about the suitability of the training offered by the colleges. It was for these reasons that the college principals asked for an independent investigation of the situation. This was undertaken by a small group under the chairmanship of Sir Bernard de Bunsen and its report was published in 1968.[19] After it had surveyed the current problems, the group built up a series of educational arguments for reorganization, first by exposing the inadequacy of the traditional staffing of a college by a principal and two or three colleagues, and secondly by noting the increase in university departments of theology from five to thirteen during the previous thirty years. Against

---

[19] *Theological Colleges for Tomorrow.*

the educational and financial background, the group made four recommendations. First, it was desirable to have fewer colleges, each containing more places, and it recommended 120 students as an optimum. Secondly, most of the colleges should be in or near universities, where there were departments of theology and other educational resources. Thirdly, as a general rule older and younger ordinands, graduates and non-graduates, should be trained together. Fourthly, ecumenical ordination training ought to be developed and at least one integrated ecumenical theological college should be established without delay.

The college principals welcomed the proposals for some larger colleges, but rejected size as a sole criterion for all colleges. Their solution was that in some centres a group of smaller colleges, not necessarily all Anglican, should be 'clustered', should work out a common programme of training, and share staff and teaching facilities. The Church's Council for Ministry endorsed the group's judgement that the theological and other facilities of the universities should not be neglected by the Church, but believed that there was still a proper place for 'self-contained' colleges, although these should be of the larger sort. The Church refused to be rushed into rapid reorganization. The possible fate of individual colleges elicited from those institutions the expected and understandable defence of vested interest and tried worth. There was, above all, the desire to avoid any appearance of direction or control from 'the centre' and it was hoped that the colleges themselves would work out schemes which would reduce the number of places to correspond with the drop in demand. There is no need to follow the subsequent events, some of which were traumatic to certain institutions. It is sufficient to record the results of the rationalization process. Ten years after the de Bunsen report the number of residential colleges had been reduced to fourteen. Of these, one represented a union of Ripon Hall and Cuddesdon at Oxford and another the amalgamation of Salisbury and Wells. At Cambridge, Ridley Hall and Westcott House, together with Wesley College, a Methodist foundation, formed a 'cluster' for the sharing of resources. In 1970 Queen's College, Birmingham, became the first ecumenical theological college, although a number of other colleges appointed non-Anglicans to their staff. The two pre-theological colleges of Brasted and Bernard Gilpin in Durham were closed, as also were the colleges for older men at Rochester and Worcester and the two colleges linked with the religious communities at Mirfield and Kelham. All the colleges formed links with the theological department of a nearby university and most of them had women training alongside men as well as students who were not proceeding to ordination. By 1978 there had also come into existence a number of official part-time courses for the increasing number of men whose training had to take place while they continued in their secular employment and who later served either in the full-time ordained ministry or as non-stipendiary priests.

## 5. Synodical Government

The Enabling Act of 1919 had inaugurated the Church Assembly. This consisted of the two Convocations of Canterbury and York, which formed the House of Bishops and the House of Clergy, together with a House of Laity, the members of which were elected by the laity of the dioceses. The Convocations continued to meet separately and dealt with matters of doctrine and worship and debated moral, social, and international issues. The Church Assembly dealt primarily with administrative and financial matters and, as a legislative body, it legislated by Measures which, when they had been approved by Parliament and had received the Royal Assent, had the force of statute law. As time passed it became apparent that there were serious weaknesses in this dual system. The time involved for bishops and clergy attending both Convocation and the Church Assembly was burdensome and excessive; there was an increasing overlap or duplication of business transacted by the two bodies; the Church Assembly, with some 750 members, was too large for good debate and the efficient dispatch of business; and the lack of communication between the Assembly and the dioceses led to accusations of remoteness from the places where the Church's work was done. Above all, there was the lack of full participation by the laity in discussions and decisions on the Church's doctrine and worship.

The subject of synodical government, with particular reference to the association of a lay element with the Convocations, was ventilated in a series of debates in the Convocation of York in 1952. When the Archbishop of Canterbury, at an early stage in the process of canon law revision, assured the House of Laity of the Church Assembly that it would be consulted throughout the revision, he made it clear that this was a concession and was not founded on any constitutional right of the laity to partici-pate in the making of canons. This brought home forcibly to the laity that in respect of certain important functions of Church government they had no established rights. Moreover, the House of Laity, having received this gracious concession of con-sultation, soon experienced considerable difficulty in dealing with the canons because they had had no part in the discussions which had preceded their formulation. In 1953, therefore, the Church Assembly requested the archbishops to appoint a com-mission 'to consider how the clergy and laity can best be joined together in the synodical government of the Church'. When it reported[20] the Commission took as its basis the conclusion of a joint committee of the Convocation of Canterbury, in a report published in 1902,[21] which it summed up as follows: 'Theology justifies and history demonstrates that the ultimate authority and right of collective action lie with the whole body, the Church, and that the co-operation of the clergy and laity in Church government and discipline belongs to the true ideal of the Church.' That was to be the theological basis of synodical government. The Commission proposed that the House of Laity of the Church Assembly be divided into two on a provincial basis and each attached to the Convocation of its province, having rights equal to those possessed by the Lower Houses of Convocation. The Church Assembly would remain, primarily for the purpose of passing Measures and for transacting financial business. The reactions to this proposal were highly critical. On the one side there were those who believed that the implication of the proposal would construct a system more cumbersome and time-consuming than the existing one and regretted that sug-gestions had not been made for a national synod which would supersede the Convocations. On the other side were those to whom the proposals represented an invasion of the traditional rights of the Convocations and would destroy the distinctive character of those bodies. In 1962 a very significant change was made to this proposal by a committee set up by the Convoca-

[20] *The Convocations and the Laity*, 1958.    [21] *The Position of the Laity.*

tions. It found it difficult to isolate any piece of Church business which could be said to be the exclusive concern of the clergy and which did not affect the laity and it criticized the 1958 report because it had left intact the dual system of Convocation and Church Assembly. The committee recommended 'that the Convocation and the Assembly be integrated in one system and that there should be one General Synod which had the final decision in legislative and similar matters'. This single body should assume the functions of the Assembly and also the process of making canons which hitherto had been the function of the Convocations. At the same time the Convocations should remain in existence, they should meet regularly at least once a year to discuss matters of concern, and certain types of canons and Measures should come before them for discussion and report before they went to the General Synod. A minority of the committee was unable to accept the proposals because it regarded them as removing from the clergy, in their Convocations, the power of final veto in matters of doctrine and worship. It proposed, instead, that the Convocations and the Church Assembly should continue as separate bodies, but that the law should be changed to enable the laity as of right to *discuss* matters at present reserved for Convocation, the basic right of veto remaining with the Convocations.

When the Convocations debated these new proposals in 1963 both Upper Houses and the Lower House of Canterbury (by a small majority) accepted them, but the Lower House of York (by an even smaller majority) adopted the minority scheme. Thus deadlock was reached and in order to discover a way through the two archbishops met with representatives of both points of view and with members of the House of Laity and subsequently presented to their Convocations a compromise scheme in 'an effort to create a synthesis of the former Majority and Minority view'. The majority scheme was accepted as the starting point, but one significant alteration was made. Instead of giving the Convocation the right only to *discuss* and *report* on certain matters before they were finally approved by the General Synod, they should have the right to *approve* such matters. On the other hand, to prevent one House from holding a permanent veto it was provided that the action of one House only might delay, but not finally block, a matter. These proposals were accepted by both Houses of the Convocation of Canterbury and by the Lower House of York: this time it was the Upper House of York which rejected them, preferring the original majority scheme. Nevertheless, it was clear that a substantial majority of all four Houses favoured the creation of a General Synod and wished also for the continued existence of the Convocations. York remained adamant about the latter because it was the possession of its own provincial Convocation which both symbolized and consolidated its identity as a distinct province of the Church of England. In November 1963 the Church Assembly indicated that the archbishops' compromise had the greatest approval and a commission was given the task of working out the details of a scheme on the general lines of these proposals and to draft legislation to give effect to them. When the commission reported[22] most of its recommendations were accepted and during the next three years the Assembly passed the Synodical Government Measure through all its stages and it received the Royal Assent in 1969.

The Measure not only was concerned with the central government of the Church but also it established a pattern of synodical government throughout the Church of England at national, diocesan, and deanery level. The General Synod, which was inaugurated by Queen Elizabeth II in November 1970, consists of three houses—bishops, clergy, and laity. The clergy, however, are elected not to the General Synod but to the Lower Houses of their respective Convocations, which can meet separately if they wish. The Convocations have the right to withdraw certain matters of doctrine and worship for separate discussion and a single House could delay considerably the passage of legislation on these matters, although hitherto the right of withdrawal has never been exercised. The General Synod is a legislative body with power to make canons and to pass Measures. It is responsible for the relationship of the Church of England with other Churches at home and abroad and with national and international Church organizations—notably with the other provinces of the Anglican Communion and the Anglican Consultative Council—and with the national and international ecumenical bodies of which the Church of England is a member,

[22] *Government by Synod*, 1966.

such as the British Council of Churches, the World Council of Churches, and the Conference of European Churches. It has the function of providing forms of service for use in the Church, it is responsible for financing the central administration of the Church and it is the forum for expressing the Church's views on public issues. Its Boards and Councils are the official channels whereby the Church exercises its corporate responsibility in the fields of education and social affairs, relates to the Church over-seas and to the other Churches, and implements policy for the selection and training of the clergy and other ministers.

The General Synod is a body considerably smaller than the Church Assembly and there are clear lines of communication between it and the Church in the dioceses. Elections to the House of Laity, for example, are made at deanery, not diocesan level, so that more people, closer to the parish situation, are in-volved. Moreover, any permanent change in the services of Holy Baptism, Holy Communion, and Ordination and any scheme for the constitutional reunion of Churches in this country must first have the approval of a majority of the diocesan synods, and consultation with the dioceses on other major matters can and does occur. It is also possible for a motion to be moved in the General Synod which has made its way up from parish, deanery, and diocese. In such ways the General Synod is considerably less remote than its predecessor.

Under the Synodical Government Measure a diocesan synod was established in every diocese and a duty was laid upon each bishop to consult with his synod on matters of general concern to the diocese and clear lines of communication were made between diocesan synods and the deanery synods, which took the place of the somewhat moribund ruri-decanal conferences and which have their own constitutional position in synodical government. The purpose of this new and comprehensive system was to ensure that there was widespread opportunity for bishops, clergy, and laity at all levels to participate in discussions and decisions on Church policy and thus give substance to the basic concept that 'the co-operation of clergy and laity in Church government and discipline belongs to the true ideal of the Church'.

# 8
# LITURGIES, MUSIC, AND CATHEDRALS

For nothing of humane composure can be much, especially in a thing of this nature, where process of time and alteration of circumstances frequently produce a necessity for correction, as most certainly in our Liturgy they very often doe. For the language in which it is wrote being constantly in fluxu, as all other living languages are, in every age some words that were in use the former grow obsolete...and always to continue these in our Liturgy without correction would be to bring a disparagement upon the whole, and expose to contempt the worship of God among us. Besides there are several things... which may be proper of Prayer at one time which may not be so in another, and all these things call for alterations and amendments whenever they happen. And therefore I am so far from assenting with some of our brethren in this particular, that our Liturgy ought not to be altered, and I think it absolutely necessary from the above-mentioned particulars that it be always at least once in 30 years brought to a review for this purpose. I am sure that this hath been the judgement of the whole Christian Church from the beginning until this time.

Humphrey Prideaux, *Letter to a Friend*, 1690

## 1. The New Services

IF THE nineteen-fifties saw the official bodies of the Church of England preoccupied with canon law revision, the sixties and seventies found them preoccupied with the more relevant task of liturgical revision, which absorbed a phenomenal amount of the time of the Convocations, the Church Assembly, and the General Synod and which culminated in the publication of the Alternative Service Book in November 1980. The task was worth while because, although the official bodies became immersed from time to time in minutiae and although the procedural machinery was not designed for the handling of liturgical texts, it dealt with what is fundamental to the life of the Church and of the worshipping congregations in the parishes. If the worship of God is the primary purpose of the Church then it is important that the public forms in which that worship is articulated should be meaningful, relevant, and corporate, conveying both the transcendence and immanence of God, expressing the fulness of Christian belief, linking together both the traditional and the contemporary, and reflecting the Church's life and witness. A species of 'curtain raiser' to future liturgical revision appeared in 1963 with the publication of *The Revised Psalter*.[1] This was the work of a commission under the chairmanship of the Bishop of Bradford, Dr Donald Coggan, which included T. S. Eliot, C. S. Lewis, a Hebrew scholar, and two eminent Church musicians. The sole task of the group was to revise the text of Coverdale's psalter which the Church of England had retained in the 1662 Book of Common Prayer, and not to make a new translation. Full weight was given to the new insights of modern Semitic scholarship, however, and the needs of congregations in both the singing and saying of the psalms received special consideration. Two years later the Prayer Book (Alternative and Other Services) Measure received the Royal Assent. The object of the Measure was to enable the Church to embark lawfully upon liturgical reform and it allowed services alternative to those of the Book of Common Prayer to be authorized, after certain procedures had been complied with, without recourse to Parliament.

Two series of services were presented to the Church Assembly at a two-day liturgical conference in February 1966. The first, which was called 'Series I', had been drawn up by the bishops and embodied many of the variations from the 1662 Prayer Book which were already in use in many Churches. It represented an attempt to bring these variations within the law and these services were duly authorized later that year. The Liturgical Commission produced a second series of services ('Series 2'), which included Morning and Evening Prayer, occasional intercessions, a service of Thanksgiving after Childbirth and the

[1] First part published in 1961.

Burial of the Dead, all of which were fairly conservative revisions of the 1662 services and prayers and ignored fundamental questions which were being asked about liturgical structures and language. The series also contained a form of Holy Communion, described as 'a draft' because the Commission wished to do more work on it and it was not strictly for official consideration. Although the other services, apart from the Burial Service, were received with general approval, it was this draft form of Holy Communion which stirred the imagination and was received with enthusiasm. Members of the Assembly pleaded for haste in its authorization, one speaker[2] describing it as 'one of the most exciting things to come out of the Church since the Reformation'. The main characteristics of the new service were that there was no attempt to retain the structure of 1662, old and familiar material lay alongside the new and unfamiliar, familiar material retained traditional language and new material was in a style consistent with the old. The concentration on the cross, so characteristic of the 1662 rite, had been broadened to include the other mighty acts of God in Christ, and these were placed within the framework of creation and the return of Christ in glory. The note of thanksgiving, muted in 1662, was restored and the *pax* was re-introduced as an integral part of the service. The four-fold eucharistic act[3] of taking, giving thanks, breaking, and distributing, obscured in the 1662 rite, was made explicit. Provision was made for an Old Testament reading, for the use of psalmody and for flexibility in the form of intercession. These features were to remain characteristic of all subsequent revisions of the service. Series 2 Holy Communion was authorized for experimental use in 1967, to be followed by the authorization of Series 2 Baptism and Confirmation.

On two issues there was strong opposition to the Commission's draft services. Dissension about prayers for the departed led to the failure of the Series 2 Burial Service to secure authorization. Many anglo-catholics could not regard as theologically acceptable a service which did *not* allow prayer for the departed, while many evangelicals could not regard as theologically acceptable a service which *did* allow prayer for the departed even on

[2] The Revd. C. Dymoke-Marr (Oxford), cf. *The Liturgical Conference 1966: Report of Proceedings*, 1966, p. 79.
[3] Cf. above, pp. 68ff.

an optional basis. With the knowledge that further liturgical revision might founder on this rock of dissension, the Archbishops' Commission on Christian Doctrine was asked to prepare a study of this subject. The Commission recognized[4] that there was common ground in that prayer is an expression of common solidarity before God and that there should be considerable theological reserve in speaking of the condition of the departed. Its solution to the problem was a prayer expressing the unity in Christ of living and departed. The words in the draft eucharistic canon of Series 2—'we offer unto thee this bread and this cup'—was the second point of controversy, for evangelicals regarded it as an unacceptable implication that the service was a sacrifice. An amended form of words, together with an undertaking to the anglo-catholics that the matter would be reconsidered at further revision, secured approval to the service.

In 1964 Dr Ronald Jasper, then a lecturer at King's College, London, had been appointed chairman of the Liturgical Commission.[5] He was to hold this office for some twenty years and bore the heavy and often controversial burden of piloting all the new services through the Church Assembly and the General Synod. In 1968 he became a Canon of Westminster and in 1975 he was appointed Dean of York. Although no latter-day Cranmer, it is perhaps to him more than to any other person that the Church of England is indebted for the production of its new services. As chairman of the Commission he stimulated its work, injected new ideas and knit together the varied outlooks and foibles of the other members. Throughout its work the Commission was in close touch with the other Churches, for liturgical revision was a preoccupation of many parts of the Christian Church. Ecumenism was to express itself in this field as in others, with the liturgical treasures of the various Churches opened to enrich the worship of them all. In 1963 the Archbishop of Canterbury was instrumental in bringing into being the Joint Liturgical Group, representing the Church of England, the Church of Scotland, the Episcopal Church of Scotland, the Baptist Union, the Congregational Church, the Methodist Church, the Presbyterian Church of England, and the Churches

---

[4] *Prayer and the Departed*, 1971.
[5] He was already known as a writer on liturgy, cf. *Walter Frere: His Correspondence on Liturgical Construction*, 1954, *Prayer Book Revision in England, 1800-1900*, 1954.

of Christ, together with an observer from the Roman Catholic Church. Its chairman was the Dean of Bristol, the Very Revd D. E. W. Harrison, and Dr Jasper was its secretary. Its first task was the production of an agreed rationalization of the Church's Calendar and Lectionary.[6] This was followed by an agreed Daily Office[7] and in 1971 the Group published a book of Holy Week services.[8]

There were those who were critical of the Series 2 services because they retained a language too reminiscent of the sixteenth century and failed to use contemporary English. The Liturgical Commission, in the preface to its report on the services of Baptism and Confirmation, in 1966, acknowledged its awareness of 'the desire for the use of language that is alive in contemporary society' and announced that it was preparing texts to meet that demand. In 1968 it published the *Gloria in excelsis*, the Creeds, *Te Deum*, and the Gospel canticles in contemporary English, together with a modern text of the Holy Communion Service.[9] The most striking—and to some the most shocking—feature of these texts was that throughout God was addressed as 'You'. This publication marked the genesis of the modern form of the future Series 3 services. Other Churches, however, were engaged on similar projects. In the Roman Catholic Church there was a body known as the International Committee on English in the Liturgy. The advisory committee of that body met with representatives of the major churches throughout the English-speaking world and in due course an international and interdenominational group was established, called the International Consultation on English Texts (ICET), of which Dr Jasper was one of the two joint chairmen. ICET produced an agreed set of texts of the Lord's Prayer, the Creed, the *Te Deum* and the congregational parts of the Holy Communion Service,[10] which were presented to the Churches for experimental use. With certain important amendments the ICET texts were to be incorporated in the Series 3 revisions.

---

[6] *The Calendar and Lectionary*, 1967.
[7] *The Daily Office*, 1968.
[8] *Holy Week Services*.
[9] *Modern Liturgical Texts*.
[10] *Prayers We Have in Common*, 1970.

## 2. New Versions of the Bible

In the Church of England the reading of Scripture is an integral part of every act of worship and it is therefore not surprising that, as the services were revised and the desire grew for the use of contemporary language in worship, the need was expressed for versions of the Scriptures in modern translation. Until 1961 the 'Authorized' Version of 1611 was in common use. Between 1881 and 1885 the *Revised Version* of the Bible had been produced under the authority of the Convocation of Canterbury but, although it was a more accurate translation and made clear many of the obscurities of the Authorized Version, it did not gain widespread support. A number of private and unofficial translations of the whole Bible or parts of it had appeared from time to time, the best known and most widely used being those by James Moffat,[11] Ronald Knox,[12] and J. B. Phillips.[13] Then, between 1946 and 1957 the *Revised Standard Version* was published in America by the National Council of Churches, taking account of current scholarship and changes in language, jettisoning archaisms which were misleading and yet preserving a dignity of style suitable for use in public worship. The RSV was widely used in this country for private and public reading.

At the meeting of the General Assembly of the Church of Scotland in May 1946 a resolution recommended that a translation of the Bible be made in the language of the present day. The following October delegates from the Church of England, the Church of Scotland, and the Methodist, Baptist and Congregationalist Churches recommended that the work be undertaken and that it should be a completely new translation rather than a revision of any earlier version. These Churches then established the Joint Committee on the New Translation of the Bible and invited representatives of the Presbyterian Church of England, the Society of Friends, the Church in Wales, and the Church of Ireland, together with the British and Foreign Bible Society and the National Bible Society of Scotland to join them. It was not possible for the Roman Catholic Church to be repre-

[11] New Testament, 1913; Old Testament, 1924; final revision of the whole Bible, 1935.

[12] New Testament, 1944; Old Testament, 1948-50.

[13] *Letters to Young Churches*, 1947; *The Gospels*, 1952; *The Young Church in Action*, 1955; *The New Testament in Modern English*, 1958.

sented but at a later stage it appointed an observer. The Bishop of Truro, Dr J. W. Hunkin acted as chairman until his death in 1950, when he was succeeded by the Bishop of Durham, Dr A. T. P. Williams, who guided the enterprise for eighteen years. After his death the Archbishop of York, Dr Donald Coggan, was appointed chairman. Although much of the success of the project was due to this succession of very able chairmen, there was one man who was the presiding genius and who gave outstanding leadership and guidance against the background of his own profound Biblical scholarship and his sensitiveness to the nuances of theology and language. This was the vice-chairman and general director, Dr C. H. Dodd, the Congregationalist scholar and theologian, who at the start of the enterprise had just retired from the Norris-Hulse Professorship of Divinity at Cambridge. The translators were scholars from various British universities whom the Committee believed to be representative of competent biblical criticism at that time. There was also a panel of literary advisers to which the work of the translators was submitted for scrutiny in order to secure a tone and style of language appropriate to the different types of writing found in the Bible. The object of the translation was two-fold. First, it was to be an accurate translation, making use of the new discoveries of ancient manuscripts, the advances of biblical criticism, and the fresh understanding of the language and background of the Bible. Secondly, it was to break away from the dignified prose of the seventeenth century and, by making use of modern speech, to restore something of the impact which the original books made upon their first readers. It was to provide English readers with a faithful rendering of the best available texts 'into the current speech of our own time, and a rendering which should harvest the grains of recent biblical scholarship'.[14] 'We have conceived our task to be that of understanding the original as precisely as we could...and then saying again in our own native idiom what we believed the author to be saying in his.'[15] The New Testament was published in March 1961 and received a great deal of attention from a wide public. The amount of

[14] 'Introduction' to the New Testament, p. vii.
[15] Ibid. For an account of the translators' methods of working, cf. Geoffrey Hunt, *About the New English Bible*, 1970. Cf. also F. W. Dillistone, *C. H. Dodd: Interpreter of the New Testament*, 1977, Chapter 18.

space devoted to it in the secular press was unusual and it rapidly
became a bestseller. The popular view was favourable; here was
a Bible which was authoritative, eminently readable, and attrac-
tively produced. Scholars questioned some of the renderings but
their assessment was mainly favourable. There were some attacks
from those who were wedded to traditional language. The Old
Testament and the Apocrypha were published in 1970 and thus
completed a great enterprise of ecumenical co-operation, great
scholarship, and sympathetic publishing. What Dr Michael
Ramsey affirmed of the New Testament translation in 1961
could be said of the whole *New English Bible*. 'It is no exagger-
ation to say that it brings out the meaning of the story with a
new vividness; it does this because the translators have achieved
a new and scholarly grasp of what the Greek [or Hebrew] really
means, and have conveyed this to a degree which their predecessors in English versions have often missed....The New Bible is
found to give fresh historical vividness to a whole narrative....It
carries meaning across from ancient author to modern reader.'[16]

There appeared in English in 1966 *The Jerusalem Bible*, an
annotated edition of the complete Bible by a group of English-
speaking Roman Catholics, based on the work of the French
biblical scholars at the École Biblique at Jerusalem and first
published in French. This too was distinguished for its historical
accuracy and a resolute attempt to translate into a modern style
of English, and it was well-liked by many Anglicans who began
to use it in public worship. In 1965 the Church Assembly passed
the Prayer Book (Versions of the Bible) Measure which enabled
the authorization for use in public worship of any version of the
Bible approved by the Church Assembly (and later the General
Synod). Under this Measure the *Revised Version*, the *Revised
Standard Version*, the *New English Bible*, and the *Jerusalem
Bible* were authorized for public use in addition to the Authorized Version of 1611. In 1978 there was added to the list *The
Bible in Today's English Version* (TEV), usually known as 'The
Good News Bible', which had been published in 1976 and of
which, by 1978, fifty million copies of the New Testament had
been sold in Great Britain alone. The aims of this version were to
provide a faithful translation of the original text and to express
that translation in words and forms that were widely accepted by

[16] *York Journal of Convocation*, May 1961.

people who use English as a means of communication—that is, in standard, everyday, natural English, avoiding words and forms not in current and widespread use.

## 3. Music and Worship

An important ingredient of public worship is music and the Church of England possesses a great heritage of Church music. Since the war, however, there have been important developments in the tradition and the liturgical changes of the sixties and seventies evoked new forms of music and caused some consternation in the ranks of many traditional Church musicians. The post-war period saw composers of the eminence of Sir Arthur Bliss and Benjamin Britten composing music for Church services. The former wrote a *Te Deum* for the Coronation of Queen Elizabeth II in 1952 and a version of the Beatitudes for the Consecration of Coventry Cathedral in 1962, while the latter's *Te Deum* and *Jubilate* have become part of the repertoire of many Cathedrals. Edward Rubbra's *Magnificat* and *Nunc Dimittis* are worthy to stand besides those of his predecessors. Michael Tippett, Malcolm Williamson, Geoffrey Bush, William Matthias, and Peter Anson, who are fully at home in the world of secular music, have made their contribution to the music of the Church. The Royal School of Church Music, founded in 1927 by Sidney Nicholson, established its headquarters at Addington Palace in 1954 and during the next ten years the membership of affiliated choirs doubled and courses of all kinds flourished. The credit for this must go to Dr Gerald Knight, who was director from 1952 to 1973, when he was succeeded by Dr Lionel Dakers. By 1970 it was promoting the highest standards of teaching for Church musicians, it had established a network of communications with the parishes, it sponsored large festivals of Church music, and it had become both world-wide and ecumenical.

There was, however, a widespread questioning of accepted axioms about Church music which generated a more popular type of music. In 1956 Geoffrey Beaumont produced his *Folk Mass* which, following a broadcast from St. Augustine's, Highgate, attracted considerable attention. As music the work had no particular merit, but Geoffrey Beaumont wrote it because he believed that it was something he could offer to God as a means whereby those unfamiliar with traditional forms might enter into the worship of the Church. It led to the formation of the Twentieth Century Church Light Music Group, which produced a number of popular hymns, but whose best-known work was Patrick Appleford's *Mass of Five Melodies*. Sydney Carter was a significant figure in writing and popularizing new songs for Church worship, the best known being 'The Lord of the Dance', 'When I needed a neighbour', and 'No use knocking on the window'. Along with the new material went the introduction of vocal and instrumental (usually guitar) groups to lead worship.

The liturgical revisions of the traditional services posed considerable problems for traditional Church musicians. It was possible to adapt the traditional settings to Series 2 Holy Communion, but this could not be done with the Series 3 texts which were authorized in 1973.[17] One of the casualties was the Merbecke setting to the Communion Service, composed in 1550 and hitherto commonly used in many churches. A number of settings to Series 3 were composed but many of them were trivial and uninspiring. Among the better ones were those by Peter Anson, by Christopher Dearnley and Alan Wicks, by Alan Gibbs, and by Peter Hurford, although the most popular setting was the one by John Rutter. The emphasis was on unison settings for congregational use, although Francis Jackson and Bryan Kelly composed more elaborate, cathedral-type versions. The period also witnessed an upsurge of hymnody—new hymn books, supplements to standard hymn books, and a multitude of home-grown parish booklets. In 1965 the *Anglican Hymn Book* was published, although its title is misleading because it served the needs of Anglican evangelicals rather than those of Anglicans as a whole. The following year *100 Hymns for Today*, a supplement to *Hymns Ancient and Modern*, was produced and sold over a million copies. It was a 'middle of the road' production, steering a middle course between the traditional and the modern, and included hymns by older writers such as Philip Doddridge and Charles Wesley as well as by new writers like Sydney Carter and Patrick Appleford. Not to be outdone, the proprietors of the *English Hymnal* published a supplement, *English Praise*, which again combined hymns that were well

[17] Cf. below, p. 239.

known and available in other books and some by modern writers. *Youth Praise*[18] and *Psalm Praise*[19] were the production of a small group of evangelicals under the chairmanship of Michael Baughan and contained a considerable amount of new material, although with some exceptions the music was all much in the same superficial style. Some churches made use of the Gélineau Psalter, used by the ecumenical monastic Community of Taizé in France in their Daily Office and adapted into English largely under the sponsorship of Dom Gregory Murrey of Downside Abbey.

## 4. The Cathedrals

It is in the cathedrals that the Anglican choral tradition is most strongly and excellently maintained and since 1945 standards continually rose, although many cathedrals gave encouragement to new forms of music sung by groups which used those buildings for their services and concerts. Cathedrals, however, are much more than centres for music. They represent the architectural achievements of the past, they embody the history of the ages and they are living centres of a worship which has persisted unbroken since their foundation. The cathedral is the mother church of the diocese, it can influence the local community, it can be a centre of education and, in more recent years, it has become a place of pilgrimage for tourists from all parts of the world.

In 1961 the report[20] of a commission appointed by the Church Assembly to make proposals for the better functioning of cathedrals in the modern age, acknowledged the importance of the ministry of a cathedral.

Cathedrals both old and new become places of pilgrimage far in excess of anything previously known. Not only do tourists arrive in vast numbers at the Ancient Cathedrals, but also in modern Cathedrals parties from schools and societies arrive on pilgrimage....More and more secular organisations seek the privilege of regular or occasional services....Far from being outmoded, the Cathedral Churches of England have never before served as living centres of worship for such a wide variety of ordinary Church members.[21]

[18] Vol. 1, 1966; Vol. 2, 1969.     [19] 1973.
[20] *Cathedrals in Modern Life*.     [21] Ibid., pp. 4-5.

Hitherto, however, the cathedrals had suffered from two disadvantages. The first was financial, with the responsibility of keeping in repair a large and ancient building, of maintaining heavy running expenses and of paying reasonable wages and salaries to its lay and clerical staff. The second was the problem of staffing, because in most cathedrals the residentiary canons were also employed in diocesan work. The Cathedrals Measure 1963 helped to overcome some of the problems by laying down that every cathedral was to have a dean or provost and two residentiary canons to be paid by the Church Commissioners and the two canons were to hold no other benefice or demanding diocesan office but were to be engaged solely in cathedral work. In this way the Church acknowledged that modern circumstances had laid upon cathedrals fresh and heavy ministerial responsibilities. The Measure also contained provisions for improving the financial and administrative arrangements of cathedrals.

There is no doubt that these provisions gave the cathedrals a new lease of life. A hundred years previously they tended to be unchanging, insular, and remote institutions, where the world outside appeared to be tolerated rather than welcomed and where, amid much idleness, works of scholarship were produced. Today, however, the buildings are in constant use, the staff is over-stretched and new facilities are being provided to welcome and interest the thousands of visitors. What is cause for some regret is that this increase in activity bids fair to extinguish the tradition of the cathedral as a home of sacred learning. The interests of the increasing number of visitors are varied. Some come out of a simple desire 'to look'—to experience beauty and space. Some are moved by what they see—a reaction which may not be a Christian response but which is nevertheless a 'religious' one. Some have spoken or unspoken pastoral needs which may or may not be met. In order to welcome tourists and to help them as much as possible a number of cathedrals have provided ancillary facilities such as gift shops, guides in various languages, visitors' centres, treasuries, refectories, exhibition areas, car parks, and lavatories. In 1978 it was estimated that in a single fortnight in August at least 1,127,000 people visited twenty-seven of the cathedrals of this country, many from overseas. This great influx has caused management problems and considerable wear and tear to the fabric. While it is clear that visitors make an

increasingly important financial contribution towards the maintenance and repair costs of cathedrals it is totally inadequate
and the question of charging for admission has been often discussed.[22]

Vast sums of money have been required in recent years by
cathedrals for the upkeep of the fabric because, unfortunately,
too many of these huge and ancient buildings had been allowed
to lapse into a dangerous condition. In 1967 an appeal for York
Minster was launched involving the immense sum of two million
pounds.[23] It was followed by appeals for St. Paul's, Canterbury,
Wells, Lincoln, Norwich, and many others. At the same time
the post-war years have seen the building of a new cathedral at
Coventry, the completion of new cathedrals at Guildford and
Liverpool and the enlargement of the cathedrals at Bury St.
Edmunds and Sheffield. On the night of 14-15 November 1940
the City of Coventry was bombed by the German Luftwaffe for
eleven consecutive hours. Large parts of the City became a mass
of rubble and the medieval cathedral, one of the most beautiful
churches in England, was reduced to a blackened shell leaving
only the spire intact. After the war the authorities started
building anew and the winning design, which was open to com-
petition, was won in 1951 by Basil Spence.[24] His cathedral was
to be set at right angles to the old one, the shell of which served
as a forecourt. Its basic shape was traditional, with the altar at
the 'east' end, separated from the nave by a chancel. Basil
Spence gathered together a team of artists whose work resulted
in the imaginative use of materials which was a main feature of
the building. The great tapestry of Christ in Glory over the high
altar was the responsibility of Graham Sutherland. John Piper,
Lawrence Lee, Geoffrey Clarke and others designed the stained
glass and the engraved glass was the work of John Hutton. Outside the entrance stood a sculpture of St. Michael and the Devil
by Jacob Epstein. The font consisted of a natural boulder from
Bethlehem. Attached to the cathedral was the Chapel of Unity,
the floor of which was basically a star containing the continents

---

[22] Salisbury Cathedral became a centre of controversy when, in 1974, it began to
make a charge for admission. A number of cathedrals make a charge for admission to
parts of the building.

[23] In 1972 a second appeal was launched.

[24] Cf. Basil Spence, *Phoenix at Coventry*, 1962.

and the emblems of the evangelists, with the symbol of the Holy Spirit at the centre. The cathedral was consecrated in 1962 and within a year it had received three and a half million visitors. Under the leadership of the Provost, H. C. N. Williams, Coventry Cathedral became a centre for new patterns of ministry. His vision was that, as the old cathedral had been destroyed by hate, the Christian response must be that of reconciliation—reconciliation between nations and reconciliation within the community in which the cathedral was situated. He brought together a large staff, members of which had responsibility towards industry, commerce, the social services, the civic and administrative life of the city, ecumenical enterprises, the ministry of healing, education, the care of tourists, the music of the cathedral and its worship, drama, and international youth work. This extensive ministry was facilitated by an undercroft which allowed the ample provision of suitable 'plant'. The cathedral thus became the base for a team of priests and laymen ready to experiment in order that people from a wide variety of backgrounds might express their faith and aspirations through the cathedral.[25] The most outstanding work of the cathedral, however, was its fostering of international reconciliation and the links of friendship which it established with Germany which had been responsible for the destruction of the former cathedral.[26] The cross of nails—nails from the burnt beams of the old cathedral tied into the form of a cross—was the Coventry symbol expressing the message: 'From Crucifixion through Forgiveness to Reconciliation.'

The building of Guildford cathedral, designed by Sir Edward Maufe, had been commenced in 1936 and had been interrupted by the war. It was completed three years after Coventry cathedral. Its design was an unadventurous and simplified version of traditional Gothic in red brick made from the clay of the hill on which the cathedral stands in a dominating and solitary position away from the centre of the city. The austere exterior was in contrast to the cool spaciousness of the interior, but it possessed little of the excellencies of materials—glass, tapestry, and woodwork—of Coventry cathedral. In the autumn of 1978, in the

---

[25] Cf. H. C. N. Williams, *Twentieth Century Cathedral*, 1964.
[26] Cf. W. E. Rose, *Sent from Coventry*, 1980.

presence of Queen Elizabeth II, Liverpool cathedral celebrated its completion, seventy-five years after the laying of its foundation stone by King Edward VII. This building had been designed on so vast a scale that it is the fifth largest cathedral in the world, accommodating a congregation of more than four thousand people and costing five million pounds. Giles Gilbert Scott designed it on a fine site on a high rocky ridge overlooking the Mersey. Built of local sandstone with copper roofs, it is a Gothic building of enormous scale and tremendous spaciousness. The best that stained glass artists, engineers, glaziers, embroiderers, and carpenters could produce contributed to its magnificence. John Betjeman has defined this cathedral's unique quality as 'the art of enclosing space', yet within its majestic structure there are facilities for a mobile altar, choir stalls, and organ console to make the building adaptable to a variety of needs and occasions.[27] The building is more than a great edifice; it is a centre of compassion and concern and a place where music, preaching, drama, and exhibitions, find a home. Here great youth events, services for every kind of occasion, international gatherings, and ecumenical meetings take place. The impact of the cathedral has been due to the vision and open-mindedness of a succession of deans—F. W. Dwelly, F. W. Dillistone and E. H. Patey.

When the diocese of St. Edmundsbury and Ipswich was formed in 1914, the parish church of St. James, Bury St. Edmunds, had been designated as the cathedral. In 1945 Stephen Dykes-Bower was appointed architect and produced an elaborate plan for enlarging the cathedral. A porch and cloisters were built and in 1964 the foundation stone of the new choir and lady chapel was laid. In 1970 the hallowing of the crossing completed the project.[28] At Sheffield a new sanctuary and other buildings had been added to the parish church cathedral before the war and in 1942 a new quire aisle and a crypt were consecrated. After the war an extension to the nave, a new west porch, a tower, and new chapels were added. Thus a modest parish church was converted into a cathedral worthy of the diocese.[29]

[27] Cf. J. Riley, *Today's Cathedral*, 1978.
[28] Cf. Leslie Brown, *Three Worlds: One Word*, 1978, pp. 195ff.
[29] Cf. Mary Walton, *A History of the Diocese of Sheffield*, 1981, pp. 44-6, 72, 118, 138-9.

# 9
# THE CONTINUING SEARCH FOR UNITY

> For the majority of English people there are only two
> religions, Roman Catholic, which is wrong, and the
> rest which don't matter.
>
> Duff Cooper, *Old Men Forget*, 1953

> The vision which rises before us is that of a Church,
> genuinely Catholic, loyal to all truth, and gathering
> into its fellowship all 'who profess and call them-
> selves Christians', within whose visible unity all the
> treasures of faith and order, bequeathed as a heri-
> tage by the past to the present, shall be possessed in
> common, and made serviceable to the whole Body of
> Christ. Within this unity Christian Communions
> now separated from one another would retain much
> that has long been distinctive in their methods of
> worship and service. It is through a rich diversity of
> life and devotion that the unity of the whole fellow-
> ship will be fulfilled.
>
> Lambeth *Appeal for Reunion*, 1920

## 1. The Anglican-Methodist Unity Scheme

DELEGATES ASSEMBLED at the Faith and Order Conference at
Nottingham in September 1964, under the auspices of the
British Council of Churches, challenged the Churches in Britain
'to covenant together to work and pray for the inauguration of a
union' by Easter Day 1980. They also called upon the Churches
to designate 'areas of ecumenical experiment' at the request of
local congregations or in new towns and housing areas. Finally,
they urged that 'negotiations between particular churches
already in hand be seen as steps towards the goal' of unity.[1] The
challenge about covenanting was not immediately accepted by

---

[1] Cf. *Unity Begins at Home: Report of the Faith and Order Conference of the BCC at Nottingham*, 1964.

the Churches and was not taken seriously until after the failure of the Anglican-Methodist reunion scheme; the establishment of areas of ecumenical experiment began soon after the conference;[2] 'negotiations between particular churches' clearly referred to the Anglican-Methodist conversations.

After the acceptance by those two Churches of the *Interim Report* in 1958[3] the representatives of the two Churches published a definitive report,[4] which recommended unity by two stages. During the first stage the two Churches would retain their distinctive life and identity but would be in full communion with each other. This would involve three things. First, the formal recognition of the two Churches would take place in a 'Service of Reconciliation', which would include 'the integration by reciprocal action of their respective ministries'. Secondly, the Methodists would accept episcopacy, Methodist bishops would be consecrated, and all subsequent ordinations of Methodist ministers would be by bishops. Thirdly, provision would be made whereby the two churches would co-operate together 'by consultation, common action and common devotion at all levels'. The Methodists would accept episcopacy provided that such acceptance was not construed as implying that there was any defect in its own ministry and provided that Methodists had as much freedom of interpretation as Anglicans had in determining the meaning of episcopacy.

Stage One might last for ten, twenty, or thirty years, but clearly it could not last indefinitely for 'the existence of two parallel Churches, side by side, in full communion, would be anomalous and unsatisfactory except as a stage towards and a means of achieving the ultimate goal of union'. Stage Two, the details of which were deliberately left vague, would be the complete integration of the two Churches. All the Anglicans signed the report but four of the Methodists, led by Professor Kingsley Barrett, objected that the implementation of the recommendations would lead to certain division in the Methodist Church and to possible division within the Church of England. Episcopacy, in the sense of the strict invariability or ordination by bishops in the apostolic succession, was unacceptable and the

[2] Cf. below, pp. 175ff.    [3] Cf. above, p. 82.
[4] *Conversations Between the Church of England and the Methodist Church*, 1958.

view of priesthood enunciated in the report endangered the doctrine of the priesthood of all believers. Within the Methodist Church a number accepted these objections and therefore opposed the scheme. They formed their own organization, known as the 'Voice of Methodism', although none of the four signatories of the note of dissent took part in the movement. After two years' discussion in the Churches, the Convocations of the Church of England and the Methodist Conference agreed by large majorities that the proposals represented the right way forward. Further conversations were initiated to clarify some important issues, to draw up a detailed scheme for the coming together of the two Churches, to revise the proposed Service of Reconciliation and to produce a common Ordinal.

Hitherto the debates on the scheme had been proceeding almost entirely at the official, national level and do not appear to have raised great interest among the ordinary members of the two Churches. After the acceptance of the two-stage scheme, however, a considerable volume of hitherto latent opposition began to emerge. Archbishop Geoffrey Fisher, from his place of retirement, began to bombard his successor, the press, members of the commission, and many others with letters opposing the scheme and to publish pamphlets setting out his views.[5] He regarded plans for reunion as both premature and unnecessary and considered that intercommunion was all that was required. He also feared that reunion with the Methodists would bring about the end of the Church of England as the Established Church of the country and as the centre of the Anglican Communion.

The latest commission published its report[6] in 1968. It included the text of a common Ordinal, which was generally accepted with warm approval. The commission's revision of the Service of Reconciliation made it clear that, in the laying-on of hands on each minister of both Churches, the prayer was offered that 'the Holy Spirit may be sent upon "each according to his need"'. Inexplicit this might be, but the intention was not in doubt. 'It was to secure that every minister taking part should

[5] Cf., e.g. *The Anglican-Methodist Conversations and the Pattern of Church Unity*, 1964; *Covenant and Reconciliation: A Critical Examination*, 1967.

[6] *Anglican-Methodist Unity: 1. The Scheme; 2. The Ordinal.* This has been preceded by an Interim Report, *Towards Reconciliation*, 1967.

receive whatever he might lack of the gifts and graces bestowed upon the ministers of the other Church.' It was open for anyone who so desired to regard the laying-on of hands as an ordination but that was not the inevitable or necessary implication. Thus we approach the rock upon which the scheme ultimately floundered. Indeed, Dr James Packer, a leading Anglican evangelical, was unable to sign the report because he could not accept a Service of Reconciliation which could in any way be construed by anyone as an ordination. On the other hand, many Anglicans believed that 'ambiguity' was no new feature of Anglicanism and that the Book of Common Prayer contained statements construed differently by different schools of churchmanship. In the unprecedented situation of two Churches coming together they were convinced that, if this was ever to become a realized situation, ambiguity had to be accepted and that there was nothing equivocal, evasive, or dishonest about this. Nobody could presume to know in this situation exactly what graces were required and it was therefore right for Methodists and Anglicans to cast themselves upon God in humility and faith and to receive what, in His eyes, it was necessary for them to receive. There were two groups, however, for whom ambiguity was anathema, but for opposite and irreconcilable reasons. Anglo-Catholics (but not all) opposed the scheme because the Service of Reconciliation did not make it explicit that the traditional catholic priesthood was being conveyed by the laying-on of hands. The evangelicals (but not all) opposed the Scheme because the Service of Reconciliation seemed to them to suggest that the traditional catholic priesthood *was* being conveyed. The first group rejected the service because ordination was not made clear, the second group rejected it because non-ordination was not made clear, and neither group could see that a totally logical solution was impossible. Both, by implication, denied the historic fact of the widely comprehensive nature of the Church of England. Moreover, the anglo-catholics, by rejecting the proposed method, were rejecting what had become the official approach of the Anglican Communion to unity schemes largely because of pressure from anglo-catholics who had been so opposed to the South India method.[7] Finally, there was a growing number of

[7] Cf. above, pp. 89f.

churchmen who began to question the whole concept of reunion by schemes initiated and implemented centrally. Groups of experts may have been discussing plans for reunion for sixteen years, but the average Anglican and the average Methodist still knew too little about each other. Again, the climate of opinion had changed so much since conversations had begun between the two Churches in 1955 that many believed that the proposed scheme ought to be replaced by a multilateral approach to unity by all the Churches in Great Britain. Meanwhile, within the Methodist Church the Voice of Methodism persuaded groups of Methodists that the scheme struck at the very heart of Methodism and that in no circumstances ought this Church to accept the historic episcopate. Although it never succeeded in becoming more than a minority movement, it seemed to many Anglicans to be more representative than it was and this caused some to hesitate and others to use it as an argument against proceeding with the scheme.

In May 1969 the Convocations agreed that there was sufficient doctrinal agreement for the two Churches to enter Stage One, that the Service of Reconciliation was adequate and that the common Ordinal was satisfactory. It had been earlier decided that there should be a referendum of the clergy and this produced a result in favour of the scheme but with a large minority against it. More than a third of the clergy indicated that they would be unwilling to take part in the Service of Reconciliation. The opinion of the dioceses was also sought and the voting at the Diocesan Conferences revealed that, while most dioceses were in favour of the scheme, the majorities were far from conclusive. It was arranged that the final decision of each of the Churches should be made on the same day. In its desire to carry the whole Church—or as many as possible—the Church of England had decided that a 75 per cent majority would be required in the Convocations, and the Methodist Conference accepted this for its own voting. On 8 July 1969 the Methodist Conference met at Birmingham and, despite a powerful speech in opposition by Professor Kingsley Barrett, approved the scheme by a majority of 76 per cent. On the same day the Convocations of the Church of England, meeting in joint session at

Westminster, failed to secure the required majority.[8] This was in spite of the well-argued and heartfelt advocacy of Archbishop Ramsey who exposed the anomaly of the Convocations rejecting a scheme the doctrinal soundness of which they had affirmed only two months before.

For some time supporters of the scheme had been pressing their opponents to produce an alternative scheme. Now, in 1970, two of the anglo-catholic opponents—the Bishop of Willesden, the Rt. Revd Graham Leonard, and Dr E. L. Mascall—and two of the evangelical opponents—Dr James Packer and the Revd Colin Buchanan—published a book entitled *Growing into Union*. It was unfortunate that the tone of this work was arrogant, polemical, and even abusive and that the authors displayed such self-satisfaction with the rightness of their views. They dealt with what they regarded as the weaknesses and confusions of the scheme, the Service of Reconciliation being described as 'a bog of illogic' and a 'magnificent double-think'. The three positive criticisms of the scheme were its lack of local support, its failure to produce a reformed as well as a united Church, and its agnosticism about Stage Two. The authors argued that reunion should emerge from local agreement. Once local Churches could reach doctrinal agreement they could proceed to unite in an episcopal Church without any service of reconciliation or unification of ministries. The united Church would thus be inaugurated 'in a piece-meal way territorially, leaving the existing denominations to exist alongside each other in every place where conscience might so agree'. The parent bodies would slowly cede their members into the life of the united Church. The authors proposed that members of non-episcopal Churches should simply be 'adopted' into the ministerial structure of the united Church and its ministers would appear before the bishop for 'recognition and acceptance as a presbyter in the Church of God into the presbyterate of the united Church'. The reaction to *Growing into Union* was unenthusiastic in both the Church of England and the Methodist Church. Many anglo-catholics were as unhappy about the

[8] Upper House of Canterbury: 27 for, 2 against (93%)
Lower House of Canterbury: 154 for, 77 against (67%)
Upper House of York: 11 for, 3 against (78%)
Lower House of York: 71 for, 34 against (68%)
Total Vote: 263 for, 116 against (69%)

authors' proposed method of dealing with non-episcopally ordained ministers as they were about the original scheme. There
were also numerous practical objections, for the implementation
of the proposals could lead to administrative, financial, and
legal chaos. Fundamentally, however, the whole concept of the
local, 'piece-by-piece' approach was regarded as untheological,
highly divisive, and productive of little more than a form of
congregationalism.

The supporters of the original scheme made a second attempt
to secure the approval of the two Churches and when the
scheme came before the General Synod in May 1972 further
voting in the diocesan synods had shown that less than 63 per
cent of the clergy favoured the scheme and less than 68 per cent
of the clergy and laity together. Speeches by the Archbishop of
Canterbury at the beginning and end of the debate were loudly
applauded, but all was in vain and once again the scheme failed
to obtain the 75 per cent majority.[9] There was a certain irony in
the fact that, immediately before this debate, the Synod had
approved the proposal for the Church of England to enter into
full communion with the Church of North India and the
Church of Pakistan. These two Churches had been inaugurated
in 1970 and each represented a union between the Anglican
Church and certain Free Churches, including the Methodists,
where the act for the unifying of ministers bore very close resemblance to the act of reconciliation in the Anglican-Methodist
scheme. For many this questioned the whole credibility of the
General Synod, for as Dr Ramsey said, 'what sort of a God is it
who was willing and able to answer the prayer with laying-on of
hands in the North India scheme and is not willing to answer the
prayer in the Anglican-Methodist Service?'

Thus ended twenty years' negotiations between the Church of
England and the Methodist Church and there was much agoniz-
ing in seeking the cause of the failure. It is superficial to suggest
that subconsciously the opponents were possessed of fear of
basic change, insecurity, and reluctance to 'launch out into the
deep' and were thus deficient in faith and hope. Most of the

[9] House of Bishops: 34 for, 6 against (85%)
House of Clergy: 152 for, 80 against (65.52%)
House of Laity: 147 for, 87 against (62.82%)
Total Vote: 333 for, 173 against (65.81%)

opponents based their stance on considered theological and practical issues. Dissatisfaction with the Service of Reconciliation, though for entirely opposite reasons, led to an unlikely but powerful alliance against the scheme between the anglo-catholics and the evangelicals. Some anglo-catholics objected also because of their conviction that union with the Methodists would make union with Rome more remote. Others in the Church, although they accepted the soundness of the scheme, after listening to those who in conscience were unable to co-operate, failed to vote for it because of the fear that the result might fragment the Church. This is the main reason why the scheme obtained a smaller majority in 1972 than it did in 1969. Fundamentally, however, the result reflected the divisions—particularly on the theology of ministry—which existed within the Church of England and indicated that until there was reconciliation within itself that Church was unready for reconciliation with another Church. Finally, there had grown up an increasing weariness with schemes, which only emphasized the gulf which can divide official policy and local conservatism. There were pleas for a multilateral approach to unity in England and for this there were those who were willing to jettison the years of negotiation with the Methodist Church which had been the one Church to respond to the Church of England's invitation in 1950.

The day after the final rejection of the scheme the bishops unanimously urged increased co-operation between the Anglican and Methodist Churches at the local level and it is salutary to record that, in spite of the bitterness, sadness, disappointment, and disillusionment that was felt by many, this call was heeded. Nevertheless, some were disheartened and weary; hasty and harsh judgements were made and there was no more talk of schemes.

## 2. Ecumenical Co-operation

The most promising outcome of the abortive Anglican-Methodist scheme was the impetus it gave to ecumenical relationships at local level. In 1967 the British Council of Churches had launched a programme of study called *The People Next Door*. It was for use by ecumenical groups throughout the country and one of its purposes was 'to test the relevance of the ecumenical insights in the local church situation'.[10] The BCC hoped that some six hundred thousand people would participate in the programme, but in the event only 85,000, of which 35,000 were Anglicans, took part. Where the project was taken seriously it did much to remove misunderstandings about the beliefs and practices of the various Churches and made friendships across denominational boundaries. The growth of ecumenical relationships throughout the country led to the emergence of three demands. The first was that intercommunion should be officially authorized, the second was that the sharing of church buildings should be made legally possible, and the third was that machinery for establishing areas of ecumenical co-operation on an official basis should be established. Rumblings about the stringency of the regulations governing intercommunion had been heard for some considerable time. There had been an attempt in the debates on canon law revision to include a reference to these regulations in canon B15 but in 1965 the part of the canon dealing with this was withdrawn under pressure from those who believed that its provisions did not go far enough. This pressure for change had been given a powerful impetus by the publication in November 1961 of an 'Open Letter to the Archbishops on Intercommunion', signed by thirty-two Anglicans, mainly concerned with the teaching of theology and related subjects and including the heads of six theological colleges and the deans of eight Cambridge colleges. The letter

urged the necessity of an immediate readiness on the part of the Anglican Communion to acknowledge the authenticity of the sacramental ministry of those churches, which had rejected the historical episcopate, and whose ministers had in consequence not received episcopal ordination. This attitude should express itself in a readiness on the part of Anglicans (in appropriate circumstances) to avail themselves of such sacramental ministrations and to admit, without let or hindrance, to Communion at Anglican altars all persons who (although not episcopally confirmed) were recognised as full members of their own churches, and who desire to receive the holy sacrament at an Anglican celebration of the Eucharist.[11]

[10] *Agenda for the Churches. A Report on PND Progress*, 1968, pp. 15ff.

[11] D. M. Mackinnon, *The Stripping of the Altars*, 1969, p. 62. A month later another 'Open Letter' on the subject, which sought to refute the arguments in the original letter, was sent to the archbishops, signed by fifty-three members of the House of Laity of the Church Assembly.

In 1968 a commission of the Church Assembly published a report[12] which considered the theological and practical aspects of intercommunion and, after debate in the Assembly and its successor, the General Synod, canon B15A was promulged, which admitted to Holy Communion in Anglican Churches all communicant members of other Churches which subscribed to the doctrine of the Holy Trinity and who were 'in good standing', although the canon required the incumbent ultimately to set before a regular communicant from a non-Anglican Church the normal requirement in the Church of England for episcopal Confirmation. Although this fell short of full intercommunion, it meant that Free Church members, as guests, could come freely to Anglican altars.

In 1969 the Sharing of Church Buildings Act was passed and this allowed the use of existing Anglican Church buildings by other denominations and made it lawful to build new churches on a shared basis, although the Act imposed certain limitations and conditions. Areas of ecumenical co-operation were being established, most commonly in new towns and in housing areas which lacked the weight of inherited tradition characteristic of the established parishes. None the less, in some localities well-established denominational patterns were breaking down in favour of ecumenical ones. In Cotham, Bristol, for example, a joint Baptist, Congregational, and Methodist Church began in 1946, while in 1968 at Desborough in Norfolk, a small town of five thousand inhabitants, Anglicans and Methodists began working towards a united congregation, a team ministry and a single set of Church premises. It will be recalled that one of the challenges of the 1964 Nottingham Conference had been a call to member Churches 'to designate areas of ecumenical experiment, at the request of local congregations or in new towns and housing areas'. Later these were defined as areas where, under responsible authority, certain denominational traditions were suspended for a period in order that new patterns of worship, mission, and ministry could be undertaken. In 1969 the British Council of Churches published *The Designation of Areas of Ecumenical Experiment*, which recommended that for such experiments a 'sponsoring body' should be established as the responsible authority under which the operation should take

[12] *Intercommunion Today.*

place. The composition of this body would depend on the area in question, but would normally consist of official nominees of the Churches involved in the experiment, and its object was to ensure that the experiment had the official commitment of the Churches involved, to give support and security to the team operating the experiment, to guard against the experiment causing the establishment of a 'new denomination', and to evaluate the experiment. This proposal was accepted by the Churches and in 1973 all the main Churches had set up a Consultative Council for Local Ecumenical Projects in England as an advisory body for local ecumenical projects. By 1974 there were some forty-six designated areas in Great Britain and the number rose to 289 in 1977, 241 of which involved sharing of buildings, 191 the joint working of congregations and 194 a sharing of ministers. The Church of England was a partner in 188 projects, the Methodists shared in 241, the United Reformed Church in 153, the Baptists in 41 and the Roman Catholics in 26. There can be little doubt that these local activities have done more to promote Christian unity than centrally devised schemes, for they have involved ordinary Christians personally in ecumenical life and worship. At the same time, problems have emerged. There is a sense in which, in spite of the work of Sponsoring Bodies, local ecumenical projects possess an ethos so different from that of the participating denominations that there is a serious danger of isolation. This is accentuated in a mobile society when a member of an ecumenical congregation moves out of the Area and finds himself faced with the divided Church in his new locality. In this new setting, to which Church is he to belong? This is paralleled by the problem raised within an Area when those coming for the baptism of their children or for admission to full membership are obliged to choose one denomination out of those involved in the united project. There has been considerable use of the bishop's dispensing power to give authority for local ecumenical projects to go beyond normal limits of Church of England practice, but there is no unanimity among the bishops themselves about the extent of their dispensing powers and this has resulted in wide divergences between them and a change of bishop can lead to a change of policy and in permissions given. Some areas ignore authority, justifying this on pastoral grounds and by the conviction that rules and traditions must not hamper the mission of the Church. It is in these situations that the danger of 'separatism' arises. All these problems demonstrate that, while local ecumenism is fundamental, it is no substitute for a continuing search for organic union between Churches at national level. These are the two sides of the single coin.

## 3. The Roman Catholic Church

Roman Catholics participated in these ecumenical activities as fully as the discipline of their Church allowed and the fact that by the end of the sixties this co-operation extended as far as it did was due to the immense changes that took place in that Church after the ecumenical estrangement of the fifties. The most important cause was the election in 1958 of Pope John XXIII. He was no revolutionary nor was he an original thinker and his knowledge of the Church of England was unreliable, but he possessed something more crucial than any of these. 'He was able to pick up, as it were, on his spiritual attenae, the Holy Spirit's promptings which led to the Second Vatican Council.'[13] Within the first year of his pontificate he announced the calling of an 'Ecumenical Council of the Universal Church' and as part of the preparation for this he established a new Secretariat for the Promoting of Unity among Christians. One of the first results of this new openness was the visit, at his own instigation, in 1960 of the Archbishop of Canterbury, Dr Fisher, to Rome as part of an ecumenical journey which also took him to Jerusalem and to Istanbul. It was the first time an Archbishop of Canterbury had visited Rome since 1397. His proposed courtesy call on Pope John was viewed with grave suspicion by the Vatican officials who treated the whole affair 'like a guilty secret'..[14] They did their best to discourage the visit and when they failed they attempted to keep publicity to a minimum. Afterwards, Fisher wrote of his visit: 'We talked as two happy people.'[15] At one point the Pope read to him a passage from a recent address which included the phrase, '...the time when our separated brethren should return to the Mother Church'. At once the

---

[13] Bernard and Margaret Pawley, *Rome and Canterbury*, 1974, p. 331.
[14] Peter Nicholls, *The Politics of the Vatican*, 1968, p. 314.
[15] Quoted, William Purcell, *Fisher of Lambeth*, p. 283.

Archbishop interjected, 'Your Holiness, not *return.*' 'Not return?' asked the Pope, 'Why not?' To which the Archbishop replied, 'None of us can go backwards. We are each now running on parallel courses; we are looking forward, until, in God's good time, our two courses approximate and meet.' After a pause, the Pope commented, 'You are right.' Fisher later said that 'from that moment, so far as I knew, he and the Vatican never talked about our returning to past situations and looking backwards for our objectives'.[16] It was a suitable climax and close to an archiepiscopate which had been notable for Fisher's endeavours for Christian reunion.

One of the positive achievements of the Archbishop's visit was that, with the agreement of the Vatican, he decided to send a representative to live in Rome to study the preparations for the Vatican Council, to keep the archbishops informed of progress, and to be at the disposal of the Secretariat for Unity for supplying information about the Church of England. The officer appointed was Canon Bernard Pawley of Ely Cathedral, who took up his appointment in 1961. It was thus officially accepted that mutual understanding was essential and that efforts must be made to appreciate the theology, liturgy, spirituality, and pastoral methods of each other's Churches. During this period there was a marked improvement in Anglican-Roman Catholic relations in this country under Cardinal John Heenan of Westminster and the Apostolic Delegate, Eugene Cardinale.

The Second Vatican Council opened in October 1962 and ended in December 1965. A notable feature was the invitation to the Church of England and other non-Roman Churches to send observers who had the right and duty to make comments and suggestions. Several documents having the official approval of the Council revealed a changed attitude to liturgy, theology, and Church order. The importance of Scripture, the use of modern critical methods of scholarship, a more balanced view of the role of the Blessed Virgin Mary, the collegiality of bishops, the pastoral office of the priesthood and the essential role of the laity were all emphasized. Most important was the more liberal attitude towards the status of the non-Roman baptized. The Decree on Ecumenism recognized a special relationship with the

---

[16] Quoted, ibid.

fellowship of the baptized, a common inheritance in the Scriptures and a bond in the celebration of the Eucharist, and it declared that 'among those in which some Catholic traditions and institutions continue to exist, the Anglican Communion occupies a special place'. Nevertheless, it cannot be overlooked that the Decree also reiterated the exclusive claim of the Church of Rome, under the papal primacy, as the source of the fulness of the means of salvation.

During the Council Pope John died and was succeeded by Cardinal Montini of Milan as Paul VI. He was liberal in his outlook and has been described as the most open-minded Pope of modern times. Moreover, he had visited England and was not unfamiliar with Anglican ways. His first allocution to the Vatican Council contained a memorable passage in which he spoke of 'the inexpressible consolation and reasonable hope that their [i.e. the non-Roman Catholic observers] presence stirs up within us, as well as...the deep sadness we feel at their prolonged separation. If we are in any way to blame for that separation, we humbly beg God's forgiveness, and ask pardon too of our brethren who feel themselves to have been injured by us.'

In August 1965 the Secretariat for Promoting Christian Unity indicated informally that a specific proposal for a visit from the new Archbishop of Canterbury would be welcomed. This visit, which occurred in March 1966, was in marked contrast to that of his predecessor and this indicated the radical change which had occurred in the relationship between the two Churches. Whereas Dr Fisher's was a 'courtesy call' on the Pope, planned to receive the minimum of publicity, Dr Ramsey's was an official and public event. He had emphasized that he was visiting in his capacity as head of the Anglican Communion and he was received formally by the Pope in the Sistine Chapel, where he was embraced as a brother patriarch. 'You are building a bridge', the Pope told him, 'which for centuries has lain fallow, between the Church of Rome and the Church of Canterbury', and the Archbishop spoke of the hope of 'increasing dialogue between theologians, Roman Catholic and Anglican, and of other traditions'. The Pope and the Archbishop promulgated a Common Declaration[17] on 24 March declaring their intention 'to inaugurate

---

[17] 'The Common Declaration by Pope Paul VI and the Archbishop of Canterbury, 24th March 1966', in the Anglican-Roman Catholic International Commission, *Final Report*, 1982, pp. 117ff.

between the Roman Catholic Church and the Anglican Communion serious dialogue which...may lead to that unity in truth
for which Christ prayed'.

Two important steps followed quickly upon the Archbishop's
visit. Within a month the Anglican Institute was established in
Rome,[18] with the Revd John Findlow, former Anglican chaplain
in Athens, as its first director. Its purpose was to establish a
channel for the extension of relationships already achieved and
it was a meeting-place for members of the Anglican Communion
and other Churches, particularly the Roman Catholic Church,
for discussion and prayer. It also gathered a library of Anglican
history, theology, and liturgy, thus providing working facilities
for Anglican scholars in Rome. Secondly, as a first step in imple-
menting the Common Declaration, the archbishops and the
Pope set up an Anglican-Roman Catholic Joint Preparatory
Council out of which was born the Anglican-Roman Catholic
International Commission (ARCIC) which in due course published three important statements—on the Eucharist (1971), on
the ministry (1973) and on authority (1976).[19] In England also a
dialogue began in 1970 between the Archbishop's Commission
on Roman Catholic Relations and representatives of the Roman
Catholic Ecumenical Commission for England and Wales. In
1974, after the Archbishop's Commission had become part of
the General Synod's Board of Mission and Unity, it joined with
a sub-committee of the Roman Catholic Ecumenical Commission to form an 'English ARCIC' for the furtherance of Anglican-
Roman Catholic relations in this country. In those early days it
devoted most of its time to the vexed question of 'mixed marriages'.[20]

A discordant note was struck in 1968 when the Pope issued
the encyclical *Humanae Vitae*, which reiterated the traditional
prohibition of all artificial methods of birth control. The intransigence of this pronouncement was in sharp contrast to the views
accepted by most Anglicans and set out in the resolutions of the
1958 Lambeth Conference. The 1968 Lambeth Conference met
shortly after the publication of the encyclical and Archbishop
Ramsey declared that 'the changes in human society and world
population, as well as the means available for contraception,

---

[18] Now known as the Anglican Centre in Rome.
[19] Cf. below, pp. 268f.          [20] Cf. below, p. 271.

which have occurred since 1958, seem to me to re-enforce rather than to shake the argument and the conclusions reached at the Lambeth Conference of 1958'. In due course the 1968 Conference declared that it found itself 'unable to agree with the Pope's conclusion', and reaffirmed the view of its predecessor.

In addition to official forms of co-operation Vatican 2 marked the beginning of a number of unofficial contacts between the two Churches and a greater willingness of Roman Catholic priests to share pastoral and liturgical functions with Anglicans. Since 1945 Roman Catholic observers had been appointed to the British Council of Churches and it became commonplace for Roman Catholics to share in local Councils of Churches. At the same time, not all Roman Catholics were enamoured of the new ecumenism and, indeed, in some of their dioceses bishops of the old school kept clergy and laity, much to the frustration of many, on a tight rein. The liturgical reforms of the Roman Church, coinciding with the parallel process in the Church of England, was a further bond between the two Churches, and the Roman Church was represented on the International Consultation on English Texts[21] and had an observer on the Joint Liturgical Group[22] in Great Britain. Finally, the Instruction to the Pontifical Biblical Commission of 1964 led to a more liberal approach on the part of Rome towards biblical studies with the result that their biblical scholars were brought into closer contact with non-Roman scholars and this drawing together on the basis of Scripture formed a most helpful basis for ecumenical relations.

Perhaps there was no better indication of the spirit existing between the two Churches at the close of the decade than the words of Pope Paul at the canonization of the English and Welsh Martyrs in 1970. They were written by the Pope himself, who added them to his address at the last moment.

Their devotion to their country gives us an assurance that on that day when—God willing—the unity of faith and life is restored, no offence will be inflicted on the honour and sovereignty of a great country such as England. There will be no seeking to lessen the legitimate prestige and usage proper to the Anglican Church when the Roman Church... is able to embrace firmly her ever-loved sister in the authentic communion of the family of Christ.

[21] Cf. above, p. 155.
[22] Cf. ibid.

## 4. Lambeth 1968

Relations with other Churches was the subject of one of the sections of the 1968 Lambeth Conference and among the Conference resolutions was a reaffirmation of the Lund principle that 'we should do together everything which conscience does not compel us to do separately'. The bishops called for experiments in ecumenical co-operation at the local level and at the same time commended the ecumenical significance of the World Council of Churches. They urged greater freedom for intercommunion and they welcomed the Anglican-Methodist Scheme for Great Britain. Finally, the Conference supported the signs of progress in Anglican-Roman Catholic relations, recommended the establishment of a joint commission of Anglicans and Roman Catholics to consider the theology of ministry and intercommunion, and commended the discussions in progress about mixed marriages. Bishop Lakdasa de Mel, Metropolitan of India, Burma, and Ceylon, gave considerable offence to some of the English bishops by suggesting that many affirmed their belief in unity provided they were not obliged to put their words into practice. 'There are a great many dear people', he said, 'who cheer from the sidelines and wave on all the innocent Africans and Asians, saying, "We will have Christian union to the last Indian."' According to Bishop Leslie Brown, he went on to say that, 'when the Church of England was actually confronted with the possibility of union, they scuttled like rabbits into a hedge', and Dr Brown commented: 'What he said hurt because it was true.' Bishop de Mel's outburst was prompted by the Bishop of Peterborough's (Dr Cyril Eastaugh) desire that the resolution acknowledging that the proposed Service of Reconciliation was 'theologically adequate' should not be put, on the ground that many of the overseas bishops did not understand the situation in England. Bishop Eastaugh was, understandably, outraged by Bishop de Mel's outburst, and feelings against him were so high that some members of the Conference threatened to absent themselves from the closing Eucharist at which de Mel was to be the preacher.[23]

One of the far-reaching decisions of the Conference was to establish an Anglican Consultative Council to take over the res-

[23] Leslie Brown, *Three Worlds: One Word*, 1981, pp. 217-18.

ponsibilities of the Lambeth Consultative Body and the Anglican Council on Missionary Strategy. The body was to include clergy and laity representative of the Churches of the Anglican Communion and was to share information, advise on provincial structures, develop policies for the world mission of the Church, and advise Anglican Churches on matters arising out of union negotiations. It was to meet every two years in various parts of the world and its first session was held in Lumuru, Kenya, early in 1971.

One of the resolutions of the Conference recorded 'gratitude for the concept of Mutual Responsibility and Interdependence in the Body of Christ, and for the renewed sense of responsibility for each other which it has created in our communion'. This concept (MRI) was invented by a group of bishops which met before the third Anglican Congress which was held at Toronto in August 1963. The delegates at the Congress accepted the scheme, the aim of which was to mobilize the resources of the Anglican Communion in such a way that help could be given where and when it was most needed. It advocated a comprehensive study of needs and resources throughout the Communion and called upon each Church to commit itself to increased financial and manpower support. Archbishop Ramsey described the purpose of the scheme as a realistic expression of the New Testament concept of 'sharing one another's burdens', for 'no man liveth to himself and no man dieth to himself'. The scheme was commended to all the Churches in the Anglican Communion and, in order to implement the proposals, a number of regional officers were appointed in different parts of the world, whose concern was to encourage the partnership of Anglican Churches in their region and also to open up means of co-operation between the Anglican Church and the other Churches. In this country the Revd Barry Till, formerly Dean of Hong Kong, was commissioned to make known the theme of MRI and the Revd D. M. Paton was appointed Regional Officer for the British Isles. Their first task was to try and make the mission of the Church more central to the life of the Church of England. The operation, 'No Small Change', was a major effort to do this, with the result that many lay people acquired a new sense of the centrality of mission in the life of the local Church.

In the years following the launching of MRI most of the prov-

inces of the Anglican Communion made their needs known to
their sister Churches in the form of 'Directories' containing lists
of projects which they hoped to implement in the next five
years. In this way the other Churches were invited to share in the
advance in mission for which each Church was hoping. Over a
thousand new projects were listed and these were over and above
the Churches' existing commitments. In order that the former
should be implemented and the latter maintained, the independent missionary societies in England established a committee to
co-ordinate this work and, as an example of its activities, it
accepted for the Church of England the responsibility of raising
£304,471 and finding forty-five new people over and above
existing commitments.[24] A new Overseas Development Fund
was established which made once for all grants towards buildings and equipment needed overseas. Individual dioceses were
encouraged to undertake a project for some area of the Church
overseas. The response was not encouraging. The economic climate in this country was steadily deteriorating and, in the event,
although a number of dioceses responded generously and produced a considerable amount of new giving, others not only
failed to produce new money but actually fell behind in their
existing overseas commitments. It is true that the 'No Small
Change' programme helped people to think afresh about the
Gospel and the Church's mission, but the connection between
this and the actual needs of the Churches overseas was seldom
made effectively in the parishes. Above all, however, the failure
symbolized the spiritual inertia of the Church of England. A
distinguished Ghanaian sociologist, Dr K. A. Busia, undertook
a survey of the Churches in a suburb of Birmingham, entitled,
*Urban Churches in Britain*,[25] in which he used phrases like,
'their membership is so small', 'winning so few converts', 'foot-
dragging towards unity', and he wrote that 'the strongest impression the evidence leaves in my mind is not that the Churches
are irrelevant, but that they lack the boldness that is born of
conviction and faith; they seem unable to take drastic steps away
from the apparent security of established tradition to meet new
situations.' A generalization based on insufficient evidence this

[24] Cf. Barry Till, *Changing Frontiers in the Mission of the Church*, 1965.
[25] Quoted in *One Mission: A Report of the Missionary and Ecumenical Council*,
1968.

may be, but if it contained any large element of truth it was not from such a source that there was likely to emerge the wide vision, the global concern, and the self-sacrifice implicit in Mutual Responsibility and Interdependence in the Body of Christ.

# PART III

# THE SEVENTIES

# 10

# CHURCH AND NATION

The irregular combination of fanciful invention may
delight awhile, by that novelty of which the common satiety sends us all in quest: but the pleasures
of sudden wonder are soon exhausted, and the mind
can only repose on the stability of truth.

Samuel Johnson, *Preface to Shakespeare*, 1765

As THE final years of the sixties gave way to the seventies, the
excitement, the iconoclasm and the idealism of those years were
gradually supplanted by an uneasiness, weariness, and pessim-
ism which were to characterize the feelings of many in the seventies. It was a time of frustration in politics, in the arts, and in
many other fields. The violence in Northern Ireland continued
unabated and there seemed to be no solution to a situation
which baffled politicians of all parties. Another apparently
incurable disease was inflation, which prefaced the worst economic recession since the war. Throughout the period prices and
wages rose but production remained stagnant and neither politicians, unions, nor employers appeared to possess either the
ability or the will to grapple with the problem. The optimism
which hitherto had characterized the twentieth century began to
wane and the expectation that in spite of everything the human
race through the mastery of science and technology was pro-
gressing from ignorance and poverty to enlightenment and
material abundance began to have a hollow ring. When he came
to power in the sixties Harold Wilson had promised a 'classless
dynamic new Britain' forged out of 'the white heat of technology'. In the seventies those bright hopes had not only begun
to fade but were coming to be viewed as undesirable.

Since 1945 the chief and overriding purpose of the majority of
our countrymen had been the creation of a materially comfort-
able life on an ever-increasing scale. Everyone had the right to a
higher standard of living, there was no upper limit to that
standard; to maintain and increase that standard meant greater

happiness, and the chief aim of government should be the growth of material prosperity and the maintenance of affluence. In the seventies these dogmas led to a Gadarene-like rush to obtain higher and higher wages to acquire more gadgets and comforts in the face of ever-rising prices. During the decade prices trebled and money seemed almost to have lost its meaning as economists and politicians talked of 'billions' and government borrowing increased on a scale which would have astonished our forefathers. To this economic crisis was added in 1973 the rise in the price of oil by the Arab oil-producing countries. The trade unions were unable or unwilling to accept the fact that expectations could be fulfilled only if wages bore some relationship to production, to hard work, to the ability of industry to pay, and to competitiveness with other nations. The various 'pay policies' of successive governments had no effect on the high wage demands of the Unions. Mr Edward Heath's Industrial Relations Act of 1971 produced the 1974 Three-Day Week, with power-cuts, food shortages, and industrial chaos. The subsequent period of socialist government ended with the 'winter of discontent' in 1978-9, when the ports were brought to a standstill, hospitals were closed, ambulance services were withdrawn, water supplies and sewage were shut off and bodies remained unburied. It is not surprising that there was disillusion with politics and economics. The government of Edward Heath had failed to halt inflation. Harold Wilson, in his second administration, lost touch and interest and James Callaghan's inability to cope with industrial unrest led to the defeat of Labour in 1979.

Another strand in the unease of the seventies was represented by the muted voice of the enthusiastic liberalism of the previous decade. Like the author of Ecclesiastes, people had become weary of the frantic search for the new, the daring, and the outrageous. It had to stop because there was nothing new to do and few moral frontiers left to cross. As licence failed to satisfy, people gradually began to feel that perhaps the restraints and standards of the past which they had rejected with such enthusiasm, might have had value. Certainly the seventies saw an unprecedented interest in, and nostalgia for, the past. The television series, 'Upstairs, Downstairs' was a notable popular success, as was also Sir Kenneth Clark's series, 'Civilisation', in 1969-70, while *The Country Diary of an Edwardian Lady*, published in 1977, became a best seller. In reaction to the post-war destruction of historic buildings and areas, the concrete anonymity of much modern architecture and the despoiling of the countryside, people became interested in conservation and amenity societies began to flourish. Allied with this trend were the various movements which reflected dismay at the effects of technology on the environment and the world's natural resources. At the end of the decade, the Brandt Report, the work of an international committee,[1] once again brought these and other pressing world problems to public notice.

A major concern in the seventies was the question of equal opportunities for the coloured immigrants in this country. After the war many West Indians had settled in Britain and they were later joined by people from India and Pakistan, so that by 1952 there were some 82,000 immigrants in this country—a figure which by 1975 had increased to 189,000. Many of them had established their own communities, particularly in London and the Midlands. Under the 1965 Race Relations Act the Race Relations Board had been created to devise methods for alleviating racial tensions and to deal with complaints of discrimination. From time to time acute tension arose between immigrants and the white population, while charges of racial discrimination in jobs, housing, and education were frequently made. Some people indeed described racialism as the major evil in British society.

When it was founded the European Economic Community (EEC) had as its vision a united Western Europe but in the event it was its economic aspects which remained at the forefront. Great Britain has always been an uneasy partner in the EEC, the nation being divided about the wisdom of being a member at all. The series of national economic problems which beset Britain ministered to its insularity because some of the blame for them was placed upon membership of the EEC. It is doubtful whether Britain has played the role in Europe which she could have done had she been less half-hearted. There has at the same time been a growing awareness of the denial of human rights in all parts of Eastern Europe where Communism reigns,

---

[1] *North-South: A Programme for Survival*, 1980.

in Southern Africa and in parts of South America. Nevertheless, there has been a greater willingness to denounce atrocities committed in countries governed by right-wing regimes than those in a left-wing society. For many people, the Helsinki Agreement of 1975, which included a commitment by both East and West to uphold basic human rights, was a notable achievement. Others were more sceptical and the subsequent sad history of *détente* has done little to undermine their scepticism.

It was against this background of growing disillusionment, the frantic search for material prosperity in face of inflation, the evidence of racial tension, and the canker of insularity, that the Church of England, along with the other Churches, attempted to respond to the problems facing the nation. This it did by attempting to assess the problems, to bring to bear upon them the insights of Christian theology and moral principles, to inform churchmen and others of their implications, to initiate discussion in the Church, and where appropriate to influence governments and government departments. In his final presidential address to the British Council of Churches, shortly before his retirement, Archbishop Michael Ramsey challenged the British Churches to take a more serious interest in the life of the nation and its social, economic, and political issues.[2] The words fell on fertile ground and by the end of 1975 a scheme was put before the BCC Assembly for the Churches to examine the British situation under the general theme of 'A Christian Hope for our Time'. This was rejected by the Assembly as too ambitious and expensive and a more modest plan was initiated.

In 1975 Dr Ramsey was succeeded as Archbishop of Canterbury by Dr Donald Coggan, Archbishop of York, and Dr Stuart Blanch, Bishop of Liverpool, was translated to York. Dr Coggan was a scholar and a pastor, whose goodness, integrity, and friendliness shone through his words and actions. His courage and his Christian confidence, amid the threats and uncertainties of the seventies, were greatly valued, but—as so often happens to those whose great qualities are simplicity and goodness—Dr Coggan sometimes displayed a simplistic and naïve approach to national and economic questions. Very soon

---

[2] Trevor Beeson, *Britain Today and Tomorrow*, 1978, p. 11.

after his appointment a steady stream of letters began to arrive at Lambeth urging the new Archbishop to call for a Day of Prayer for the nation. They came from people who believed that the national situation was deteriorating and that, if their longing for a better Britain was to materialize, a spiritual lead was imperative. The Archbishop himself believed that, if such a call to the nation was to be made at all, it must be done immediately and that, therefore, in his view this urgency meant that the suggestion that the leaders of all the Churches in Britain should produce an agreed message was not feasible. Not everyone agreed with this and the fact that it was not attempted may well have detracted from the force of the message. However, the 'Call to the Nation' was made by the two archbishops alone, but with the goodwill of the leaders of the other Churches who had been informed of what was afoot. The Call was launched from Lambeth Palace on 15 October 1975 with full press and television coverage. It was accompanied by a Pastoral Letter to be read in all Churches on the following Sunday. Misunderstanding arose because the latter was seen as the main message from the archbishops whereas, in fact, it was no more than a supplementary document to the main message which was given through the media at Lambeth.

The Call was addressed not only to the Church but to 'all those who are concerned for the welfare of the nation', and who recognized that materialism is not enough. The archbishops made five statements—each person counts; a strong family life means a strong nation; good work matters; others must be put before self; and a right attitude to money, to materials and machines, and to life itself is vital. No detailed analysis of, or answer to, the national problems was offered, but 'unless there is a concentrated effort to lift our whole national debate up into the moral sphere...we shall never find the answer'. Finally, groups of people all over Britain, of all denominations and none, were invited to face two questions—'What sort of society do we want?' 'What sort of people do we need in order to achieve it?' In the ten months that followed 27,000 letters poured into Lambeth from all sections of the community, showing that many were indeed looking for a lead and were glad that the archbishops had spoken out. On the other hand, the response was far from enthusiastic among many 'ordinary people', for whom the sense of God was vague and the consciousness of sin, in the Christian sense, was meaningless. Where Christian conviction is lacking the voice of prophecy falls on deaf ears. Moreover, the Call was in generalities, with the absence of any suggestions about how the complex problems of national life might be approached. People were suspicious of simple answers to problems which everyone knew to be complicated and many detected that behind the archbishops' questions lay a simplistic view of the nation's predicament and the Church's response to it.

The basic flaw in the Call was that too much emphasis was placed on the responsibility of the individual and nothing was said about the structures of society which condition the individual. A third question was required: 'What kind of structures are needed to produce the kind of people we need?' This criticism was voiced by the Bishop of Southwark, Dr Mervyn Stockwood, in the *Morning Star* on 31 October.

A man's character [he wrote] be it good or bad, is partly, if not largely determined by his environment, by the social and economic circumstances in which he is placed...It is this system, more than any other single factor, that is producing the evils that Dr Coggan so greatly deplores. If he is right in thinking that our country is heading for disaster let him draw the attention of the nation to the system that is largely responsible for it.

Dr Stockwood was taken to task-for using a communist newspaper to make his criticism of the Archbishop, but his reply was that critical remarks had already been made in that journal and that he was seeking to give its readers a more balanced view. He was also accused of disloyalty to the Archbishop, but the latter did not see it that way, for if his Call produced controversy that was good because one of the reasons for the Call was to initiate a debate on the issues raised by it. In the view of many, however, the Bishop of Southwark went sadly wrong in his statement elsewhere in the article that under a truly socialist system pornography and the other evils of London's West End would be eliminated overnight. It was this statement which hit the headlines and led many to interpret the bishop's words as advocating a communist system. But he had made only what in his judgement was a statement of fact and in doing so neither approved nor disapproved of the communist regime. Neverthe-less, it had the effect of deflecting public discussion away from the main issues in the Archbishops' Call to a pro- and anti-communist argument.[3]

The two questions in the Archbishops' Call encouraged the British Council of Churches to proceed with the project to help the Churches to think seriously about the kind of issues implied by the questions. This was the 'Britain Today and Tomorrow' project, which selected certain important subjects for investi-gation, analysis, and discussion. The result was that, through a series of working parties, a number of Church leaders, clerical and lay, gave substantial attention to most of the major problems facing the nation, viewing them in a world perspective and relating them to the insights of the gospel. Britain's changed role in the world, racism, the relationship between poverty and powerlessness, the growth of violence, the problem of unem-ployment, and the recent trends in education were among these concerns. Trevor Beeson has said that the result of this agenda was to drive Church leaders 'firmly in the direction of change and aligned them with what may, at the risk of misunder-standing, be described as the progressive forces in society'.[4]

Like the other British Churches the Church of England has consistently held the view that coloured people in this country are entitled to equal respect and opportunity and to protection against discrimination. It supported legislation, such as the Race Relations Act 1976, which enabled the Commission for Racial Equality to act directly against discriminatory acts and speeches and to ensure equality of opportunity. In 1977 the General Synod positively accepted the fact that Britain was an irrevo-cably multi-racial society and recognized that the presence of immigrants enriched the British way of life. The Race Relations Project was established by the British Council of Churches, one of the objects of which was to seek ways in which coloured people could be helped to develop a sense of self-respect and self-help. In November 1978 the Project was commended to the General Synod which in the previous year had urged the

[3] Cf. Mervyn Stockwood, *Chanctonbury Ring*, 1982, pp. 183-9. On the Archbishops' Call, cf. John Poulton, *Dear Archbishop*, 1976.

[4] Op. cit., p. 15.

Government to adopt 'policies of positive discrimination' to prevent the perpetual deprivation of coloured people. Finally, in 1980 the Church of England supported the establishment by the Board of Social Responsibility of a Resource Group to assist churchpeople to respond and contribute to a multi-racial society based on a plurality of cultures. This was a necessary step in view of the fact that, in spite of what had been done by the Church in the national sphere and by a large number of Churches in the local situation, far too many churchmen remained unconcerned about racialism.

The problems of racial harmony in Britain had a counterpart in the far more violent disturbances in Northern Ireland, where the task of creating new initiatives for political and social life were immensely complicated by the extremist goals of both the IRA and the Protestant 'loyalist' para-militarists. The General Synod debated the issue in 1977,[5] but apart from this the Church of England has been as bemused as the rest of the country about the solution to this intractable problem. Archbishop Coggan visited Northern Ireland three times to study the situation and to show the Church of England's sympathy with the people of the province.

Probably no one has done more to make the Church of England aware of the environmental problems caused by modern technology than the Bishop of Birmingham, the Rt. Revd Hugh Montefiore. In 1969, when he was Vicar of Great St. Mary's, Cambridge, he delivered three theological lectures at the Queen's University, Belfast, under the general title, 'Man's Dominion',[6] in which he set forth the brutal facts about resources, pollution, and health, and saw the crisis as a spiritual one because only the perspective of eternity could give man a sufficient motive and strength of will to be responsible for future generations.[7] The inauguration of 1970 as European Conservation Year brought these problems forcibly to people's notice, but in the meantime the Standing Committee of 'The

---

[5] The debate was on a document, *The Irish Problem and Ourselves,* by Giles Ecclestone and Eric Elliott, 1977, published under the auspices of the Board of Social Responsibility.

[6] Published as *The Question Mark,* 1969.

[7] Other works by Bishop Montefiore on the same theme were, *Can Man Survive?* 1970, *Doom or Deliverance,* 1972, *Apocalypse; What Does God Say?* 1976.

Countryside in 1970', virtually the English branch of the European Conservation Year Project, had invited the Church of England Board of Social Responsibility to prepare a statement on the theological, philosophical, and ethical basis for the use and conservation of natural resources of land, air, water, and wild life. The result was the publication in 1969 of a document entitled, *Man in his Living Environment*, which later appeared in a more popular form and was widely studied, receiving very favourable comment as a constructive contribution by the Church to European Conservation Year.

In the first of his Belfast lectures, Bishop Montefiore had devoted some space to radioactive pollution, with particular reference to the disposal of nuclear waste. Since 1969 the world had become increasingly alarmed by this problem and it was brought to a head by the Government's plan to build a Fast Breeder Reactor and to extend reprocessing facilities at Windscale. The Board of Social Responsibility produced a study paper[8] which set out the issues fairly and called upon our society to clarify the nature of its goals and priorities, to insist that the public is made aware of the real issues and to balance short-term need against long-term consequences.

In the early sixties the Ecumenical Centre for the Church and Society had been established in Brussels by a number of Christians working in the EEC in order to provide a setting for social and chaplaincy functions and for the informal exploration of European questions from a Christian standpoint. The Church of England participated in the Centre, which also provided a variety of services to the Church through the supply of information, the organizing of conferences, and liaison with the EEC Commission. After the elections to the European Parliament the Centre established contact with members of the Parliament. After 1973 the Centre became the executive arm of the Commission of the Churches of the European Community, which in the main consisted of representatives of the national councils of Churches, although the Church of England was one of three Churches represented separately. It meets twice a year and these meetings offer opportunity for studying some aspect of EEC

---

[8] *Nuclear Choice*, 1977.

policy and its implications for the Churches. In 1980 the Commission became formally responsible for the Brussels Ecumenical Centre so that the activities of the latter were effectively unified with the work of the Commission, which changed its name to the Ecumenical Commission for Church and Society in the European Community.

The relationship between the Church of England and Europe became closer in 1980 when the Diocese of Europe was created. Hitherto, jurisdiction over Anglican Churches and chaplaincies in Europe had been two-fold. First, since 1633 the Bishop of London had the Jurisdiction of North and Central Europe, although for some ninety years he had devolved the day-to-day responsibility for episcopal oversight upon a suffragan, usually the Bishop of Fulham. Secondly, the Bishop of Gibraltar, an extra-provincial diocese created in 1842, was responsible for the oversight of Anglican centres in territories bordering on the Mediterranean and in other parts of Southern Europe. The situation was altered somewhat when, in 1970, the Bishop of Fulham was appointed to be Bishop of Gibraltar as well. There was another Anglican presence in Europe. This was the Convocation of American Churches in Europe, comprising six congregations under the charge of an American bishop who worked closely with the Bishop of Fulham and Gibraltar. Partly because of Britain's membership of the EEC and partly because of the greater mobility between distant places, the Churches in Europe saw advantage in a complete integration of the work of these three areas of jurisdiction. In 1980 a Measure to establish the Diocese of Europe received the Royal Assent. The Bishop of London's jurisdiction of North and Central Europe and the Diocese of Gibraltar came together to form the new diocese and synodical government, modified by the absence of a diocesan synod, was established in the diocese, which is represented in the General Synod by its bishop and by representatives of the clergy and laity. Thus the Anglican Church in Europe was integrated as fully as was possible into the Province of Canterbury. To the regret of many the new diocese did not include the American Churches. These Churches, which were always more integrated with their home Church and had representation on its General Convention, were hesitant about modifying or weakening that relationship. Again, the ethos of the European and

American Churches is very different and it was felt that the way forward was through close and growing co-operation between bishops, chaplains, and congregations, rather than by constitutional integration.

Since the war the Churches of Eastern Europe have found it difficult to develop links with Western Europe and the Conference of European Churches, officially constituted in 1964 and recognized by the World Council of Churches as the regional ecumenical conference for Europe, is one of the ways in which the problem has been overcome. The Conference had been unofficially in existence for five years before and had held its first meeting in 1959, as the result of many years' preparation by the then Bishop of Sheffield, Dr Leslie Hunter, Dr Egbert Emmen of the Dutch Reformed Church, and Praeses Ernst Wilm of the Evangelical Church in Germany. Private discussions during meetings of the Conference remain one of the few ways in which Churches from East and West can meet. The Conference, which is based in Geneva, has a membership (in 1980) of 112 Churches in almost all European countries, and slightly under half come from Eastern Europe. Probably no other body, secular or religious, provides such a bridge between the divisions of Europe. The Conference is also an important meeting-place for Orthodox, Old Catholics, and Protestant Christians and, although it is not a member, the Roman Catholic Church is represented by a strong group of observers.

In 1974, at the request of the British Council of Churches, and with the assistance of a group under the chairmanship of Sir John Lawrence, Trevor Beeson, Vicar of St. Mary's, Ware in Hertfordshire, published a book on the religious situation in Russia and Eastern Europe, entitled *Discretion and Valour*. It revealed the continuing strength of religion and the deep spiritual life that exists in many Eastern European countries in spite of discrimination and persecution. The work was written in a popular style, its first printing of 16,500 was soon sold out and it was translated into a number of languages. The document was debated in the General Synod, which assured the Churches in the oppressed circumstances of Eastern Europe of the deep and continuing fellowship of prayer between them and the Church of England. On more than one occasion the Church of England has expressed its solidarity with individual Christians and upholders of human rights who have had action taken against them. Mention must be made of the Centre for the Study of Religion and Communism, established in 1969 at Keston, near Bromley in Kent, which is a research centre specializing in the study of religion in the USSR and Eastern Europe. It publishes its findings in a quarterly journal, *Religion in Communist Lands*, and its extensive archives are regularly at the disposal of government departments, Church leaders, and the media.

South Africa, with its unjust system of apartheid, has been another area of deep concern for the Churches and in the seventies this was focussed largely on the matter of British investment in companies which were involved in business and trade in South Africa. In 1972 the World Council of Churches urged all member Churches outside South Africa to press corporations to withdraw investment, not only from South Africa, but also from Namibia, Zimbabwe, Angola, Mozambique, and Gune-Bissao. Britain was a major foreign investor in South Africa, the largest market for South African exports and the third largest supplier of South Africa's import needs. Some people maintained that the only proper Christian course was to withdraw investments as the WCC urged. The majority, however, favoured the continuance of investment because it was only thus that Britain could assist in producing change for the better in South Africa. The General Synod in 1973 advised members of the Church of England who were shareholders in firms with South African interests to put all possible pressure on those firms to work for the closing of the gap between white and black employees. It also urged that no funds controlled by the Church of England should be invested in any companies which disregarded the interests of its black workers. The policy of the Church Commissioners has been consistent and has been a blend of discouragement and constructive engagement. They do not invest in companies operating wholly or mainly in South Africa and this represents their witness against apartheid. With multi-national companies, however, it is virtually impossible not to be involved in some way in investment in Southern Africa. It is here that the Commissioners' constructive engagement has operated. This implies a commitment to keep closely informed of the policies and practices of these companies and to use their influence to encourage and support progressive policies.[9] In 1979 the British Council of Churches called for a radical change in attitudes and supported the WCC's proposal of 1973 for complete disengagement on the ground that the existing policy had not worked, for although working conditions had improved, the fundamental economic and political system had remained unchanged.[10] The General Synod was not prepared to endorse this policy,[11] the reason being the belief that recently significant improvements had been achieved in the wages and conditions of black employees.

Returning to Great Britain itself, one of a series of problems was centred on work and industry. The Church of England's Industrial Committee of the Board of Social Responsibility kept churchmen aware of the political, moral, and theological issues concerning 'the closed shop', unemployment, and the impact of technological change, especially that associated with microprocessors, on job opportunities in Britain.[12] In 1978 there was pressure on the General Synod to declare itself uncompromisingly against the closed shop, but it was unwilling to do more than to urge tolerance and a liberal interpretation of the law. On another occasion the Synod called upon the Churches to develop means for the care of the unemployed and to make provision for the creative use of leisure. Finally, in 1979 the Synod urged the Government to develop policies which would encourage the creation of new jobs, minimize the fear of adapting to change, and to help to provide a better deal for the Third World.

'For millions of people television has become the most important influence in their lives.'[13] This was the view of the Church of England Broadcasting Commission established in 1970 to prepare evidence on behalf of the Church for submission to a committee which the Government proposed to set up to enquire into broadcasting prior to the expiry of the Charter of the

---

[9] Cf. report in *The Times*, 27 October 1978.

[10] *Political Change in South Africa: Britain's Responsiblity*, 1979.

[11] November 1979.

[12] Cf. *Understanding Closed Shops*, 1977; *Work or What?*, 1977; *Work and the Future*, 1979.

[13] *Broadcasting, Society and the Church: The Report of the Broadcasting Commission of the General Synod of the Church of England*, 1973, p. 3.

BBC and the statutory constitution of the Independent Television Authority. In the event an extension was granted to
both until 1981 and the government committee was not established until 1974. The report of the Church's commission was
then submitted in evidence. It covered all aspects of broadcasting and television. It maintained that producers could not
be neutral or disclaim responsibility for attitudes they helped to
propagate and the advertising element in TV helped to create
unrealistic desires and expectations which could deaden responsibility for the real needs of the world. Comparatively little was
said about the portrayal of sex and violence on the screen, although the commission recommended the use of a symbol to
mark programmes between 8 p.m. and 10 p.m. which were unsuitable for family viewing. On religious broadcasting the commission urged that the majority of religious programmes should
be Christian in character, that those on TV should continue to
be placed at peak viewing time on Sunday, and that Christian
broadcasts 'should be more evidently grounded in the fundamental Christian affirmations and a more sustained attempt
must be made to relate the biblical message to the human
situation'.[14] There should be more documentary programmes
about Christian work and more Christian material in children's
programmes. The commission called upon the Church to invest
more time and money in training people for the media and
urged that 'the Church as a whole needs to be awakened to the
importance of broadcasting as a formative element in society
and should seek to create an alert and discriminating public'.[15]
When the government committee reported in 1977[16] it passed
certain strictures on the Churches' use of broadcasting. The
Churches seemed less than clear what they should be doing.[17]
'The efforts of clergymen not to put off their audience by dwell-
ing on what is integral to Christianity are far from edifying.'[18] It

[14] P. 79.
[15] P. 81. In 1974 the Social Morality Council, which brings together humanists and
religious believers of various faiths, published its views on the subject in *The Future of
Broadcasting*. It excluded religious broadcasting from its brief, but covered a wider
canvas than the Church of England's commission and, in the view of many, produced
a more thoughtful and workmanlike report.
[16] *The Report of the Committee on the Future of Broadcasting* ('The Annan Report').
[17] Ibid., p. 319.
[18] Ibid., p. 322.

also recognized the difficulties of religious broadcasting. People's expectations of a religious programme were so different that some are always going to be disappointed and critical. The answer that the Central Religious Advisory Committee (CRAC) gave to the Commission's question about the objectives of religious broadcasting indicated that CRAC had departed fundamentally from its original aims. Instead of attempting 'to reflect the worship, thought and action of those Churches which represent the mainstream of the Christian tradition in this country', CRAC's objectives had widened to include non-Christian traditions and views 'which are evidently related to a religious interpretation or dimension of life'.[19]

The Abortion Act of 1967 legalized abortion on a number of grounds, but many people became increasingly concerned about the so-called 'social clause' which extended legal abortion to a consideration of 'the patient's total environment actual or reasonably foreseeable'. There was consternation as the Act was increasingly interpreted in a very liberal way. In the first year of the working of the Act there were 54,819 abortions, but by 1972 this had risen to 156,741, which represented 15 per cent of all live births. Moreover, there was further disquiet about undue pressure being placed upon doctors and nurses who held conscientious objections to abortion. Commenting on the letters received at Lambeth after the Archbishops' Call, John Poulton noted that, 'of all the causes taken up in this correspondence, abortion received far and away the greatest attention'.[20] Such was the unease about the working of the Act that in 1971 the Government appointed a committee to enquire into the matter. It recommended ministerial action to check abuses, but concluded that the Act had been a salutary piece of legislation by reducing human misery and eradicating illegal abortions.[21] In the year that this report was published the General Synod affirmed its view that the Government should improve the law and practice of abortion and, in particular, ensure the non-victimization of doctors and nurses who were unable, on conscientious grounds, to perform these operations. In 1975 the

[19] Ibid., p. 319.        [20] Op. cit., p. 105.
[21] *Report of the Committee on the Working of the Abortion Act* ('The Lane Report'), 1974.

Synod declared its support of a private member's bill, presented by Mr James White, for the amendment of the Act. The two archbishops had already declared the support of the Church of England for this bill, which was regarded as going some way to correct the abuses of the Act, but unfortunately it lapsed at the end of the parliamentary session. The Synod then urged the Government to make time available for the discussion of another private member's bill on the subject, sponsored by Mr John Corrie in 1979-80, but this also lapsed through lack of time.

In 1976 there was a proposal to show in this country Thorson's film, *The Many Faces of Jesus,* the subject of which was the alleged sex life of Jesus, involving both homosexual and hetero-sexual acts. It was condemned publically by the Prime Minister and the Archbishop of Canterbury, while the General Synod expressed the hope that 'no action will be taken by Her Majesty's Government, the film industry or film distributors which would facilitate the appearance of the film'.[22] As a result of this op-position the film was banned. It was one of the few occasions when there was a massive public concern over a moral issue. It is interesting and significant to compare this with what happ-ened the following year when *Gay News* published a poem by James Kirkup which depicted a homosexual relationship be-tween a Roman centurion and the crucified body of Jesus in physically sensual terms. *Gay News* was convicted for offences under the blasphemy laws, but Mrs Whitehouse who led the opposition was unable to obtain the support of Church leaders to the extent that they would be prepared to enter the witness-box. There were three reasons for this. In the first place, some believed that public evidence of this nature would be counter-productive. Secondly, others feared that to attack the poem would be misconstrued as an attack on homosexuality itself. Thirdly, there were those who believed the laws of blasphemy to be archaic in modern conditions and an unnecessary check upon freedom of expression. On the other side there were many who regretted the absence of outright condemnation by the Church and some who supported the blasphemy laws and favoured their extension to religions other than Christianity.[23]

[22] *Report of Proceedings*, November 1976.
[23] In 1981 the Law Commission advocated the abolition of the crime of blasphemy and the strengthening of the laws against abusive and insulting behaviour in places of worship by the provision of a new offence of threatening, abusive, and insulting

Homosexuality itself was a controversial issue facing the Church in the seventies. Following the 1967 Sexual Offences Act there was greater freedom in society generally to discuss homosexual behaviour publicly and there was a considerable increase in the number of people seeking advice on the subject. The Gay Liberation Front began a campaign for a greater acceptance by society of the homosexual. For some 'gay people', however, the Church seemed to be one of the main obstacles to their aspirations. Nevertheless, some leading Christians were deeply involved in the Homosexual Law Reform Society and as sponsors of the Charter for Homosexual Rights, while there were specific Christian movements such as the Open Church Group and the Gay Christian Movement. The latter was active in the universities, and its influence was felt in those theological colleges which had strong university links. In 1974, therefore, the Conference of Principals of the Anglican Theological Colleges asked the Board of Social Responsibility to prepare a study of 'the theological, social, pastoral and legal aspects of homosexuality'. The working party set up in response to this request produced a unanimous report,[24] but it caused some consternation within the Board, which had to decide whether or not it should be published. In the end, in face of the Board's inability to agree, it was published with the addition of a section of 'critical observations'. The report maintained that the problem of homosexuality could not be solved by appeal to biblical texts which reflected an age when the nature of homosexuality could not be known. With regard to homosexual marriage, heterosexual union as the norm was reaffirmed, whereas in an intimate homosexual relationship one strand—the biological complementarity of the partners—is lacking. On the other hand, either to condemn or to forbid such a relationship entered into by a Christian after a responsible decision would be insufficiently sensitive to the predicament of the homosexual. For the Church

behaviour in any recognized place of worship or cemetery—*The Law Commission Working Paper No. 79: Offences against Religion and Public Worship*. The response of the Archbishop of Canterbury to this proposal was that the blasphemy laws should remain, but they should be reformed in certain respects and be extended to religions other than Christianity—*Blasphemy*, 1981.

[24] *Homosexual Relationships: A Contribution to Discussion*, 1979. Cf. also Peter Coleman, *Christian Attitudes to Homosexuality*, 1980.

to accept homosexual unions, as an alternative to heterosexual marriage, 'would involve the repudiation of too much that is characteristic...of Christian teaching about sex'. Nevertheless, it was impossible to deny that there may be circumstances where individuals may justifiably enter into homosexual relationships similar to marriage. The Group could see no good reason, apart from scandal, for excluding from Church membership and Holy Communion those who in good conscience had entered into a regular and stable homosexual union, but a homosexual priest who openly acknowledged living in sexual union with another man could not expect the Church to accept him as if he were married. The report met with a mixed reception. The Campaign for Homosexual Equality and the Gay Christian Movement were disappointed because of the absence of more firm agreement with their aims and ideals, but many churchmen were equally dismayed by what they regarded as a betrayal of traditional Christian standards.

Another subject of discussion during this period was the moral issues involved in the treatment of terminal illness and the place, if any, which euthanasia has in the sick room. In 1975 Baroness Wootton introduced in the House of Lords a private member's bill, the effect of which would have enabled an incurable patient to decide to end his life and to make it un-lawful for anyone to interfere with that decision. On the other side was the 'hospice movement', pioneered by Dr Cicely Saunders at St. Christopher's Hospice, Sydenham, which inter-preted 'euthanasia' in its strict meaning of 'dying well' and which, through the controlled use of drugs, demonstrated that it was possible for a terminally ill patient to die with dignity, free from pain and possessing a quality of life. In 1975 the Board of Social Responsibility published a document produced by a working party which included theologians, doctors, and lawyers, entitled *Dying Well*. Its thesis was that modern know-ledge of drugs is such that there need be little or no pain in terminal sickness and that euthanasia, as popularly understood, is unnecessary. It may be that the use of such drugs may shorten life, but in some cases it may lengthen it and in all cases it will enhance it. The group called for greater understanding of the needs of the dying and for more instruction on terminal illness in medical and nursing schools. The document had a wide circulation and it was discussed in the General Synod and throughout the Church, in diocese, deanery, and parish. It did much to educate public opinion and, since its publication, the hospice movement has grown and other schemes for treating the terminally ill have emerged. This was the subject which the Archbishop of Canterbury chose when, in 1976, he was invited by the Royal Society of Medicine to deliver the Edwin Stevens Lecture.[25]

[25] *On Dying and Dying Well*, 1977.

# 11

# GOVERNMENT BY SYNOD

I look with terror on any admission of laity into
synods. It at once invests them with an ecclesiastical
office, which will develop itself sooner or later, I
believe, to the destruction of the Faith.

E. B. Pusey, 1852

Theology justifies, and history demonstrates, a co-
ordinate action of clergy and laity as integral parts of
the whole Body of Christ, that the ultimate authority and right of collective action lies with the whole
body, the Church, and that the co-operation of
clergy and laity in Church government and discipline
belongs to the true ideal of the church.

*The Convocations and the Laity*, 1958

AT ITS inauguration in 1970, many churchmen hailed synodical
government as a panacea for the many ills that beset the Church
and, like their predecessors after the establishment of the
Church Assembly in 1919, were doomed to disillusionment and
frustration. There were an astonishing number of candidates for
election to the first General Synod. Some 500 electoral places
had to be filled and about 2,500 candidates offered themselves
to the electorate. In November 1969 a group of people called
together by the Earl of March, had set up the New Synod
Group, the object of which was to counter the danger of party
candidates, either evangelicals or anglo-catholics, being returned
as a result of organized electioneering, which, in the face of the
hitherto unorganized efforts of 'middle-ground' candidates,
had led to a Church Assembly not truly representative of theological and ecclesiastical opinion in the Church. The Group
sponsored 'middle ground' candidates, dispatched some 25,000
letters to the electorate and published a pamphlet, *The Church
and the General Synod: An Electoral Manifesto for the New
Synod Group*. When the result of the election was announced it
was discovered that many well-known and useful members of

the old Church Assembly had not been returned and, that half the members of the House of Laity and some two-thirds of the House of Clergy had been elected for the first time. The new members included a number of reforming candidates such as Bishop John Robinson, Canon Eric James, the Revd Paul Oestreicher, and among the laity, Robert Beloe and Priscilla Cornwell-Jones. In the House of Laity, over two-thirds of the members were over forty years of age and nearly a quarter were over fifty.[1] Nevertheless, it was a considerably younger House than its counterpart in the former Church Assembly. Fewer came from public schools and considerably more from grammar or direct grant schools. There was a drop in the number of retired service officers and an increase in the numbers from the field of education. There were no representatives of the skilled or unskilled manual workers. A similar survey of the House of Laity in the second General Synod, elected in 1975, revealed that there were 10 per cent more women than in the first Synod, that there was a fall in the number of younger members, and that there were more members with educational backgrounds other than public schools. As before, there was no representative of skilled or unskilled manual workers. Professor Kathleen Jones, who conducted the survey, concluded that the Synod was more like a body of experts—'an ecclesiastical British Academy'—than a representative body and she commented on the fact that, because of this, there were few members who could 'provide more than a personal anecdote' in debates on such crucial issues as 'the immigrant population of Britain, the brawling and increasingly influential world of the trade unions and the poor and the rootless'.[2]

For the most part the Synod was not the radical body which many feared and for which many hoped. As a result some of the new members experienced a sense of frustration and impotence. There were complaints about the length of time required to get a Measure on to the statute book or to authorize new services, about the Synod's preoccupation with its own affairs instead of

---

[1] Kathleen Jones, 'The House of Laity in the General Synod', in *Crucible*, July/Aug. 1971.

[2] Kathleen Jones, 'The General Synod: 1975 Version', in *Crucible*, October/December 1976. Cf. also George Moyser, 'Patterns of Representation in the Elections to the General Synod in 1975', in *Crucible*, April/June 1979.

giving a lead to the Church and the nation on the political and social problems of the world, or about its failure to be a force for the evangelization of the nation. Such criticisms arose largely from false expectations and from a misunderstanding about the nature and purpose of the General Synod. The Synod was a legislative body, recognized as such by parliament, and any ecclesiastical matter which impinged upon existing statute law had to pass through the appropriate legal stages. If Measures did not have the Synod's full scrutiny, the Synod would lose the confidence of parliament which is responsible for recommending that its Measures should receive the Royal Assent. Secondly, delay was due to an essential feature of synodical government, because one of the purposes of its introduction was to enable the dioceses and the deaneries to play an integral part in the Church's decision making and this by its very nature lengthened procedure. Thirdly, synodical government was not democratic government but aimed—particularly on important issues—to obtain consensus in such a way that neither the bishops, the clergy, nor the laity could be overriden by a majority of the other Houses. Finally, the Synod was not an evangelistic body; its task was to serve and ease the task of those whose responsibility it was in the parishes. The provision of new services, changes in the law affecting pastoral reorganization, the appointment and payment of the clergy, the sharing of church buildings and most of the other administrative, financial, and legislative decisions of the Synod removed obstacles and facilitated changes which, in turn, assisted the primary task of the Church in the parishes.

The weakest link in the synodical system was the deanery synod. In theory, the establishment of deanery synods ought to have enhanced the importance of the deanery itself. There were many instances where a deanery synod became both a co-ordinating and initiating agent, providing training schemes for the laity, visitors for the local hospitals, or making representations to local government departments on such matters as housing, planning, amenities, and the social services. Nevertheless, far too often in many areas the deanery synod failed to inspire and this was due partly to the fact that, unlike the diocesan and the General Synod, it had no power to make final decisions and had no control over finance. There may have been a more fundamental reason. Anthony Russell[3] has pointed out that Church people are committed to the local parish as 'the unit of participation' and to the diocese as 'the unit of identification', and he concludes that 'into this pattern the deanery fits at best uneasily. It seems artificial in the sense that it does not correspond to the pattern of commitment, and at the same time it is too large an area to be the unit of participation in any real sense'.

If, in spite of the presence in its midst of a number of reformers, the first General Synod was in no sense a radical body, the second General Synod was, by comparison, a conservative one, and this reflected the change of mood of the Church of England. From 1970 onwards the voice of the radicals was heard less and the ferment of the sixties gave place to a more muted call for change. It has to be remembered that at the heart of the Church's life there lies a deep conservatism, which means that, while some change is acceptable, radical methods of reform stand little chance of success. Where then, in the seventies, had all the reformers of the sixties gone? Where was that organized and cohesive body of opinion which challenged the conservatives in the Church and which brought liveliness to debate and discomfort to ecclesiastical leaders? The staying power of radicals does not match that of those who are concerned to maintain the status quo. On the other hand, radicals are by nature impatient people and age modifies impatience just as it questions the validity of quick solutions to problems, and the radicals of the sixties were ten years older in the seventies. Fundamentally, however, they were up against the fact that the majority of bishops, clergy, and laity believed in evolution rather than in what they regarded as revolution and that for them 'gradualness' was preferable to radicalism.

A notable feature of the first General Synod, apart from the catholic-evangelical coalition against the Anglican-Methodist Scheme in 1972, was the absence of that party pressure which had so often been apparent in the days of Convocation and the Church Assembly. There appeared to be a greater willingness on the part of members to seek mutual understanding and to judge

---

[3] 'The Countryside and the Church', in *Crucible*, April/June 1976.

issues on their merits. Once again this was a reflection of what was happening within the Church itself. At local level, catholic and evangelical ministers and congregations were discovering fellowship where before there had been separation. Among the younger clergy there was a greater openness and sensitivity between those who differed theologically. There was less defensiveness, a greater willingness to understand a different point of view and more humility. Undoubtedly the liturgical changes were doing much to remove barriers. In the sixties and seventies the anglo-catholics noted Rome's call for the simplification of language and ceremonial in their own Church and they found in Series 2 and 3 services of Holy Communion a revision which had parallels with that of Rome. Throughout their history anglo-catholic worship had centred on the Eucharist. After the Keele Congress in 1967 evangelicals began to see the Holy Communion as 'the main service of the People of God' and determined to work towards 'the practice of a weekly celebration...as the central corporate service of the Church'.[4] They too used the Series 2 and 3 services of Holy Communion. Thus both groups saw the centrality of the Eucharist, and both groups were using, for the first time, a common form of service.

An important phenomenon in the life of the Church of England during this period was the new-found self-confidence of the evangelicals, who were more powerful, articulate, and intelligent than they had been for many years. They no longer felt threatened and there was therefore no need for them to continue to adopt defensive positions with hard-and-fast 'tests' of party loyalty. In the pre-war and immediate post-war years many evangelicals had been more concerned with preserving their own purity of doctrine than with attempting to co-operate with others in evangelism and the ecumenical movement and were too parochially orientated to take any influental part in the higher councils of the Church. It was the attitude of a depressed minority which regarded themselves as a group apart, as almost a Church within the Church.[5] As long as this attitude persisted

---

[4] The Congress Statement, par. 76.

[5] E.g. '"Party" fellowship was a great deal stronger in the diocese than the recognition of the common fellowship in the Body of Christ.' This was in the St. Albans diocese between 1920 and 1945. cf. Michael Furse *Stand Firm*, 1953, p. 112.

there was little chance of evangelicals becoming an effective force in the Church of England. During the nineteen-fifties, however, a gradual change took place and this was largely due to the status and influence of one man. John Stott was a person of wide vision and deep understanding, and very persuasive. A gifted expositor of the Bible, a prolific writer[6] and an evangelist, he was also a statesman who possessed the ability to understand other points of view. He was vicar of All Souls, Langham Place in London from 1950 to 1977 and under his leadership that church became the heart of evangelical Anglicanism.

During the years that followed evangelicals began to shed their cloak of separation and elitism, became aware of the comprehensiveness of the Church of England, and saw that within that Church they had an important part to play. Their appeal to Scripture became less rigid and fundamentalist as they recognized the need to understand the language of the Bible in terms of the context in which it was written and saw that the debate between the Bible and tradition, between Scripture and reason, was an important issue. The doctrines of atonement and redemption and concern for personal conversion had tended to be so central to many evangelicals that other aspects of doctrine and spiritual experience had been ignored or relegated to the periphery of theology. Now they began to rediscover the doctrine of creation and become aware of the need to concern themselves with Christian enterprise and influence in the world, recognizing that church-based teaching, preaching, and evangelism could be no substitute for concern with issues of politics, economics, social and racial justice, and industrial relations. Here they were greatly influenced by the leading layman of that school, Mr (later Sir) Norman Anderson, particularly by his book *Into All the World,* published in 1968. Norman Anderson was a distinguished academic lawyer who had been a missionary in Egypt and who brought his deep evangelical faith, his theological knowledge, and his gift of lucid exposition to meet the challenge of biblical criticism and to lead his fellow evangelicals

[6] E.g. *Epistles of St. John,* 1971; *Understanding the Bible,* 1972; *Christian Mission in the Modern World,* 1975; *Christian Counter-Culture,* 1978 *I Believe in Preaching,* 1982.

to see the implications of their faith for social and political issues.[7]

This new-found confidence found expression in the National Evangelical Anglican Conference at Keele University in 1967, attended by a thousand delegates. There was a much greater willingness to take seriously the existence of the views of those in the Church of England who were not conservative evangelicals and to make a commitment to the ecumenical movement. 'The outstanding effect of Keele', wrote John King, 'was to deal a death blow to the idea of an evangelical unity existing as a kind of alternative to the ecumenical movement.'[8] Of the most far-reaching importance, however, was the fact that Keele 'set the Church of England Evangelicals squarely in the historic Church. Loyalty to the historic Church...came before loyalty to Evangelicals wherever they might be found.'[9] The Church of England now had to take the evangelicals seriously, with the result that they have played a full part in the life of the Church at both diocesan and national level. Two outstanding example are the Revd Colin Buchanan and Norman Anderson. Both became influential members of the General Synod, Colin Buchanan serving with great effect upon the Liturgical Commission and Norman Anderson becoming Chairman of the House of Laity in 1970. The latter, by his membership of the Anglican Consultative Council and his multifarious activities in the central councils of the Church, was symbolic of the era which saw the full participation of evangelicals in the institutional life of the Church. The post-Keele confidence was also reflected in the evangelical theological colleges which have remained constantly full and have produced ordinands of high quality, most of whom while preserving their deep evangelical convictions have sought to understand the convictions of others and sit lightly to many of the badges beloved by their predecessors. In the late seventies there were not enough benefices with evanglical patronage to accommodate the number of evangelical clergy. The result has been that some have gone into

---

[7] Works by Norman Anderson include: *Christianity and Comparative Religion*, 1970; *Issues of Life and Death*, 1976; *A Layman Among the Theologians*, 1978; *God's Work for God's World*, 1981.

[8] John C. King, *The Evangelicals*, 1969, p. 120.

[9] Ibid., pp. 120-1.

parishes of other traditions and it is significant that they have
been content to proclaim the evangelical gospel without necessarily radically changing the tradition of the parish. Evangelical
parishes became some of the most vigorous in the country with
large congregations, flourishing Pathfinder groups for young
people, house churches, Bible study groups and determined
efforts to meet the uncommitted and the deprived. These
parishes have produced many ordination candidates and missionary volunteers. Evangelicals thus became a vigorous group
ready to seize fresh opportunities wherever they might be found
in the Church of England.

The self-confidence of the evangelicals was in contrast to the
waning influence of the anglo-catholics. The various catholic
societies reached a low ebb and the literature published by
catholics compared unfavourably both in quality and range with
that being published by the evangelicals. Moreover, a great
deal of what anglo-catholics had fought and stood for in the
past—a theological view of the nature of the Church, the
centrality of the Eucharist, a liturgy which was less tied to the
theology of the reformers than that of 1662—had been assimi-
lated into the Church of England so that the anglo-catholics no
longer appeared to stand for a distinctive view of these matters.
Finally, anglo-catholics had traditionally looked to the Western
Church as its norm, which, until Vatican 2, had appeared to be
adamantine and unchanging. After Vatican 2 the Roman
Liturgy was revised in the same direction as the Anglican liturgy,
many rules, such as those about fasting and evening Communion, were relaxed, while a uniform way of doing things gave
place to legitimization of variety. As Rome thus 'became more
Anglican', so the ground was cut from under the feet of anglo-
catholics who had hitherto copied Roman ways. Vatican 2, it has
been said, 'pulled the carpet from under anglo-catholics'. No
wonder many catholics felt threatened and disillusioned. In
such ways anglo-catholicism was in danger of losing its cohesiveness and distinctiveness. Nevertheless, the Catholic stance was
still of importance to the Church in order to help to preserve
within Anglicanism the sense of Church history, the continuity
of the Church through the ages, and the value of tradition
alongside Scripture. The anglo-catholic is more conscious than
others of the links of our Church with the Church of the West

and the Church of the East. He will stress the transcendent nature of religion, the objectivity of the sacraments, and the place of order and beauty in the worship of God. If the evangelicals keep the Church aware of the centrality of the atonement in Christian theology and life, the anglo-catholics keep it aware of the equal centrality of the incarnation.[10]

In spite of the stalwart leadership of Dr Graham Leonard, Bishop of Truro, and Dr John Moorman, Bishop of Ripon, anglo-catholics themselves were conscious of the malaise that had descended on them and were experiencing a feeling of isolation. On Ascension Day 1977 the Bishop of Chichester, Dr Eric Kemp, announced that he believed that the time had come for a renewal of catholicism and that arrangements were being made for a conference in the following Easter Week at Loughborough University.[11] This met with an enthusiastic response, over a thousand delegates attended and a movement for Catholic Renewal in the Church of England was launched. The conference passed no resolutions but raised questions and called for a challenge to personal holiness. Its aim was not a reassertion of partisanship but a quest for catholicity, the wholeness of the gospel, of the Church and of man. Indeed, one writer asserted that 'it was not a Conference at all, but a mission, where worship and preaching came together to inspire, hearten and renew'.[12] It was criticized for its lack of intellectual content, for being predominantly clerical—although many lay people were present—and for its lack of attention to social issues. Nevertheless, the conference was an inspiration to those present and in the months that followed smaller gatherings for Catholic Renewal were held up and down the country.

[10] Cf. Alan Wilkinson 'Requiem for Anglo-Catholicism', in Theology, January 1978, pp. 40ff.

[11] Cf. Catholic Renewal in the Church of England; Loughborough Conference Report, 1979.

[12] Church of England Year Book, 1979, p. xxviii.

# 12

# CHURCH AND STATE

The fundamental and decisive argument for a change in the relationship between Church and State is scriptural and spiritual...Under the totally changed conditions of our time, it is impossible to justify by any appeal to the Scriptures the arrangement by which a Christian society can be to such a large extent controlled and governed by those who do not belong to it, who may be uninterested and ignorant of its worship and teaching, and who may even be bitterly hostile to it.

Cyril Garbett, *Church and State in England,* 1950

## 1. Steps Towards Reform

'A PERUSAL of the records of the Church for the last hundred years makes depressing reading', wrote Dr Eric Kemp in 1961, 'for the same problems have been discussed again and again at intervals of a generation, conclusions have been reached but rarely translated into effect.'[1] Of no subject was this more true than that of the relationship of Church and State. In the present century there have been four commissions on the whole subject and at least four committees or commissions dealing with particular aspects of the relationship. Nevertheless, the seventies saw a major shift in the Church-State relationship which was surprising after the many years of inaction. The two matters which many regarded as restricting the functions of the Church were the control of its worship and doctrine by Parliament and the appointment of bishops by the Crown.

No change could legally be made by the Church in matters of doctrine and worship without the consent of parliament and there was considerable feeling that it could not be right for the worship and doctrine of the Church to be under the control of a secular body, which comprised members of all Churches,

---

[1] *Counsel and Consent,* 1961, p. 196.

Jews, agnostics, and atheists. Memories lingered of 1927 and 1928 when the Revised Prayer Book, overwhelmingly approved by the Church's representative bodies, was rejected by parliament. With regard to the appointment of bishops, when a vacancy occurred the Prime Minister nominated names to the Crown. There was no procedure laid down for the choice of names, although extensive consultations were undertaken by the Prime Minister's Appointments Secretary. The consultative system was developed by Sir John Hewitt, a man rooted and grounded in the Church of England, whose courtesy and integrity made him an able servant of Church and State. He became Appointments Secretary in 1962 and was succeeded ten years later by Mr Colin Peterson, another committed churchman. The Archbishop was always consulted, but many critics objected to the cloak of secrecy which surrounded the whole process and the absence of any formal machinery whereby the diocese corporately could make its wishes known. There was also criticism of the procedure of 'election' by the dean and chapter after the appointment had been announced. The Appointment of Bishops Act 1533 was still in operation, under which the Crown sent to the dean and chapter a *congé d'élire* giving them permission to elect a bishop, but this was always accompanied by a letter missive from the Sovereign giving the name of the person they were to elect. If the chapter refused to elect, the Crown could appoint by letters patent.

Two actions on the part of the Crown in 1961 increased disquiet over its handling of appointments. The first was the nomination by the Crown of Archbishop Fisher's successor without the interval of a Sunday on which the Church could pray for the guidance of God in the choice of a fit person to occupy its highest office. The second action aroused more widespread controversy. The Very Revd Walter Boulton was provost of Guildford, where he had been a successful pastor and leader, and when the new cathedral was completed, for which he had done so much to raise money, it was generally assumed that he would be its first dean. In 1961, however, the Crown surprisingly appointed the Rt. Revd George Clarkson, Bishop Suffragan of Pontefract, and this left Walter Boulton without a job. What had seemed to the Church to be a desirable appointment had been frustrated by the Crown and, because of the cloak of secrecy, no explanation would or could be forthcoming. It is true that Boulton was a controversial figure. He had published a book[2] on marriage under the auspices of the Mothers' Union, which subsequently withdrew it as being contrary to its principles. He had his own ideas of what a cathedral should be and do, which caused some opposition. Unfortunately his bishop, who supported him, died just as the appointment was to be made. A petition was sent to the Queen from Boulton's supporters but it was of no avail and ultimately Boulton was found a small benefice in Rutland. Although this was not the appointment of a bishop, the incident cast suspicion on the whole system.

The same year the Archbishop of Canterbury in his first presidential address to the Church Assembly said that 'there is now undoubtedly a desire within the Church for a new examination of the question [i.e. of Crown appointments]...If, therefore, the Assembly...were to ask the archbishops to appoint a Commission, I am sure we would try to find as weighty and competent body as we can.'[3] A week later the Prime Minister, Mr Harold Macmillan, commented in the House of Commons: 'If it is thought desirable that this Commission should be set up again [sic] in the light of new conditions, I should welcome it.'[4] On 7 November the Church Assembly by a large majority requested the archbishops to set up a commission to consider the method of Crown appointments to ecclesiastical offices.

Lord Howick of Glendale was chairman of the commission which reported[5] in December 1964. It firmly recommended that Crown appointments should be retained but that the procedure should be modified in order to transfer to the Church the initiative in the choice of bishops. Each diocese should establish a vacancy-in-see committee with the task, when there is a vacancy, of drawing up a statement of the needs of the diocese which would be sent to the Archbishop and the Prime Minister. Consultations between the Prime Minister and the archbishops would begin and would continue until both archbishops were ready jointly to submit to the Prime Minister two or three

---

[2] *Marriage*, 1960.
[3] *Report of Proceedings*, Vol. XLI, No. 2. p. 240.
[4] *Hansard* (*House of Commons*). 11 July 1961, p. 210.
[5] *Crown Appointments and the Church*.

names. It was also proposed that election by the dean and chapter should be abolished and that the bishop's appointment should be by letters patent. This would mean that the outmoded legal formalities of the confirmation of the election would not be required and this should be replaced by a public Ceremony of Record.

The report was received by the Church with disappointment because of its timidity, its theological inadequacy, its refusal even to give consideration to any radical reform of the present system, and its cavalier dismissal of possible alternatives. It was felt that its proposals would give the archbishops too much power and that there was too much bland talk about agreement being reached by goodwill on both sides. When the Church Assembly received the report it accepted its proposals for vacancy-in-see committees in each diocese, but it did not approve the abolition of election. Throughout the debates there was a clear note of dissatisfaction and there was great reluctance to make minor changes in the existing system lest this should postpone a more thorough consideration of constitutional change. Consequently, the Assembly postponed further consideration of the subject and asked the archbishops for another commission to examine the constitutional relationship of Church and State and to suggest modifications which were desirable and possible, bearing in mind the effect of that relationship upon the steps being taken to secure greater unity between the Churches.

This new commission, under the chairmanship of Professor Owen Chadwick, reported in 1970.[6] It was a fascinating document, gathering together a mass of information on the history and law of the Church-State relationship. Lucidly and sensitively written, it possessed an ecumenical and sociological awareness absent from previous reports on the subject. The commission believed that the time had come for the Church to be freed from controls and it considered that this could be done without disestablishment. It made two major radical recommendations. First, all matters affecting the worship and doctrine of the Church should be subject to the final authority, not of parliament, but of the General Synod. Secondly, bishops should no longer be nominated by the Prime Minister but by a committee

[6] *Church and State.*

or electoral college, representing both the diocese and the Church at large. The General Synod, having accepted the report, asked the dioceses to make their views known on the question of introducing a Measure to transfer the control of doctrine and worship to the General Synod. The dioceses were almost unanimous that early action along these lines should be taken. A majority of dioceses were also in favour of giving the Synod power to replace the 1662 Prayer Book by another book, but it was a much smaller majority and a substantial element of unease about this was evident in the diocesan debates.

## 2. Worship and Doctrine

After the Church of England (Worship and Doctrine) Measure was introduced in the Synod in November 1972 disquiet was expressed throughout the country that it gave insufficient safeguards to the 1662 Prayer Book. Steps were therefore taken to increase these safeguards and the final Measure ensured that it should remain in use until the Synod asked parliament for its replacement. None the less, although the Synod gave final approval to the Measure in February 1974 by an overwhelming majority[7] criticism continued unabated and was to reach its culmination on the floor of the House of Commons. In its final form the Measure authorized the General Synod to approve, amend, continue, or discontinue forms of service, although the services in the Book of Common Prayer were to remain permanently available for use. The form of service to be used in a parish was to be the joint decision of the incumbent and the Parochial Church Council and if there was disagreement between the two the services should be those of 1662, unless during the previous four years another form had been in use for at least two years in which case the PCC might require that form to be used. The Measure also gave the Synod power to make provision concerning the obligation of clergy and others to assent or subscribe to the doctrine of the Church of England and it was under this clause that in 1975 the Synod authorized a new form of Declaration of Assent.[8]

The Measure was debated in the House of Lords on 14 Nov-

---

[7] 346 for the Measure; 10 against.          [8] Cf. below, p. 235.

ember 1974 when it was introduced by the Archbishop of Canterbury on his seventieth birthday and on his last day in office. After four hours' debate, during which a considerable amount of criticism was levelled both at synodical government and at liturgical revision, approval was given to the Measure. The real test came, however, on 4 December when it was introduced in the House of Commons. During a heated debate it appeared that the necessary majority might not be forthcoming, but Labour members rallied to the support of their colleague, Mr Terry Walker who, as Second Church Estates Commissioner, had the task of moving the motion. Forty Labour MPs were among the 140 members who voted for the Measure; of the forty-five opponents, forty-four were Tories and their UUU supporters. The debate threw a fascinating light, not only on the Church-State relationship, but also upon the very nature of the Church of England itself. Much was said about the merits of the 1662 Prayer Book and 'the beautiful mystery' of its words. The opponents appeared impervious to the need expressed by a large section of the Church for a liturgy in a language which had at least some affinity with that used in the contemporary world. Opponents could find nothing good in the new services. 'A sort of gibberish', said Mr John Stokes; 'sterile bureaucratic words of modern usage', said Mr David Mudd. Many saw the Book of Common Prayer as a bastion against change. 'We do so desperately need stability and continuity', declared Mr Patrick Cormack, 'We deeply need both the anchor and the beacon which the Book of Common Prayer provides.' The General Synod came in for some rough criticism and was accused by Mr Ivor Stanbrook of being 'a small group of activists many of whom cannot escape...the charge of self-interest', and it was charged with being unrepresentative and out of touch with 'the man in the pew'. Much was said about the nature of the establishment and Mr Enoch Powell affirmed that all Members of Parliament, whether or not they were members of the Church of England, had the responsibility of regulating the worship and doctrine of the Established Church.

What emerged most significantly from the debate was the fact that there appeared to be two 'Churches of England'. One was composed of committed members, who were regular worshippers, who were dedicated to mission and who played their part in synodical structures. The other was the 'vague mass', who attended worship spasmodically, who took no part in the Church's mission, and who held aloof from the synodical structures, but who nevertheless regarded themselves, rather than the first group, as 'the Church of England'. The Worship and Doctrine Measure polarized the two and posed the question: Which of these two is the real Church of England?

### 3. Appointment of Bishops

The General Synod had already turned its attention to the other major proposal of the Chadwick Commission on Church and State and in July 1974 had expressed its view that, in order that the Church should have a more effective voice in the appointment of bishops, a small body representative of the vacant diocese and of the wider Church should choose a suitable person and submit his name to the Crown. The Archbishop of Canterbury and Sir Norman Anderson, chairman of the House of Laity, embarked on consultations with the Prime Minister and with the leaders of the other main political parties and it was discovered that as the matter concerned the royal prerogative there would be no need for legislation. On 8 June 1976, in a parliamentary answer, the Prime Minister stated that, although there was good reason why the State could not divest itself of a concern with Crown appointments, there was a case for changing the existing arrangements 'so that the Church should have, and be seen to have, a greater say in the process of choosing its leaders'. Bishops would continue to be appointed by the Crown, who would, as now, receive final advice from the Prime Minister. The Church would appoint a small committee to assess a vacancy and possible candidates for it and to submit two names, which might be given in order of preference, but the Prime Minister would retain the right to recommend the second name or to ask the committee for a further name or names. Following the acceptance of the Prime Minister's proposals, the Synod established a Crown Appointments Commission, which consisted of twelve members—the two archbishops, three members elected by the House of Clergy and three elected by the House of Laity, together with four members appointed by the vacancy-in-see committee of the vacant diocese. Some people felt that the new system was not radical enough, for the actual appointment continued to lie with the Prime Minister and not with the Church. Given the fact, however, that the Church had wished to retain the ratification of a new bishop's appointment by the Sovereign, and given the fact that the Sovereign can act only on the advice of her ministers, the position of the Prime Minister had to be retained and he, in turn, would expect to be able to exercise some element of choice. Nevertheless, the heart of what the Church sought was inherent in the new system for it was a method whereby a representative body could share in consultations and, by making decisions on names, have a decisive voice in the final choice, for the only name that the Prime Minister could finally choose was one which emerged from the Commission. Never again could a bishop be appointed without the approval of the Church, acting through its own representative body.

## 4. Establishment

The Worship and Doctrine Measure and the new method for the appointment of bishops produced a real transfer of power, but they did not change the principle or the reality of the Church-State relationship itself. It was noticeable that during the period when these changes were taking place little was heard of the question of disestablishment, although if the negotiations on the appointment of bishops had failed or if parliament had refused to approve the Worship and Doctrine Measure, the question might well have become acute. It was generally felt, however, that provided these two questions could be solved satisfactorily there was value in the Church of England continuing as the National Church. On the other hand, there were those who argued that in a pluralist society such as Britain had become it was questionable whether the concept of a National Church, which had the nominal allegiance of 50 per cent or less of the nation,[9] was a realistic one. In what sense does the National Church now affirm that the nation intends to be a Christian society or maintain that it is an expression of the

[9] *Religion in Britain and Northern Ireland: A Survey of Popular Attitudes*, ITV, 1970. According to this survey, 22% of Britons denied membership of any Church. Of 78% who *did* claim membership, only 50% were members of the National Church.

nation's recognition of religion? It is significant that on the most important national issues it is the Churches *together* who approach the Government or make pronouncements.

It is not altogether surprising that the history of the Church of England since 1945 shows that it has become gradually more autonomous, more sharply defined and less diluted by its national role. This has been due to two factors. The first has been the natural reaction of the Church to take up a defensive position and to emphasize its distinctiveness as it finds itself ministering in a pluralist society and whose position has been one of increasing weakness. The second factor is more positive, for today 'a man who involves himself with the Church, who practises his faith, does so not with but against the conventions of society and increasingly against his cultural inheritance.'[10] Commitment now carries greater weight than convention and this inevitably marks off the committed Churchman from the nominal churchman, who remains out of touch with the ethos of the committed, and from the non-Christian, who does not wish to be committed anyway. Some of the landmarks indicating the gulf can be discerned. Perhaps the earliest was the marriage regulations of 1938, which in a particularly clear way indicated that the discipline of the Church on this issue differed sharply from the law of the State. Another was the Worship and Doctrine Measure and the new forms of service, together with the reaction they provoked. A third was the more rigid baptism policy adopted by the Church (made even more rigid in some parishes), which saw the sacrament more in terms of commitment than in terms of a missionary opportunity towards the uncommitted. Synodical government and some of the Measures it has passed have sharpened the Church's consciousness of itself as an autonomous institution.

There is loss as well as gain in this. The Bishop of Durham confessed in 1976 that 'there is no foreseeable possibility of the Church of England, or even a united Church, continuing as the Church of the nation in anything but a very attenuated sense', but—he added—'this is no excuse for simply writing off the values inherent in the old system', and he urged that steps should be taken to counter this by 'careful attention to local roots', and by ensuring 'that local Christian communities

---

[10] Valerie Pitt, 'Memorandum of Dissent', in *Church and State*, 1970, p. 74.

continue to recognise their responsibility to the large mass of people who do not share their strength of commitment'. His conclusion was that 'a Church which believes in its responsibility to the whole of society and which refuses to define itself too precisely, makes great demands on the spiritual integrity of those who stand at the centre of its life. But its witness is all the more valuable at a time when other forces in society tend increasingly towards polarisation and fragmentation.'[11]

## 5. Marriage, Divorce, and the Family

We have already noted the fact that the Church of England's discipline on the remarriage of divorced people is one indication of divergence of view between the National Church and the nation. Inevitably the Church came under criticism from those who were nominal members and, indeed, it is the most rigorist of all the Churches on this issue. This dissatisfaction was illustrated in 1955 when Princess Margaret was contemplating marriage with Group-Captain Peter Townsend, who was divorced from his wife. In the end she decided not to marry him and in a statement issued on 31 October she gave her reasons— 'Mindful of the Church's teaching that marriage is indissoluble, and conscious of my duty to the Commonwealth, I have resolved to put these considerations before any others.' Although she stated that she had reached the decision entirely alone, many people preferred not to believe this and shared the view of the *Manchester Guardian* that the decision had 'plainly been come to after subtle pressure' and it was firmly believed that Archbishop Fisher was at the centre of the pressure. This was untrue, for at no time did the Archbishop even discuss the matter with Princess Margaret nor was he invited to do so, and when she went to see him on 27 October it was not to consult him but to tell him of her decision.[12] Nevertheless, 'the winds of dis-

---

[11] John Habgood, 'Directions for the Church of England', in *Theology*, May 1976, pp.132ff.

[12] The picturesque description by Randolph Churchill, in the *Spectator* (23 May 1958), of the Archbishop awaiting Princess Margaret's visit with 'all his books of reference around him carefully marked and cross-referenced' and Princess Margaret's saying, 'Archbishop, you may put your books away; I have made up my mind already', is apocryphal. Archbishop Fisher told his biographer, William Purcell, 'I had no books of any sort spread around...She never said, "Put away those books", because there were not any books to put away.' Cf. Purcell, *Fisher of Lambeth*, p. 248.

approval for a time blew very hard indeed upon Fisher'.[13] Thus did 'the world' respond to an act of self-sacrifice to uphold the Church's discipline on Christian marriage.

In the years that followed the promulgation in 1957 of the Act of Convocation forbidding the marriage in Church of a divorced person whose partner was still living, the divorce rate continued to soar. There were many factors contributing to this, among them the lack of Christian commitment, early marriage, longer life expectancy, the decline of parental authority, the break-up of the family, the changed position of women in society, the higher expectation of personal and social fulfilment in marriage, and the effect of the universal availability of contraception.

The most potent influence on the divorce rate, however, was the change in the law of marriage and divorce, coupled with the establishment of the Legal Aid Fund. In 1956 a Royal Commission on Marriage and Divorce reported, and one member urged the adoption of a new principle to replace that of the matrimonial offence, namely 'irretrievable breakdown of marriage', defined as a situation in which 'the facts and circumstances affecting the lives of the parties adversely to one another are such as to make it impossible that an ordinary husband and wife would ever resume cohabitation'.[14] It was this concept which was to form the basis of a radical revision of the law on divorce. In 1963 Archbishop Ramsey, in a speech in the House of Lords, announced that he was asking some of his fellow-churchmen to investigate the possibility of finding 'a principle at law of breakdown of marriage which was free from any trace of consent'. The outcome was the appointment of a group, under the chairmanship of Dr Robert Mortimer, Bishop of Exeter, which issued its report, *Putting Asunder: a Divorce Law for Contemporary Society,* in 1966. It is to be emphasized that the report advocated no change whatever in the Church's fundamental teaching on the sanctity of life-long marriage. It maintained, however, that the Church had the task of concern for the welfare of those in the community who did not share its own views and with the provision which the State might make

[13] Purcell, op. cit., p. 242.
[14] *Royal Commission on Marriage and Divorce: Report 1951-1955,* 1956, 'Statement of his views by Lord Walker', p. 340.

for them. 'It is right and proper', said the group, 'for the Church to co-operate with the State...in trying to make the divorce law as equitable and as little harmful to society as it can be made.' The Group proposed the abolition of the concept of the matrimonial offence and the establishment in its place of a doctrine of the irretrievable breakdown of marriage. The existing accusatorial process should be replaced by a procedure by inquest—i.e. an enquiry into the past history and present state of the marriage, with a view to discovering whether any relationship remained between the parties. The group empha-sized that they were not advocating divorce by consent because it would not be the parties themselves but the court that would decide whether the marriage should be dissolved. Endorsement of these proposals was given by the Church Assembly in Febru-ary 1967 and by the Methodist Conference the following year.

The Law Commission, to which the report was referred by the Lord Chancellor, was critical of the proposals and rejected the procedure of inquest as 'procedurally impracticable', as distress-ing and humiliating to those involved, and as greatly increasing the cost of divorce. As a result members of the group and of the Commission met to see if a compromise could be found and the result was embodied in the Divorce Reform Act 1969, which indeed provided that breakdown of marriage should replace the matrimonial offence, but in place of procedure by inquest the courts should be directed to infer breakdown, in the absence of evidence to the contrary, on proof of the existence of certain matrimonial situations—namely, adultery, unreasonable behaviour, desertion for two years, separation for two years where this is agreed by both parties, and separation for five years without the agreement of one party. Many churchmen were critical of two of these situations, believing that the avail-ability of divorce after two years' separation would lead to 'trial marriages' and that unilateral divorce after five years was unjust to the faithful spouse who refused divorce for conscientious reasons. The majority of people, however, saw the Act as a realistic and honest approach to a major human problem and regarded the increase in the rate of divorce that followed as but the open recognition of what hitherto had remained hidden. Increase there certainly was. In 1970 there were 25,000 divorces; in 1972, the year after the Act became effective, there were

119,000, while in 1975 this had increased to 121,000.[15] Divorce
had become easier than parliament had intended when it passed
the Act and such safeguards as the Act contained were eroded by
the courts, for between 1973 and 1977 special procedures were
introduced enabling the majority of divorces to be obtained on
affidavit without either party attending court, thus changing
judicial enquiry into administrative process.

Inevitably, the new concept of irretrievable breakdown and
the rapid rise in the divorce rate caused many Christians to
question the Church's regulations, which appeared to represent
a lack of compassion for the hurt and damaged individuals involved in divorce proceedings and a failure to recognize that
people can and do make mistakes. Within the Church, however, there appeared to be no consensus. The reason for this was
that there are three views within the Church on the nature of
marriage and divorce. The first is that marriage is by nature indissoluble and *cannot* be dissolved; the second is that, although
marriage is in intention indissoluble and *ought* not to be dissolved, yet in a sinful world marriages do die and evidence
shows that second marriages can be fulfilling—such second
marriages should, with due safeguards, be solemnized in
Church; the third starts from the same premises as the second,
but concludes that to solemnize second marriages in Church
would weaken the Church's witness to marriage as a life-long
commitment. Because of these different views and because of
the pressure to relax the Church's discipline, the archbishops
appointed a commission 'to prepare a statement on the Christian doctrine of marriage'. The commission came to the conclusion[16] that when a first marriage had irretrievably broken
down and divorce had followed, there could be no theological
objection to a second marriage, but it argued that this was a
judgement that had to be made by the Church of England
itself, which should seek to discover whether there was 'a moral
consensus' on the legitimacy of second marriages and on the
propriety of the solemnization of such marriages in Church.
If such marriages were to take place there should be certain

---

[15] *Marriage and the Church's Task: The Report of the General Synod Marriage Commission*, 1978, pp. 12-13.
[16] *Marriage, Divorce and the Church: The Report of the Commission on the Christian
Doctrine of Marriage*, 1971.

safeguards, such as an enquiry into the disposition of the parties and their intention that the second marriage was to be life-long. The actual service should be preceded by a declaration that these safeguards had been complied with. The report did not fare well at the hands of the Church and it had rough handling in the General Synod. Those who took the indissolu-blist position felt that less than justice had been done to their point of view by a commission which they regarded as unrepre-sentative, and there was also widespread dislike of the whole concept of 'moral consensus', for the rightness or wrongness of an action could not depend on numbers. By the time of the third debate on the report the consequences of the operation of the Divorce Reform Act were becoming apparent and, in view of the dissatisfaction with the report, the archbishops were asked to initiate a further examination of the subject. A new commis-sion, under the chairmanship of the Bishop of Lichfield, the Right Revd Kenneth Skelton, began to re-tread the well-worn track.

The organization within the Church which, since its foun-dation in 1876, had done most to keep alive in the minds of Church and nation the sanctity of marriage was the Mothers' Union, a world-wide movement which in 1971 was active in 200 dioceses in the Anglican Communion. One qualification for membership was that a member was faithful to her marriage vows and declared her intention 'to uphold the Sanctity of Marriage'. It was explicitly stated that 'divorce must be regarded as a disqualification for Membership'. The Mothers' Union was frequently criticized for its rigid attitude and it was not immune from the effects of the debates in the sixties and seventies about the status of the divorced and the proposed and actual changes in the law. At the same time questions were being asked about the internal operations of the Mothers' Union and about its relationship to the Church itself. The Central Council saw the need for an independent examination of the aims, objects, and structure of the organization and in 1969 it appointed a com-mittee for that purpose under the chairmanship of the Bishop of Willesden, the Rt. Revd Graham Leonard. Among its recom-mendations[17] were two alternative proposals. The first was that the rules should be unchanged, save that women who were

[17] *New Dimensions*, 1972.

divorced and who had subsequently remarried should be eligible for membership. The second was that membership should be open to all, married and divorced, provided they were able to subscribe to the ideals and intentions enshrined in the objects. There followed a long and heart-searching discussion throughout the organization and in 1974 the second alternative was adopted and membership was opened to all those who had been baptized and could subscribe to the aims and objects, except that divorced women who remarried would require the approval of the Mothers' Union diocesan officials and of the local incumbent before they could become members.

The Bishop of Lichfield's commission reported in 1978[18] and one of the merits of the report was that it did not confine itself to problems connected with divorce but emphasized the importance of the Church's pastoral ministry to those about to be married, of supporting marriages under stress, of caring for those whose marriages had broken down, and of general teaching at all times about personal relationships. It also called for training facilities for both clergy and laity. The commission, which was more representative than the previous commission, was divided on the crucial question of remarriage after divorce. Twelve members supported the proposal—which became the majority recommendation of the commission—that the Church of England should review its regulations so as to permit a divorced person to be married in Church under certain cicumstances and following a pastoral inquiry, recognizing that such marriages would be exceptional. Four members supported the retention of the existing regulations on this issue. The commission was unanimous, however, in recommending the rescinding of the regulation forbidding those married after divorce to be admitted to Holy Communion until the bishop gave permission. The report received a warmer welcome than did its predecessor but the main recommendation failed to secure a consensus when it was debated in a full house at the General Synod in July 1978, being passed in the House of Laity by only one vote and lost in the House of Clergy by only twenty votes. On the total vote the motion was lost by seven. The Synod decided that it would proceed no further until it had

---

[18] *Marriage and the Church's Task.*

asked the Church, through the diocesan synods, to declare its mind.[19]

Alongside concern about the increase in the number of divorces, which by 1981 gave England and Wales a higher divorce rate than any other country in Europe, went anxiety about the stability of the family which appeared to be threatened by easier divorce, the growing economic and social independence of women, and the liberal attitude towards sexual relationships. It was estimated that couples divorced in 1975 had 202,475 children, of whom 145,096 were under sixteen.[20] The enormous increase in the rate of divorce was amounting to a social revolution which was affecting the whole of society and represented a vast amount of human misery. On 16 June 1976 the Archbishop of Canterbury initiated a debate in the House of Lords on the 'continuing importance of the family in the changing circumstances of Britain today'. Dr Coggan saw this as part of his Call to the Nation in which he asked, 'What sort of Britain do we want today?'[21] He saw bad housing, early marriage, unemployment, and the 'trivialisation of sex' as the four serious dangers to establishing and maintaining stable family life. The action he believed to be called for was better education for marriage, better housing, and the lowering of unemployment, and he pleaded that consideration be given to the appointment by the government of a Minister for the Family[22] to survey the present divorce law, the employment of young people, the effect of the abortion laws, and to watch the legislation which affected the teaching of religion in schools.[23] His

[19] When the dioceses reported in 1980 it was found that the result was inconclusive and that there was no clear majority in favour of change permitting remarriage in Church. Nevertheless, in the following year the Synod by a clear majority in all three Houses agreed that there were circumstances in which a divorced person might be married in Church during the lifetime of a former partner and asked the Standing Committee to set out a range of procedures for cases where it was appropriate for such a person to be remarried in Church.

[20] *The Future of Marriage: A Report by a Research Sub-Committee of the Society of Conservative Lawyers*, 1981, p. 12.

[21] Cf. above, p. 193.

[22] As did the Research Sub-Committee of the Society of Conservative lawyers in 1981—op. cit., p. 22. It was supporting a recommendation already made by a working party on marriage guidance, set up by the Home Office, in its report, *Marriage Matters*.

[23] *Hansard* (*House of Lords*), 16 June 1979, pp. 1257ff; 'The Importance of the Family', in Donald Coggan, *Sure Foundations*,1981, pp. 80ff.

proposal was received with little enthusiasm by the Government, which pointed out that the problems were so extensive that they were the responsibility of nearly every government department. There were others who saw little merit in meeting a problem of this nature by yet another government department.

# 13

# DOCTRINE, WORSHIP, AND THE LIFE OF THE SPIRIT

Since 1662 there has been change almost beyond belief in the facts and modes of English life... We are living in a new world: it is ours, if we are true to the faith that is in us, to seek to make it a better world. It is by prayer and service that we may hope to do it. But we dare not think that a Book of Common Prayer fitted for the seventeenth century can supply every want of the twentieth...New knowledge and new ways of life bring with them new customs and forms of speech unknown before. As men think upon God's wonderful works unveiled before them and are quickened afresh by the power of his Spirit, their hearts and minds frame for themselves new prayers and thanksgivings and seek new occasions of worship. It is the duty no less than the right of those who bear the burden of a great trust to see that plain needs are plainly met.

Preface to the proposed *Book of Common Prayer*, 1928

## 1. The Debate about Christ

ONE OF the first uses to be made of the Worship and Doctrine Measure 1974 was to alter the Form of Subscription to the Thirty-Nine Articles of Religion. Under the Clerical Subscription Act of 1865 any man being ordained or assuming an ecclesiastical office was obliged to assent to these Articles, unrevised since 1571, as 'agreeable to the Word of God'. They also had to be read in public by a new incumbent after his institution. Few clergymen agreed with all the statements in the Articles, which had been the product of an age of fierce theological controversy. They caused difficulty to many who contemplated ordination and there had been numerous calls for their revision.[1] On the

---

[1] E.g. W. R. Matthews, *The Thirty Nine Articles*, 1961. The Revd John Pearce-Higgins, when he was appointed a residentiary canon of Southwark in 1963, made a protest against the Articles before the bishop in the Cathedral.

other hand, there were those who strongly supported the status quo. Some saw the Articles as the bond of unity among Anglicans of diverse theological views, while many evangelicals accepted them as entirely consonant with the Word of God.[2] In 1968 the Archbishops' Commission on Doctrine proposed[3] that assent to the Articles and their public reading should cease. In their place there should be a more general assent, preceded by the reading of a Preface which would set the Articles and other Church of England formularies within the context of scripture and the creeds. The Commission advised against a revision of the Articles themselves because it considered that the difficulties of the task were too great. The General Synod accepted the proposals with minor alterations and, under a canon promulged in 1975, the clergy were to affirm and declare their belief 'in the faith which is revealed in the Holy Scriptures and set forth in the catholic creeds and to which the historic formularies of the Church of England bear witness'.

Theological debate in the seventies centred on Christology. The diverse views held about this central belief of Christians was illustrated in 1972, when a group of Cambridge theologians published a series of essays[4] emanating from a graduate seminar on Christology inaugurated by Maurice Wiles, who was then Dean of Clare College. The group had taken up the challenge in the introduction to *Soundings*[5] to do some hard thinking about the fundamental problems of Christian theology and the symposium revealed the lack of a common mind among the theologians and a wide difference of approach to this central doctrine. The following year John Robinson published *The Human Face of God*, in which he gave a frank presentation of the historical Jesus as an entirely human personality through which divinity was manifested. One sees in the man Jesus 'the *concentration* as in a burning glass...of the true light that lightens "every man"',[6] for Jesus is different from other men, not in kind, but in degree. In more radical vein Maurice Wiles

---

[2] E.g. J. I. Packer, *A Guide to the 39 Articles*, n.d. Cf. also *The Articles of the Church of England*, by J. C. de Satagé, J. I. Packer, H. G. G. Herklots and G. W. H. Lampe, 1964.
[3] *Subscription and Assent to the 39 Articles*.
[4] *Christ, Faith and History*, ed. S. W. Sykes and J. P. Clayton.
[5] Cf. above, p. 110.     [6] Op. cit., p. 209.

in 1974[7] maintained that incarnational theology is difficult if
not impossible and that we must either abandon traditional
Christology or accept incoherence. All that can be said is that
Jesus tells us something of God's eternal nature. Don Cupitt,
Dean of Emmanuel College, Cambridge, declared in 1975 that
'the Eternal God, and a historical man, are two beings of quite
different ontological status. It is simply unintelligible to declare
them identical.'[8] The television programme, 'Who Was Jesus?',
in which Don Cupitt featured, disturbed many Christians,
although this was partly due to their ignorance of the progress of
biblical studies in this century. To those with a fundamentalist
approach the normal methods of biblical criticism seemed to be
an undermining of the authenticity of Jesus, whereas Cupitt's
theme was that 'the chances today of finding out the real Jesus
are better than they have been since the beginning of Christianity'.[9] Many others were more deeply disturbed by what they
regarded as Cupitt's unorthodox assessment of the person of
Jesus, who—in his view—had never taught his pre-existence nor
the salvation of men by his sacrificial death. He 'is rightly called
saviour, mediator, redeemer, not because of what he is in himself but because he was so possessed by that to which he bore
witness. In that sense he is rightly called the absolute in time,
the one who shows the way to the perfect world.'[10] Cupitt
followed this up in 1979 in *The Debate about Christ*, in which
he reached the conclusion that 'the full coequal deity of Jesus
is nowhere taught in the New Testament',[11] and, in his view,
this is 'a doctrine incompatible with both the Jesus who started
it off and the God he believed in'.[12] The christological lists
were joined by Professor G. W. Lampe in 1976 in his Bampton
Lectures, *God as Spirit*. God as Spirit is always and everywhere
at work in the world and in men and women, and there is
nothing strange about his being in and acting through Jesus,
except that Jesus provides the focal instance and key to God's
dealings with the world and with men and women. God acted

---

[7] *The Re-making of Christian Doctrine*. Some critics regarded the book, not as the
're-making', but the 'un-making' of Christian doctrine.

[8] 'The Finality of Christ', in *Theology*, December 1975, p. 625.

[9] Don Cupitt and Peter Armstrong, *Who Was Jesus?* 1977, p. 9.

[10] Ibid., p. 92.      [11] Pp. 108-9.      [12] P. 128.

as Spirit in Jesus decisively and in unparalleled fashion, but this activity was in a totally human Jesus.

The Doctrine Commission, whose chairman was, significantly, Maurice Wiles, caused considerable comment when it produced in 1976 a document entitled, *Christian Believing*. It consisted of a joint report followed by eight essays by individual members of the Commission, which had been asked by the archbishops to say something about 'the nature of the Christian faith and its expression in Holy Scripture and the Creeds'. Although the report showed 'certain underlying agreement...about the way in which Christians need to approach questions of belief', it explicitly acknowledged 'the very considerable degree of divergence' which existed within the Commission. Its starting point was that the Christian faith and life is for all believers an adventure, 'a voyage of discovery', rather than an assurance. Fundamental differences of opinion arise because of the comprehensiveness of the Church of England. Some people, such as the religious affairs correspondent of *The Times*,[13] regarded the Commission as pushing the limits of comprehensiveness 'farther and farther as the various standards of orthodoxy have been down-graded', and many agreed with him that the report would not in the long run 'assist the Church to make up its mind where it stands or to discover whether it stands anywhere'. Professor Stephen Sykes raised an even more crucial matter when he asserted that the Church of England, which 'professes the faith uniquely revealed in the Holy Scriptures and set forth in the Catholic creeds...will find no difficulty in ordaining or commissioning persons who have serious reservations about credal beliefs or who regard them as mistaken'.[14] He judged that 'the Anglican Church has progressively shed its distinctive confessional commitment, relatively broad though that always was'.[15]

Great publicity was given to the publication in 1977 of *The Myth of God Incarnate*, which sold 30,000 copies in the first eight months. It consisted of a series of essays and the chief argument of the whole collection was that both the New Testament and the development of Christian doctrine were culturally conditioned. Readers' attention was drawn to the many

[13] 16 February 1976.
[14] *The Integrity of Anglicanism*, 1978, p. 37.
[15] P. 43.

different Christologies within the New Testament itself, Don Cupitt deplored 'orthodox' Christology, John Hick disputed the uniqueness of Jesus, Maurice Wiles thought that the idea of the incarnation might have to be abandoned and gave a careful study of the word 'myth' in modern theology. The latter was important because a great deal of the consternation aroused by the book centred on the use of this word in the title, which was unnecessarily provocative and did the authors' cause little good. Two constant themes throughout the work were the difficulty of securing historical evidence about Jesus and the rejection of the Chalcedonian Definition of Christology as unintelligible to modern man.[16] 'In the hue and cry raised after the publication of the book', wrote the Bishop of Bristol, 'one could be for-given for thinking that our Christian beliefs had only the flimsi-est basis and were so fragile that the whole Christian world stood trembling on the abyss of destruction.'[17] Wild charges were hurled against the contributors, chief among them being that they were undermining the faith of 'simple Christians in the pews'. Bishop Eric Treacy, for example, emerged from retirement to address a letter to the *Church Times*,[18] in which he flayed the contributors but admitted that he had not read the book! Few of the vociferous critics grasped the fact that the authors were being loyal to the truth as they saw it or appreci-ated that it is of no service to the laity to protect them from the results of scholarship.

Fortunately there were others who were prepared to meet the authors on theological rather than emotional terms. Before the year was out another group of theologians from both the catho-lic and evangelical camps replied to *The Myth* in a series of six essays entitled *The Truth of God Incarnate*. The presuppositions lying behind historical scepticism were criticized and the inten-tion of the New Testament writers to assert the divinity of Christ was reaffirmed. The chief weakness of the work lay in its consideration of philosophical and sociological issues, which revealed a lack of understanding of the cultural gap between the world of the first century and our own. Two other works ap-

---

[16] As long ago as 1912 William Temple had declared that the Definition was 'a confu-sion of the bankruptcy of Greek patristic theology'.

[17] The Right Revd J. Tinsley in *Three Crowns: Bristol Diocesan News*, August 1977.

[18] 5 August 1977.

peared at the time when the controversy was afoot. In 1977 Eric Mascall, from the catholic side, reasserted the orthodox doctrine of the incarnation[19] and C. F. D. Moule exposed some of the unexamined assumptions behind much contemporary New Testament scholarship and maintained that all the estimates of Jesus made by the early Church were there in embryo in the historical Jesus himself.[20] In July 1978 the seven essayists of *The Myth* met with a group of their leading critics, including Charles Moule, at Birmingham University in a number of private sessions and three public debates and the papers read on those occasions were published.[21] They revealed no resolution of the conflicting views, although there was a welcome openness to alternative opinions, with both sides more obviously eager to discover the truth than they had appeared to be in their earlier writings.

## 2. Towards an Alternative Service Book

A third series of alternative services was authorized in the seventies, beginning with Holy Communion in 1973. The most controversial characteristic of the new services was the use of modern English which involved addressing God as 'you' instead of 'thou'. The critics asserted that modern language of this kind stripped the liturgy of mystery, relegated God to terms of human discourse and relationships, and was unworthy to stand beside the great prose of Cranmer. The critics were being less than fair for, although no one could describe the language as perfect, it was certainly not the style of the *Daily Mirror* or of ordinary conversation, and many of the prayers displayed a rhythm and a syntax worthy of an act of worship. It was not always realized that the appreciation of the language of the 1662 Prayer Book was the result, not only of its literary merit, but also of long familiarity, and it is impossible to make an accurate judgement of modern language services until they too have become familiar through long usage. Moreover, the critics showed little appreciation that the purpose of using

---

[19] *Theology and the Gospel of Christ.* A defence of orthodox Christology came from the evangelical side in 1981 when Norman Anderson published *The Mystery of the Incarnation.*

[20] *The Origin of Christology.*          [21] *Incarnation and Myth*, 1979.

modern language was that, if worship was to be living and relevant, language had to make it so and must therefore not be archaic or remote from that with which people are familiar in their daily lives.

Although reliable figures were difficult to obtain, there is no doubt that the Series 2 and Series 3 services came into regular use in the majority of parishes. In 1979 Series 3 Holy Communion underwent an extensive revision. Although there was general contentment with the service and many would have wished it, with a few minor changes, to remain as it was, there were those in the Church who would never be satisfied with it as it stood. The revisers attempted to acknowledge this and, in the face of a thousand proposed amendments, revised the whole text from beginning to end, adding further enrichments and a greater choice of alternatives. They also took the radical step of including four alternative Eucharistic Prayers at the heart of the service. In doing this they weighed against the traditional Anglican principle of liturgical uniformity the evidence of the need for some degree of liberty within an ordered liturgical framework. The plea for one Eucharistic Prayer, without any alternative, had to be balanced by the fact that, as a result of sincerely held doctrinal differences about the nature of the Eucharist, there had been diversity at this point for nearly a hundred years. Nevertheless, it was emphasized that these were not 'party' prayers, nor were they the result of a 'political deal', as some asserted. Each of them expressed in different ways what was done and each of them was accepted in the General Synod by the various shades of theological opinion in the Church of England. It was hoped that each of the prayers would be used in turn in order to give a helpful variety and not principally to suit the needs of different groups.

This was virtually the last step in the process of liturgical revision which had begun twenty-five years previously. The process had been remarkable for the absence of doctrinal bitterness and controversy which was in sharp contrast to the sad discord which had accompanied the Prayer Book Revision in the years leading up to 1927. From time to time there was indeed deep difference of opinion but there was an eirenic spirit abroad and a considerable growing together as each sought to understand the other and to reach, if possible, common ground. Moreover, the revision had been by a process of consensus. In the Roman Catholic Church liturgical revision had been imposed by authority, which drove some conservatives into militancy in defence of the Latin Mass. In the Church of England the most that the General Synod did was to authorize the services for use; the decision to use them or not remained with the incumbent and the Parochial Church Council in each parish. Those who objected to the new services had the right and opportunity to make their views known at the Annual Parochial Meeting and to seek election to the Parochial Church Council. Nevertheless, some of the clergy and laity deeply regretted the movement away from the 1662 Prayer Book, particularly laypeople who were not regular Churchgoers and who found increasingly that, when they did go to church, they were faced with unfamiliar services. In 1975 the Prayer Book Society was founded 'to uphold the worship and doctrine of the Church of England as enshrined in the Book of Common Prayer' and to encourage the use of that book 'as a major element in the worshipping life of the Church of England'. A massive petition was presented to the General Synod in 1979 for the 'continued and loving use' of the Book of Common Prayer and the Authorized Version of the Bible. It was organized by Professor David Martin of the London School of Economics and the six hundred signatories represented all sections of public and academic life. They included the heads of twenty Oxford and Cambridge colleges, actors, authors, poets, politicians, diplomats, leaders of the Armed Services, cabinet ministers, and journalists. Part of the Petition was a 'St. Cecilia Petition', signed by a long list of leading musicians, including twenty-three cathedral organists, which pleaded for the recognition of the fact that 'the musical wealth of the Church is linked to classic texts, biblical and liturgical, of unique force and numinous power'. By no means all of these people claimed religious belief and a press release by the organizers revealed that 'some atheists signed with great fervour, holding that it was a national question'. The signatories had little or no conception of the need for change which lay deep in the hearts of many churchmen, of the synodical processes whereby ordinary worshippers had been able to make their voices heard, or of the tradition of liturgical scholarship which had contributed to the revision of the services. The crux of the matter, however, was whether the primary purpose of the liturgy was the preservation of great literature from the past or whether it was to be the vehicle of the living faith of the present; whether the Bible was primarily a literary ornament to be admired and reverenced or a tool explaining and illuminating the faith in a language that could be understood and based on the achievements of modern scholarship.

It had been generally assumed that the process of liturgical revision would culminate in the publication of a new prayer book as an alternative to the 1662 Book of Common Prayer and the General Synod proposed that the new book should appear in November 1980, on the understanding that for at least ten years there would be no further major revision. The contents covered the whole range of Series 3 services, together with tables of lessons and psalms, occasional prayers and thanksgivings, and a psalter. The latter was a modern translation of the psalms which had been undertaken by an ecumenical panel of distinguished scholars and musicians and had been published in 1977 by Collins.[22] Although the Alternative Service Book was published commercially by independent publishers, control of the material remained in the hands of the Church, which retained the copyright and to which a fair share of any profits was to be paid. Two days after publication a copy of the new book was ceremoniously presented to the Queen at the inauguration of the third General Synod.

## 3. The Charismatic Movement

In many parts of the Church worship has been profoundly influenced by the charismatic movement, which has been described as 'perhaps the most important single post-war movement to cut across every denominational boundary and, linking Anglicans, Baptists and Roman Catholics in England with Methodists in Africa and Catholics in South America, to bring to life an evangelistic experience of individual spiritual rebirth which unites substantial numbers of Christian people who were formerly divided'.[23] The origin of the movement lay

---

[22] *The Psalms: A New Translation for Worship.* Cf. David Frost, *Making the Liturgical Psalter*, 1981.
[23] R. Towler and A. P. M. Coxon, *The Fate of the Anglican Clergy*, 1979, p. 198.

in the pentecostalist revival which occurred at the turn of the century, especially in America, and which was characterized by two features. The first was that 'baptism in the Spirit' is a second blessing subsequent to conversion and the second was that this baptism is authenticated by 'speaking with tongues'. Within the Church of England signs of charismatic renewal became evident in the early sixties, and between 1962 and 1964 St. Mark's, Gillingham, St. Mark's, Cheltenham, and St. Paul's, Beckenham, received publicity for 'speaking with tongues'. In the latter year the Revd Michael Harper founded the Fountain Trust to inform and guide charismatic renewal in the Church by right teaching and the Trust did more than anything else to keep the renewal within the bounds of the traditional Church.[24] The Movement received much encouragement from visits from America of leading charismatic figures such as David du Plessis, Larry Christenson, Dennis Bennitt, and David Wilkerson. The revival was said to have 'come of age' in Britain when the first international conference was held under the auspices of the Fountain Trust at Guildford in 1971 and was attended by a number of theologians such as James Dunn and Simon Tugwell. In 1978 a conference for Anglican leaders was arranged at Canterbury to precede the Lambeth Conference and was attended by thirty-two bishops, two-thirds of them from overseas. The Lambeth fathers were informed that the number of Anglicans involved in charismatic renewal was 810,000 and in the mid-seventies it was estimated that half of those in theological colleges had been influenced by the movement, which cut across boundaries of theology and churchmanship. In 1975 regular meetings began between representatives nominated by the Evangelical Alliance and the Fountain Trust and in 1977 leading evangelicals and charismatics published an important joint statement, *Gospel and Spirit*. Likewise there was an increasing interest among catholics in the Church of England, particularly among those involved in 'catholic renewal' stemming from the Loughborough Conference in 1978.[25] A catholic

---

[24] The Fountain Trust closed in September 1980 because the trustees took the view that it had played its part in charismatic renewal for sixteen years and they believed it to be God's will that it should close. There was also a feeling that the Trust had become 'another institution' and that institutionalism inhibited the life of the Spirit.

[25] Cf. above, p. 216.

charismatic movement met at Walsingham for a number of years until its numbers grew so large that it had to move its location to High Leigh. The movement also built a new ecumenical bridge between the Churches and support for it came from the Church of Scotland and from the Methodist Church. The most interesting and significant feature has been the way in which the Roman Catholic Church welcomed charismatic renewal. Cardinal Suenens, primate of Belgium, became a leader in a movement which he has declared to be essential to the life of the Church. In this country a third of the delegates at the conference arranged by the Fountain Trust in 1971 were Roman Catholics.

Charismatic renewal is characterized by a high doctrine of the gifts of the Spirit and in particular those of speaking with tongues and healing. The experience of being so overwhelmed by the power of the Spirit led many to speak of it as 'baptism of the Spirit', which enabled them to witness freely to others, to express their love to each other and to speak naturally and freely to God in prayer. Coupled with this was the expectation that God would work visibly in, for example, healing and deliverance from the power of evil. Wherever charismatic revival occurred there was nearly always an increase in fellowship and prayer, a deep evangelistic concern, growth in the number of communicants and a greater giving to the Church at home and overseas. Through its meetings for prayer and worship, the renewal introduced Anglicans to forms of praying, praising, singing, and sharing which most of them had never experienced before. Chorus singing, the use of gesture and dance, ministeries of healing and deliverance carried out in the midst of the congregation, gifts of tongues and interpretation, prophecies and singing in the Spirit—all these are characteristics of charismatic worship. Nevertheless, on the whole, charismatic worship in the Church of England does not appear to have divorced itself from the official forms of worship, partly because the flexibility of the new forms authorized by the Church of England has enabled charismatics to introduce many of the features characteristic of their prayer meetings. Many parishes have been transformed and renewed by the movement, the most notable being that of St. Mary-le-Belfrey, York (once declared redundant) under the Revd David Watson.

Like all movements, however, charismatic renewal has both weaknesses and excesses. Among those involved there is a tendency to pietism and a reluctance to grapple with the social and other problems of the world. The Statement of the Theological Basis of the Catholic Charismatic Renewal issued in Rome in 1973 commented also that 'in some cases there is a real social engagement, but the involvement is superficial in that it does not touch the structures of oppression and injustice'.[26] The charismatic experience can also result in the abdication of hard theological analysis in favour of uncritical pietism. In certain parts of the movement there has been a dangerous over-dramatization of the demonic and the ministry of deliverance. Perhaps its greatest weakness, however, lies in the danger of divisiveness, springing from a feeling of spiritual elitism which can too easily result in a sectarian attitude towards fellow-Christians. In spite of its unifying influence between catholic and evangelical and between the Christian Churches, there is sometimes a reluctance to acknowledge that the Church is still the Church and a Christian is still a Christian where there is no speaking with tongues, and in some parishes congregations have been divided and disrupted. Moreover, in 1979 there were in Britain several hundred 'churches' with over 50,000 members in what came to be known as the House Church Movement. The emergence of these house churches was due to division in the local situation caused by the charismatic movement—between those who had had 'an experience' of the Holy Spirit and those who had not. When the local situation was uncongenial to the new experience of the charismatics, the latter began to seek opportunity to meet together to enjoy their newly-discovered forms of worship. These meetings were held in private houses and then expanded into larger premises. Some members of house churches retained their allegiance to their denominational churches; others lost interest and thus helped to produce what looked like a new 'charismatic denomination'.[27]

[26] Cf. *One in Christ*, 1974, pp. 206-15.

[27] Cf. 'The House Church Movement in Great Britain', by Walter J. Hollenwager, in *The Expository Times*, November 1980. The most recent studies of the charismatic movement from the Anglican point of view are a report, drafted by Canon Colin Buchanan, of a working group, entitled *The Charismatic Movement in the Church of England*, 1981, and John Gunstone, *Pentecostal Anglicans*, 1982.

## 4. Exorcism

A Roman Catholic theological memorandum on the charismatic movement warned that 'excessive preoccupation with the demonic and an indiscriminate exercise of deliverance ministries is based upon a distortion of the biblical evidence and is pastorally harmful'.[28] It is noteworthy that the sixties and seventies saw a widespread growth of interest in the occult, embracing a wide range of phenomena from astrology to spiritualism, from the ouija board to black magic. The *Sunday Telegraph* described magic as 'one of the boom industries of the last decade'.[29] The popular interest in the occult was seen in the large sales of Dennis Wheatley's books on the subject and by the large audiences at films like *The Exorcist*. With this intense preoccupation with the occult it is not surprising that demon possession and the practice of exorcism (or the ministry of deliverance) became of concern to many in the Churches. The practice of exorcism increased and a number of books were published on the theology of demon possession and on the pastoral care required in coping with such cases. Chief among these writers were Michael Harper, J. C. Neil-Smith, John Richards, Simon Tugwell, and Dom Robert Petitpierre. In 1963 the Bishop of Exeter was distressed by 'the unhealthy and near-hysterical publicity given by the national press to the question of exorcism in the Church of England' and having received a number of requests for help and advice he convened a small and distinguished commission 'to consider the theology, technique, and place in the life of the Church of exorcism'. The group completed its report in 1964 but it was not published until 1971.[30] Its main recommendation was that each diocese should appoint an exorcist and that training should be provided on a provincial basis. It stressed that it should be assumed initially that the patient's trouble had a physical or mental cause and only after the case had been referred to a psychiatrist should exorcism be undertaken.

[28] Quoted by Kenneth Leech, 'The Charismatic Movement and the Demons', in *Chrism*, November 1975.

[29] Quoted by John Richards, *But Deliver us from Evil*, 1974, p. 29. This is a valuable work on the subject of exorcism.

[30] *Exorcism: The Report of a Commission convened by the Bishop of Exeter*, edited by Dom Robert Petitpierre.

Those who adopt a sober approach to the ministry of deliverance insist that it is a part only of the Church's total ministry of healing and reconciliation. It is the investing of exorcism with the aura of the extraordinary and its isolation from the total ministry of the Church which sometimes produces tragedy. A notable example of this occurred in 1974 when an all-night exorcism was performed at St. Thomas's Church, Gawber, near Barnsley. The vicar, the Revd Paul Vincent, and a Methodist minister, the Revd Raymond Smith, together with their wives and two laymen worked for many hours to exorcize evil spirits from Michael Taylor, a man of thirty-one who was happily married with five children. During the exorcism they claimed to have cast out some forty to fifty evil spirits, but immediately afterwards Taylor returned home and murdered his wife in a most brutal manner. The Church authorities recognized the sincerity—albeit misguided—of the two clergymen but were unanimous in their condemnation of what took place at Gawber and of other exorcisms of this type which did not produce such fatal consequences. The Bishop of Wakefield, in whose diocese the incident occurred, instructed all clergy to cease from exorcism until he had received the report of a commission he had convened to advise him. The commission recommended that 'no formal rite or service purporting to deliver a person or place from evil possession or demonic attack' be permitted unless expressly authorized in each case by the bishop or his deputy.[31] In 1975 the Archbishop of Canterbury issued guidelines for the whole Church. Exorcism must be carried out only in collaboration with the resources of medicine, in the context of prayer and sacrament, with a minimum of publicity, by experienced persons authorized by diocesan bishops, to be followed by continuing pastoral care. Following these guidelines, diocesan bishops formulated appropriate regulations, all of which were characterized by a cautious approach to an uncharted sea and by the warning that sincerity and enthusiasm could never be substitutes for a qualified medical opinion. Finally, the archbishops and members of the General Synod received an Open Letter,[32] signed by sixty-five churchmen, mainly theologians from the universities and including the principals of six theological

[31] Cf. John Peart-Binns, *Eric Treacy*, 1980, p. 245.
[32] May 1975. Reprinted in D. Cupitt, *Explorations in Theology* 6, 1979, pp. 50ff.

colleges, which claimed that the Church of England was making a serious error of judgement in issuing these regulations because the effect would be to give exorcism an official sanction which it ought not to have. Exorcism, said the signatories, was alien to the whole tradition of the Church of England and ran counter to the views of modern scholarship that demon possession in the time of Jesus was conditioned by cultural factors. 'It is, we think, a mistake to suppose that loyalty to Christ requires the Church of England to re-create, in late 20th. century Europe, the outlook and practices of 1st. century Palestine. Such an attempt invites ridicule, not to mention the harm that may be done.' The letter ended with a plea that exorcism should receive no official encouragement or gain any official status in the Church of England.

# 14

# MINISTRY AND MISSION

> If the Church generally should come to take a low
> view of its ministry and think it matters little whether
> its numbers are adequate, its training sufficient and
> its discipline sound, I am very sure that the Church is
> heading for spitirual shipwreck.
>
> Hensley Henson,
> *Church and Parson in England*, 1927

## 1. The Office of Suffragan Bishop

SINCE THE passing of the Suffragans Nomination Act in 1888,
which enabled the Crown to add to the number of sees to which
suffragan bishops could be consecrated, the office had proliferated to such an extent that by 1971 there were sixty-four
suffragan bishops and full-time assistant bishops and only three
of the forty-two dioceses in England were without either. The
result was that the Church of England became concerned about
both the nature of the episcopal office and the appropriate
structures for a diocese. There were a number of other reasons
for this concern besides the increase in the number of suffragan
sees. First, the rapid increase in population, the growth of new
conurbations, the reorganization of local government boundaries, and the demand for high standards of pastoral care led
to questions about the right size for a diocese and the relationship of diocesan boundaries to local government boundaries.
Secondly, the office of suffragan bishop itself was questioned as
being theologically anomalous; the concept of the bishop as 'the
focus of unity' led many to the logical conclusion that there
ought not to be two bishops—a diocesan and a suffragan—in
one diocese and that, therefore, there must be smaller dioceses
each under a single bishop. Thirdly, in order to cope with the
population problem, to meet the need for episcopal care and to
provide proper status for suffragans, some diocesan bishops
were unofficially dividing their dioceses into defined areas of
episcopal care, although there were wide differences of opinion

and practice about the autonomy, if any, which could or should be delegated to the areas and their bishops. Experiments of this type were in operation in the dioceses of London, Oxford, Norwich, and York, and in the seventies similar schemes were being considered also in Canterbury, Exeter, and Chelmsford.[1] The area system in London was the most thoroughgoing, for the diocese had been divided into five well-defined territorial areas in which the area bishop possessed as much autonomy as the existing law permitted. The area system raised questions about its consonance with a true theology of episcopacy, the desirability of removing financial, synodical and legal barriers to a greater autonomy for areas, the control which the Church as a whole ought to exercise over such arrangements and the continuing rise in the number of suffragan bishops which such schemes involved.

In 1965 the Archbishop of Canterbury, with the agreement of the bishops of London, Chelmsford, Chichester, Guildford, Oxford, Portsmouth, Rochester, St. Albans, and Winchester, appointed a Commission to consider the reorganization of the diocesan system in London and South-East England. The Commission produced two alternative schemes.[2] The first was to reorganize London into five dioceses, which would involve reshaping the dioceses of Rochester, Canterbury, St. Albans and Chelmsford; to divide the diocese of Oxford into three dioceses; and to make certain readjustments in the other dioceses in the South-East. The second scheme was to divide the diocese of London and the other South-East dioceses into thirty small dioceses grouped in six regional areas. The proposals received little enthusiasm, although the Church Assembly showed a preference for the smaller dioceses scheme. In 1972 the General Synod invited one of its members, Canon P. A. Welsby, to prepare a document on the issues raised by suffragan bishops

---

[1] Cf., e.g. 'Episcopal Oversight Report' (Chelmsford), 1974; 'Organization and Communication in the Diocese of Canterbury', 1974; *Report of the Bishop of Oxford's Working Party on the Division of the Diocese*, 1970, followed by *Civil and Ecclesiastical Boundaries*, by the Oxford Diocesan Group for Mission, 1976; *A Report on the Diocese of York*, by John Adair, 1970; *Future Patterns of Ministry* (Diocese of Exeter), 1975. The dioceses of York, Durham, and Newcastle produced a report on *The Church in the North-East*, 1974, which had special reference to Teeside, Tyneside, and Wearmouth.

[2] *Diocesan Boundaries*, 1967.

and area reorganization. In fact Canon Welsby's document[3] concentrated on fundamentals and suggested certain questions which the Church must answer. The debate on this document revealed no general desire for any sharp break from the way in which episcopal oversight was being organized and exercised. A few members argued the case for mono-episcopacy and smaller dioceses, but that particular model had no wide attraction. On the other hand, the sharing of episcopal responsibility within a diocese was acceptable, provided the suffragan was given sufficient autonomy to exercise a true *episcope*. Indeed, it was clear that the Synod was content for there to be a variety of diocesan structures. There was, however, a desire that legal and other obstacles that stood in the way of greater autonomy for suffragans and areas should be removed and that means should be devised whereby a diocese who wished to establish an area system on a permanent basis could legally be enabled to do so.

The final outcome was the Dioceses Measure which became law in 1977. A permanent commission was established whose task was to prepare reorganization schemes for dioceses, which might include the founding of a new bishopric, the alteration of diocesan boundaries, the granting of power to a diocesan bishop to delegate certain of his powers to a suffragan, and the division of a diocese into episcopal areas, with area synods if required. No diocese could petition for the creation or revival of a suffragan see without the approval of the General Synod. Canon Welsby's document had also dealt with the question of the correspondence between diocesan boundaries and the units of local government, particularly in the metropolitan areas. There appeared to be little desire, however, for the general upheaval which such reorganization would involve.

In the diocese of London action was taken. In 1979 a scheme was approved under which the five episcopal areas—London, Kensington, Edmonton, Stepney, and Willesden—each had its own bishop and archdeacon, its own area synod and bishop's council, and the diocesan bishop transferred to the area bishops certain legal powers which they, and not he, were to exercise. The Bishop of London remained the bishop of the diocese, the administration of the diocese remained centralized and

---

[3] *Episcopacy in the Church of England*, 1973.

St. Paul's continued to be the cathedral of the whole diocese, but the area bishops were to exercise complete episcopal and pastoral authority within their areas. The diocese of London, in fact, is a small province in all but name.

## 2. Stipends and Patronage

Out of the debates on the Morley Report dealing with the deployment and payment of the clergy there emerged in due course four measures. The first was the establishment in 1972 of the Central Stipends Authority and the appointment of the Church Commissioners to be that Authority. Its task was to establish national standards of remuneration for incumbents, assistant curates, deaconesses, and full-time lay workers. The Church Commissioners' own income was insufficient to provide the money required to reach the 'target range' prescribed by the Authority and each year an increasing portion of the stipends of the clergy had to be raised by church people in the dioceses, with the result that by 1980 parishes were paying nearly one-third of the stipends. It is noteworthy that a Church which had come to depend so much upon the endowments of the past for the payment of its clergy responded so readily to this new challenge which enabled stipend levels to keep pace with inflation. Secondly, in 1975 the compulsory retirement age for clergy was fixed at seventy.[4] Thirdly, in 1977 machinery was established whereby a benefice might be declared vacant where an incumbent was unable, by reason of age or infirmity, to discharge his duties adequately and also in cases where the pastoral relationship between the incumbent and the parish had seriously broken down.[5] There has been great reluctance to use this machinery because of the undesirable publicity which such cases attract and because of the financial implications of the procedure. Fourthly, it became lawful in 1977[6] for benefice endowments and glebe to be pooled and thus to remove one cause of the wide differences of income levels.

The most intractable problem was to devise an appropriate method for the appointment of incumbents to benefices to

---

[4] Ecclesiastical Office (Age Limit) Measure.

[5] Incumbents (Vacation of Benefices) Measure.

[6] Endowment and Glebe Measure, 1976. The Measure came into operation in 1977.

replace the patronage system. The Morley Report had recommended the abolition of patronage and its replacement by a diocesan ministry committee, but this was unacceptable to the Church. A proposal that responsibility for the deployment of the clergy should rest with the diocesan pastoral committee and appointment to a parish should be made by a parish appointments committee consisting of bishop, patron, and representatives of the parish, was rejected in 1973 when, significantly, a motion in the General Synod to abolish patronage was lost only because of a tie in the House of Bishops.[7] The evidence was clear. There was no common mind in the Church on what should replace the existing method of appointment. There was no overwhelming call for the abolition of patronage, but many wished to see it replaced by a different method, and even those who saw value in the system looked for some measure of reform. The Synod, therefore, tried again and in 1978 produced the Benefices Measure, proposing a dual system whereby a priest might be appointed to a benefice. The first, 'Presentation by Patron', represented the traditional system reformed to provide for a fuller involvement of the parish in the appointment process. The second system, 'Presentation by Selectors', was a completely new procedure whereby the appointment would be made by four selectors, one of whom would be the bishop or his representative and the other three being nominated by the Parochial Church Council. It would be for each parish to decide which of the two systems should apply.

## 3. State Aid for Churches

Reference has been made to the commendable response by the laity to the challenge to raise money for clergy stipends. Another source of financial concern was the repair and maintenance of parish churches, most of them dating from many centuries past. In the case of churches no longer required for worship the redundant churches section of the Pastoral Measure, 1968, made it possible for them to be demolished or for an alternative use to be made of them. Between 1969 and 1979 nearly five hundred

[7] The voting was as follows: House of Bishops 14 for, 14 against; House of Clergy 95 for, 67 against; House of Laity 75 for, 66 against.

churches were declared redundant, of which some two hundred were demolished and some 150 were preserved by the Redundant Churches Fund.

These procedures were of no use to those whose financial anxieties centred on a church which remained in use and for some years the possibility of state aid had been under discussion. In 1976 the Government accepted in principle the case for state aid for churches in use, but in the current financial climate it was unable to give a specific date for the inauguration of the scheme. The following year the government announced its willingness to make three-quarters of a million pounds available for aid to historic churches during 1978/9, which would be increased to approximately two million pounds in 1979/80. In the long and complicated negotiations with the government the Church was ably led by the Bishop of Rochester, Dr David Say, and the result was a new form of partnership between Church and State.

## 4. Manpower

Between 1973 and 1980 the number of full-time clergy declined from 13,000 to 11,235 and between 1974 and 1979 the number of men ordained each year dropped from 348 to 303. The reduction in numbers was offset to a limited degree by the employment of deaconesses, accredited lay workers and readers, by the use of retired clergymen and by the grouping of parishes. The mid-seventies saw a fairly rapid growth in the non-stipendiary ordained ministry, but by 1980 numbers had steadied to about 120 annually. In 1970 there were only two courses available for training for this type of ministry, based at Southwark and Manchester, but by 1980 a network of courses covered most areas of the country.

The response of the Church to the problem of manpower was two-fold. First, in 1978 the bishops issued a call for an increase of men for ordination, aiming at a target of 400 to 450 candidates recommended for training each year, and this appeal was accompanied by a letter from the Archbishop of Canterbury to the clergy and laity urging renewed efforts in fostering vocations to the priesthood. The bishops also agreed on thirteen resolutions on the future of the ordained ministry and called upon the

Church to provide the resources for training and for ensuring that the clergy were adequately paid, housed, and pensioned. Furthermore, they considered it essential that the existing number of theological colleges should be retained and it granted a period of stability for an initial period of three years.

The second response of the Church to the manpower situation was to recognize that any kind of rational deployment of the available ministry over the whole country must depend on the ability to encourage men to be placed where the needs of the Church were greatest. The House of Bishops approved a scheme, known as 'the Sheffield Scheme' (because the chairman of the group which prepared the scheme was the Bishop of Sheffield), which provided a basis for establishing 'fair shares' for each diocese, thus placing the full-time clergy where the need was greatest. The Church moved towards the implementation of the scheme over a number of years and by 1980 seventeen dioceses were within 5 per cent of their Sheffield target. In 1976 it was agreed that a similar scheme should be established for the equitable sharing of newly ordained deacons.

## 5. The Ordination of Women

Throughout the post-war years a theme which surfaced with constant regularity was the ministry of women. In 1945 the Church Assembly recommended the establishment of a theological college for women and two years later Convocation very hesitantly discussed the question of authorizing qualified women 'to take special services in church and to speak at them'. It was in 1962, however, when the Church Assembly had before it another report on women's ministry,[8] that the first steps were taken which led to the great debate on the ordination of women. The report had deliberately avoided this issue, but it recommended that the reasons for withholding the priesthood from women should be thoroughly examined. Accordingly a commission was established which in its report made no judgement of the issue but set out fairly the biblical, psychological, and ecumenical considerations for and against the ordination of women.[9]

[8] *Gender and Ministry.*     [9] *Women and Holy Orders*, 1966.

The next event was the assertion in the report of another
working party on women's ministry[10] that 'until the Church
resolves this matter [of the ordination of women], it will be
almost impossible to make any clear definition of women's part
in ministry'. When the report's recommendations were debated
it was agreed that steps be taken to ensure that all accredited
lay workers, both men and women, be accorded equal status
and that accredited women should do all that readers did, which
included preaching and officiating at Morning and Evening
Prayer. The years that followed saw women playing an increasing part in worship—conducting services, reading the scriptures,
preaching and assisting with the administration of Holy Communion. Salaries, pensions, and conditions of service for women
were improved and in 1969 the order of readers was opened to
women.

The Lambeth Conference of 1968 affirmed 'that the theological arguments...for and against the ordination of women to
the priesthood are inconclusive',[11] but requested 'every national
and regional Church or Province' to study the question and to
report to the Anglican Consultative Council. In July 1973 it was
decided that before the Church of England gave an answer to
the Council the views of the dioceses should be obtained both
on the principle of women's ordination and on the desirability
of consequent action. Thus for the next two years the dioceses,
deaneries, and parishes of the Church were preoccupied with
the debate on the ordination of women. When the reports from
the dioceses were examined the verdict on the question of principle was clear. Thirty-three diocesan synods carried the motion
that 'there are no fundamental objections to the ordination of
women to the priesthood'. On the wisdom of immediate action,
however, only fifteen dioceses resolved that the Church should
proceed to remove the legal and other barriers to the ordination
of women. This was reflected in the decisions of the General
Synod in July 1975 when, after a debate of high order in a
crowded house, it agreed that there were no fundamental objections to women's ordination but failed to proceed to any consequent action. In opposing such action those who objected to the
ordination of women on principle were joined by those who,

[10] *Women in Ministry: a Study*, 1968.    [11] Resolution 34.

while agreeing with women's ordination, feared that to act immediately would damage the Church of England's relations with the Roman Catholic and the Eastern Orthodox Churches, and by those who judged that the diocesan voting indicated that the Church of England as a whole was not ready for such a far-reaching step. The latter group believed that to go forward would impose an intolerable strain on the consciences of a considerable minority and such an important departure from tradition as the ordination of women could be justified only by overwhelming support within the Church.

At the request of the Synod the Archbishop of Canterbury entered into correspondence with Pope Paul VI, the Oecumenical Patriarch and the Old Catholic Archbishop, inviting their Churches to examine the theological and other implications of the removal of the barriers to the ordination of women in the Church of England. The Pope regretfully recognized that 'a new course taken by the Anglican Communion in admitting women to the ordained priesthood cannot fail to introduce into this dialogue an element of grave difficulty' and in 1976 the Vatican Declaration on 'The Question of the Admission of Women to Ministerial Priesthood',[12] although primarily intended for Roman Catholics themselves, served as an exposition of the Pope's reasoning and declared that the Sacred Congregation judged it necessary 'to recall that the Church, in fidelity to the example of the Lord, does not consider herself authorised to admit women to priestly ordination'.[13] The Old Catholic bishops, with one exception, rejected the ordination of women and, after May 1978, they ceased to share in Anglican consecrations of bishops in those Churches which had decided to ordain women. The most acute reaction came from the Orthodox Churches and the issue seriously affected the discussions in the Anglican-Orthodox Joint Doctrinal Commission in July 1978 to such an extent that it 'brought our dialogue to a point of acute crisis'. An Orthodox statement declared that 'by ordaining women, Anglicans would sever themselves' from 'the continuity in the outward laying-on of hands and continuity in Apostolic

---

[12] *Inter Insigniores.*

[13] In 1980 the Roman Catholic hierarchy in England and Wales declared that they were not prepared to ask the Vatican to reopen the question of the ordination of women.

faith and spiritual life'. There is no doubt that the reaction of these three Churches influenced profoundly the action in subsequent debates of many churchmen who were not themselves opposed to the principle itself.

The Church of England renewed the debate in 1978. This was due largely to pressure from those who observed what was happening elsewhere in the Anglican Communion. The diocese of Hong Kong had ordained women in 1971 and it had been followed by the Church of the Province of New Zealand (1974), the Anglican Church in Canada (1975) and by the Episcopal Church of the USA (1976). The Lambeth Conference of 1978 passed an important resolution[14] declaring its acceptance both of those Churches which did and those which did not ordain women and it urged each to respect the other's convictions. It recommended that, where synodical authority was given for ordained women to exercise their ministry in provinces which did not ordain women, this should operate only where pastoral need warranted and when such ministry was acceptable to the bishop, clergy, and people of the place where it was to be exercised. The General Synod in 1978 had before it a motion asking for legislation 'to remove the barriers to the ordination of women to the priesthood and their consecration to the episcopate'. This was passed in the House of Bishops and in the House of Laity, but it was defeated in the House of Clergy by a significant majority.[15] There still remained the question of those women lawfully ordained abroad who subsequently visited England. In 1979 the General Synod was asked to approve the preparation of a *temporary* Measure, with a non-recurrable life of seven or five years, which would enable women priests ordained overseas to exercise their priesthood in this country in certain specified circumstances, on certain specific occasions, or for stated limited periods of time. This proposal was defeated; once again there was insufficient support from the House of Clergy.[16]

[14] Resolution 21.

[15] House of Bishops 32 for, 17 against; House of Clergy 94 for, 149 against; House of Laity 120 for, 106 against.

[16] House of Bishops 26 for, 10 against; House of Clergy 87 for, 113 against; House of Laity 110 for, 65 against.

## 6. Strategy for Mission

Episcopal organization, the deployment and payment of the clergy, and the ordination of women were not ends in themselves but, provided theological truth was maintained, their object was to further the mission of the Church in this country. In these years there was some uncertainty about the most appropriate methods for promoting the mission of the Church, caused partly by a failure to understand the relationship between evangelism and mission. Some saw the main thrust of mission, in a pluralist and largely secular society, in terms of influencing and penetrating the structures of society which powerfully affected men's lives. Others placed priority on the caring role of the Church, believing that Christian witness made its greatest impact when it is seen in terms of service to others. Finally, there were those who cared less for these things and saw the task of the Church in the traditional terms of the direct proclamation of the gospel and the winning of souls for Christ. Even here there was a difference of approach, some seeing this direct proclamation in local terms and as part of the day-to-day life of the Church, while others envisaged it in terms of a local campaign of limited duration or of a nationwide call to men and women to face the claims of Christ.

Traditional styles of evangelism saw two notable changes. More and more it took the form of house group meetings rather than large rallies and very frequently it was ecumenical in character. One of the most notable efforts of evangelism was the 'Call to the North' which was initiated in 1968 following a meeting between the Bishop of Liverpool, Dr Stuart Blanch, the Roman Catholic Archbishop of Liverpool, and a representative of the Baptist Church and of the united Reformed Church. In the spring of the following year all the Church leaders of the northern province met with the Archbishop of York. At this meeting and at subsequent ones in 1970 and 1972 the possibility of a united ecumenical mission to the whole of the north of England was discussed and it was finally decided to launch the 'Call to the North' in Holy Week 1973. In preparation for this, house groups were established throughout the region and these sought to influence non-churchgoers in their areas. Holy Week saw a variety of public ecumenical occasions, culminating in a

'Call' by the Church leaders. A feature of the Call to the North was the absence of central direction and the emphasis on local initiative and decision, the centre providing materials and ideas. Again, the agents of the Call were not specialist evangelists but the people in each area, which was encouraged to develop its own appropriate message and methods. In order that the Call should be seen to be relevant to social problems as well as to personal salvation, the theological emphasis was on the 'Gospel and the Kingdom'. Finally, it was made clear from the outset that this was not a traditional mission, in the sense that it was to be concentrated into a few weeks and then cease, but a continuous process the impetus of which would be maintained throughout the seventies. This did not happen, however, and the Call faded out. Nevertheless it was an imaginative vision and in those places where it was taken seriously there was a considerable increase in Christian commitment and Church attendance. It had involved lay people in active mission and in many cases, particularly in the large centres of population, there was much encouragement and enthusiasm. The North East decided to run its own mission, 'Action North East', in parallel with the Call to the North, and the creation by the Bishop of Durham, Dr Ian Ramsey, of the North Eastern Ecumenical Group was perhaps the most enduring result of the Call to the North in that part of the country. Indeed, throughout the north of England the most exciting outcome of the Call was the great improvement in ecumenical relations.[17]

In some areas local radio was used by the Church as part of its strategy for mission. The most notable example was the three Lent Courses for the dioceses of Rochester and Canterbury sponsored by BBC Radio Medway from 1979. The first series of programmes communicated with an audience of some 20,000 many of whom were in house groups comprising a mixture of active and fringe members of various denominations. Other evangelistic projects included such ventures as the mission to the quarter of a million holiday-makers who visited the Norfolk Broads each year and the ministry in the parish of St. Leonard's to the holiday-makers at St. Leonard's-on-Sea. A holiday club for children was organized by all the Churches in Chorleywood,

---

[17] For most of the information about the Call to the North I am indebted to Canon John Hunter, who was full-time officer for the Call until 1977.

Herts, where over a thousand children gathered and on a smaller scale this was paralleled in many parishes up and down the country. On the other hand, the Archbishops' Council for Evangelism[18] was disbanded in 1978 and a private voluntary organization called 'Tomorrow's Church' carried on some of the work of the former Council, particularly its concern to foster everyday lay ministry and the giving of advice at parish level.

In 1976 a series of events began which culminated in the concept of a National Initiative in Evangelism.[19] The executive committee of the British Council of Churches and the Evangelical Alliance had asked the Archbishop of Canterbury to call together a group of representatives of a number of bodies involved in evangelism. The group reached a consensus that in all the churches there was the conviction that the local congregation carried primary responsibility for evangelism and called on the Church to share in reporting and evaluating the evangelistic enterprises being undertaken by local Churches and to plan local initiatives in evangelism. The group also proposed the calling of a National Assembly on Evangelism not later than 1980. In 1977 the General Synod expressed the willingness of the Church of England to co-operate with the Initiative, although it was made clear that the emphasis must continue to be placed on local rather than national activity and that fundamental questions must be asked about the nature and practice of evangelism. The Initiative committee attempted to establish a network of local groups, based on the main local government units, to further the aims of the Initiative. These 'County Support Groups' were slow in being established and difficult for the Church of England, whose dioceses are not arranged on a county basis. Preparations went ahead for the National Assembly which was held at Nottingham in October 1980. The aims of the Assembly were to create vision and enthusiasm for evangelism among those attending, to awaken new confidence in the Gospel, to understand better the nature of evangelism itself, and to share information. It had originally been hoped that some 2,000 delegates might take part, but the unexpected slowness in establishing the County Support Groups meant that

---

[18] Cf. above, p. 49.

[19] 'National' was later changed to 'Nationwide' in order to indicate that the emphasis was on *local* initiative.

local response was poor and the final number of delegates was 822, some half of whom were Anglicans. The Assembly was not an easy one because of the varied expectations within the Churches. Alongside the majority which preferred local and regional enterprises rather than a centrally imposed campaign were a number who hoped for some kind of national mission to the nation. Two basic convictions made it possible for such a varied Assembly to take place at all. The first was an awareness of the huge missionary task in England and the second was the presence of sufficient agreement to allow the different groups to bear common witness. Evangelical and charismatic elements were present in force but the more 'liberal' elements were missing and—until a special session was arranged at the end— the Assembly ignored a large number of social concerns, such as race and unemployment, which were crucial for understanding the context within which evangelism must operate. There was some theological convergence but little hard dialogue between established evangelicals and the others. Many lay people present had their vision of the Church and its mission widened, but others had been discouraged by their participation in the County Support Groups. And all the time there was the tension between those who saw evangelism as being most effective at local level and those who yearned for a mass movement. This was highlighted by the invitation from a special committee of 100 to Dr Billy Graham to visit Britain for another national crusade.[20]

It has to be said that while the Nationwide Initiative had the official co-operation of the Church of England it failed to gain any effective and enthusiastic support in that Church. Far from implying that the Church of England was lukewarm towards evangelism, the reason was that its members were preoccupied with local evangelistic activities and could not believe that a Nationwide Initiative could do other than distract their energies from what was already going on. Dr Coggan was the driving force behind the Initiative, but his desire to see the venture launched before he retired meant that it was hastily and incompletely prepared. Nevertheless, the Assembly closed on a note of

[20] Dr Graham declined the invitation. It is understood that he is now due to come in 1984.
[21] 28 December 1980.

cautious optimism and the Archbishop of York, in a contribution to 'What I hope for in 1981' in the *Sunday Telegraph*,[21] declared that the Assembly 'was a first and important step in a united programme for evangelism that could involve many congregations throughout the country in a concerted effort to communicate the Christian faith to those who at present do not believe in it or know what it is'.

The Nationwide Initiative undertook a survey of the numerical strength of the Churches in 1979,[22] which claimed to be the most comprehensive religious census ever undertaken in this country. It revealed that 18 per cent of the total adult population were Church members and that 11 per cent of the population were regular attenders, numbering well over three and a half million. Lancashire was the highest with 16 per cent of the population attending, while (in the words of the report) 'the county most in need of Christian mission' was Humberside, with 7 per cent of the population attending church. The Anglican, Methodist, and United Reformed Churches were losing members, but the Baptists and the Pentecostalists were recording increases in church attendances. So far as the Church of England was concerned, 280 people had left the Church each year between 1975 and 1979, yet that was less than in the years 1970 to 1975. County figures showed that the decline was not confined to city areas but applied also to the West, the South West, East Anglia, the East Midlands, and the North East. In Cumbria, Lincolnshire, Cambridgeshire, Bedfordshire, West Sussex, and Dorset there were signs of increases in both membership and attendance. The Revd Gavin Reid, of the Church Pastoral Aid Society, with the prophet Elijah in mind, summed up the picture presented by these figures: 'I believe that these figures reveal that we are still in a spiritual drought in this country. I also believe that they reveal a little cloud coming up from the sea. The life-giving rain may well be coming. God knows, we are thirsty enough'.[23]

---

[22] *Prospects for the Eighties*, 1980.     [23] Ibid., p. 18.

# 15

## ONE CHURCH, ONE MISSION IN ONE WORLD

> How can the Church call men to worship of the one
> God if it is calling to rival shrines? How can it claim
> to bridge the divisions in human society...if when
> men are drawn into it they find that another division
> has been added to the old ones...A Church divided
> in its manifestation to the world cannot render its
> due service to God or to man, and for the impotence
> which our sin has brought upon the Church through
> divisions in its outward aspect we should be covered
> with shame and driven to repentance.
>
> William Temple, 1937

### 1. Covenanting for Unity

THE FAILURE of the Anglican-Methodist Scheme for Union in
1972 caused much disappointment and many ecumenical Anglicans, wearied by the battles and frustrations of the previous
years became dispirited, while others were unwilling to embark
on new negotiations for fear of another failure. It was generally
felt that a period of peace was needed before new initiatives
were taken. There was a growing conviction that the road to
unity ought not to be sought unilaterally by two Churches
acting on their own but that movements towards such an end
should have the participation of all the main Christian Churches
in this country. In 1972 the Presbyterian Church in England and
the Congregational Church came together to form the United
Reformed Church and at the inauguration of the new Church
the leaders of the other Churches pledged their Churches to
continue the quest for unity. In the following January Church
leaders met at Christ Church, Oxford, for informal and unofficial conversations, from which emerged a plan to hold 'Talks
about Talks'. It was the newly inaugurated United Reformed
Church which took the initiative in inviting the Churches to
participate in these talks, which represented an attempt to dis-

cover how unity could best be furthered. The Church of England gave a positive response to the invitation and all the other major Churches in Great Britain, including the Roman Catholic and the Orthodox Churches, accepted the invitation. These talks concluded with a proposal to establish a commission to work towards union between the Churches and 'other forms of visible unity'. Thus the Churches Unity Commission came into being in 1974. The participants were the Church of England, the Baptist Union, the Churches of Christ, the Congregational Federation (i.e. those Congregational Churches which had not joined the URC), the Methodist Church, the Moravians, the Roman Catholic Church, and the United Reformed Church. The Bishop of Manchester, the Rt. Revd Patrick Rodger, was the chairman, the Revd Kenneth Greet, Secretary of the Methodist Church, was the vice-chairman, and the Revd John Huxtable of the URC was the secretary. In January 1976 the commission issued a report[1] containing 'Ten Propositions' as an acceptable basis for continuing the search for unity and to which the constituent Churches were asked to give a reply. The Propositions reaffirmed the conviction that 'the visible unity in life and mission of all Christ's people is the will of God' and that, therefore, the Churches were willing to join in a covenant to seek visible unity. By accepting such a covenant the participating Churches would recognize each other's members as 'true members of the Body of Christ and welcome them to Holy Communion without conditions', recognize each other's ministries as 'true ministries of word and sacraments in the Holy Catholic Church', and agree that initiation in the covenanting Churches be by mutually acceptable rites. Non-episcopal Churches would take episcopacy into their systems and all the Churches would explore what further steps would be necessary 'to make more clearly visible the unity of all Christ's people'.

By 1978 the Churches had given their replies. The Congregational Federation and the Baptist Union were unable to accept the Propositions. The Roman Catholic Church, although unable to enter a covenant, saw value in other Churches, conscientiously able to do so, covenanting for unity. The Methodist Church was willing to enter the covenant as soon as the Church

---

[1] *Visible Unity in Life and Mission.*

of England was prepared to do so. The Churches of Christ and the Moravians agreed to enter the covenant, as did the United Reformed Church provided certain questions about episcopacy could be clarified. In the Church of England the dioceses were overwhelmingly in favour of continuing consultations with the other Churches but, although one-third of the dioceses desired early progress towards covenanting and the mutual recognition of members and ministries, a considerable number expressed anxieties or reservations about various aspects of the Propositions. Consequently, the General Synod, while affirming the Church of England's readiness to proceed by discussion towards covenanting on the basis of the Ten Propositions, asked for further clarification from the Churches of Christ and the Moravian Church about the authorized minister at the Eucharist, from the Churches of Christ about infant baptism and from the United Reformed Church about issues connected with episcopacy. It also affirmed that such discussions should 'in no way pre-judge the admissibility and acceptability of women to the ordained ministry of the Church of England'. Moreover, the Synod stipulated that the covenant should include incorporation of the existing ministries into the historic three-fold ministry by a prayer which made clear that such incorporation was intended, by a distinctive sign for conferring the gift of the Spirit, and by a concelebration of Holy Communion.

The replies from the Churches were followed by the establishment of the Churches Council for Covenanting which, adhering to the two-year time-table requested by the Church of England, published in June 1980 its proposals for a Covenant.[2] The Covenant would be set within a liturgical act falling into three parts—reconciliation; ordination of bishops and presbyters, the blessing of existing ministers, and the reaffirmation of baptismal promises; a joint celebration of Holy Communion. There would be a national service followed by similar regional services. Subsequently, the Churches would accept each other's members at Holy Communion and recognize each other's ministries. Future ordinations would be by a common ordinal and there would be an agreed rite of initiation. The covenanting Churches would develop methods of joint decision-making. The Commis-

---

[2] *Towards Visible Unity: Proposals for a Covenant.*

sion drew attention to one anomaly which would exist for a period up to seven years because the United Reformed Church, although in principle it accepted bishops in the historic succession and in practice would have such bishops, would not ordain its existing moderators to the episcopate. The Commission believed that this anomaly was one which could be lived with for the sake of fuller unity. On the acceptance of women ministers the Commission recognized the position of those who on conscientious grounds could not support this.

As was expected, the three anglo-catholic members of the Anglican representation on the Commission[3] were unable to accept these proposals on two main grounds. First, they objected to the provision allowing the United Reformed Church the seven-year period during which not all their leaders would be ordained to the episcopate. Such a deliberate reservation on the part of the URC was not, in their view, in accord with the belief expressed in the report that the proposed covenant provided an unambiguous method for incorporating the ministers of all the Churches in a new relationship within the historic ministry of the Church. Secondly, they believed that the recognition of women ministers of non-episcopal Churches, built into the proposed covenant, presented grave difficulties for the Church of England because it attempted to pre-judge an issue which it was the responsibility of that Church itself to determine.

When the proposals came to the General Synod in July 1980 they received a very qualified response which once again revealed the deep divisions within the Church of England. Both sides proclaimed their desire to listen and to learn; both sides affirmed their commitment to reunion. At the end of the debate, however, 117 (mostly clergy) voted against the procedural motion to 'take note of the report'.[4] When it is realized that a number of members, who were not really happy with the proposals but understood that to 'take note' committed no one to anything, voted in favour, and recognizing that a two-thirds majority would be required in all three houses before the proposals could become a programme for action, it is not surprising that

[3] The Bishop of Truro, Dr Graham Leonard; Canon Peter Boulton, Vicar of Worksop; Mr Oswald Clark, Chairman of the House of Laity of the General Synod.

[4] House of Bishops 38 for, 2 against; House of Clergy 113 for, 70 against; House of Laity 138 for, 45 against.

gloom rather than jubilation characterized the outcome. The one sign of encouragement was the strong lead given by the bishops, only two of whom voted against the motion.[5]

## 2. Rome and Canterbury

In September 1971 there emerged from the Anglican-Roman Catholic International Commission an Agreed Statement on the Eucharist[6]—the first of three such statements. The vexed question of transubstantiation was relegated to a footnote and, on the eucharistic presence itself, the authors agreed that 'the elements are not mere signs: Christ's body and blood become really present and are really given. But they are really present and given in order that, receiving them, believers may be united with Christ the Lord.' The signatories acknowledged that there could be no repetition of the sacrifice of Christ made once for all, but the eucharist proclaimed the atoning work of Christ on the Cross and made it effective in the life of the Church. An Agreed Statement on the ministry[7] followed in 1973, which recorded considerable agreement on the nature of priesthood and brought close together the ministry of the word and the ministry of the sacraments. 'Because the eucharist is central to the Church's life...the essential nature of Christian ministry, however it may be expressed, is most clearly seen in its celebration.' The statement avoided the basic question of the validity of Anglican orders. The third Agreed Statement, on authority in the Church,[8] was published in 1976 and differed from its predecessors by deliberately leaving some important problems, such as the 'divine right' of the papacy and the infallibility and jurisdiction of the Pope, still to be solved. The authority which had accrued historically to the papacy was not questioned, although it was agreed that there may have to be reinterpretation. The see of Rome was the only see which made claim to universal primacy and therefore 'it seems appropriate that in any future

[5] In 1981-2 thirty-six dioceses accepted the Covenant proposals and eight rejected them. In July 1982 the General Synod rejected the proposals because the vote in the House of Clergy and the total vote of the whole Synod failed to reach the necessary two-thirds majority.

[6] *Eucharistic Doctrine.*

[7] *Ministry and Ordination.*

[8] *Authority in the Church.*

union a universal primacy such as has been described should be held by that see'. That was the key section in the document so far as ecumenical relations were concerned.

These three statements in no way carried the authority of either Church and represented the agreement of the signatories only. They were, however, an honest endeavour, as the final statement expressed it, 'to get behind the opposed and entrenched positions of past controversies. We have tried to reassess what are the real issues to be resolved.' In 1979 the General Synod agreed that the Statements on the Eucharist and the Ministry were 'sufficiently congruent with Anglican teaching to provide a theological basis for further dialogue'. Convinced that theological discussion, however important, could not of itself bring about unity, the Synod also expressed the conviction that, 'in consultation with the Roman Catholic Church, the Anglican Communion should proceed to the implementation of the stage-by-stage progression to full communion'.

Two years previously, from 27 to 30 April 1977, the Archbishop of Canterbury, Dr Coggan, had paid an official visit to the Pope. Peter Hebblethwaite has taken the view that Dr Coggan's welcome to Rome was notably less enthusiastic than that accorded to his predecessor and that this was due to the fact that during the interval the Church of England had been debating the question of the ordination of women.[9] Dr Coggan and the Pope met privately for ninety minutes and the matters they discussed were subsequently outlined in the Common Declaration which they both signed at the end of a service in the Sistine Chapel.[10] It recommended that the International Commission should continue its work but agreed that theological dialogue must be accompanied by practical steps in the search for unity. It reaffirmed organic unity as the goal being sought as part of the Church's evangelistic work because divisions hinder the witness of the Church to the world.

Some people accused Dr Coggan of making a tactless error on the evening of his audience with the Pope. In a sermon preached in the Episcopal Church of St. Paul-within-the-Walls he re-

[9] *The Year of Three Popes*, 1978, p. 23.
[10] Cf. 'The Common Declaration by Pope Paul VI and the Archbishop of Canterbury', 29 April 1977, in Anglican-Roman Catholic International Commission, *The Final Report*, 1982, pp. 119ff.

iterated the call in the Declaration for co-operation in evangelism and then he added that this would be less than effective 'until we are able to go to that work strengthened by our joint participation in the Sacrament of Christ's Body and Blood'. The following year, at the end of the Week of Prayer for Christian Unity, the Archbishop repeated this plea in a sermon in Westminster Cathedral. The following month Cardinal Basil Hume, the Archbishop of Westminster, gave an address to the General Synod[11] which, being the first of its kind, made history. In the course of it there came a negative response to Dr Coggan's plea. The Cardinal reiterated the traditional Roman Catholic view that participation in Holy Communion was not a means towards organic union but the consummation of it and that before 'we can, as Churches, approach the Altar of the Lord together' there are other questions which must be solved. This position was reaffirmed in August 1980 when the Roman Catholic hierarchy in England and Wales stated that they were unable to approve even of occasional admission to Holy Communion of members of other Churches married to Roman Catholics.[12]

This leads us to turn to another cause of division between the two Churches—the subject of mixed marriages. In 1907, following the decree *Ne Temere,* any marriage between a Roman Catholic and a non-Roman Catholic taking place in an Anglican church, though valid in English civil law, was regarded as invalid by the canon law of the Roman Church. A mixed marriage solemnized in a Roman Catholic church was valid, provided the Roman Catholic party had obtained a dispensation from the ecclesiastical authorities, to which certain conditions were attached. The marriage service was to be reduced to bare essentials and the non-Roman partner was required to promise, normally in writing, that any children of the marriage should be brought up in the Roman Church. The Roman Catholic partner was required to endeavour to win the other to the Roman faith. This could—and did—cause much stress and tension within a marriage and, ecumenically, it was discouraging because it was evidence of the superiority which the Roman Church believed itself to possess over all other Churches. It is not surprising that

[11] *Report of Proceedings,* February 1978, pp. 135ff.
[12] *The Easter People: A Message from the Roman Catholic Bishops of England and Wales in Light of the National Pastoral Congress, Liverpool 1980,* 1980, p. 29.

after the Second Vatican Council, which acknowledged the spiritual relationship between Rome and the 'separated brethren' and which regarded all baptized Christians as 'united in Christ', the situation became easier. Progress, however, was slow. First, in 1966 the Vatican issued an *Instruction on Mixed Marriages*, which made a small concession to the new spirit by ordering that, if the non-Roman Catholic partner felt conscientiously unable to give the required promises, the bishop must refer the case to Rome which might grant a relaxation of the normal regulations. Next, in 1970 the Roman Catholic Episcopal Conference of England and Wales issued a *Directory Concerning Mixed Marriages* which considerably relaxed the position. Finally, in response to the views expressed by the Anglican-Roman Catholic International Commission, the *Directory* was revised in 1977. The revision represented a real movement towards a more sympathetic approach to mixed marriages. The Roman Catholic partner was to undertake 'as far as possible' to see that the children were brought up as Roman Catholics and had to read and sign a declaration to do this, but the non-Roman partner was no longer required to make any promise. 'For serious reasons' the Roman Catholic bishops might give a dispensation for the marriage to take place in an Anglican church before an Anglican priest, in which case the Roman Catholic priest could be present and take part in the rite, provided it was not part of the Eucharist. When the marriage took place in a Roman Catholic church within the context of the Mass the non-Roman partner was not to receive the Sacrament. With the consent of the Roman Catholic priest a non-Roman Catholic minister might be present in the sanctuary and might be invited to read passages from the Scriptures, to say prayers which are part of the Roman rite and to give an address. A service of blessing and thanksgiving in the Church of the other party was positively recommended.

In 1980 the Roman Catholic Church in this country held a National Pastoral Congress and this was followed by a message[13] issued by the Bishops of England and Wales which represented their reaction to the Congress. It contained a number of decisions which affected Anglican and Roman Catholic relations.

[13] Ibid.

Although the Congress had pleaded for the ordination of women 'to be explored seriously at this time', the bishops refused to raise the question with the Pope. They agreed to reconsider seeking full membership of the British Council of Churches, but at the end of the year they announced that they would not be joining the Council in the foreseeable future. In response to the Congress's call for a renewed theology of sex and marriage, the hierarchy endorsed the encyclical, *Humanae Vitae*, but agreed to a re-examination of the teaching on contraception.

## 3. The Anglican-Orthodox Doctrinal Commission

In 1962 Archbishop Michael Ramsey and the Ecumenical Patriarch, Athenagoras I, had agreed to the establishment of a new Joint Anglican-Orthodox Doctrinal Commission. When the full commission met in Oxford in 1973 work was delegated to sub-committees whose statements were presented to the second full joint conference in Moscow in 1976. Out of this emerged the 'Moscow Statement', which dealt with seven topics upon which agreement had been reached in principle but not necessarily on their application. Perhaps the most significant passage in the Statement was the agreement of the representatives of the two Churches on the *filioque* clause[14] in the Nicene Creed. The Anglican members accepted the Orthodox view that, because the original form of the Creed did not include that clause, because it was introduced without the authority of an ecumenical council, and because the Creed 'is the public confession of faith by the People of God in the Eucharist', the *filioque* clause should not be included in that Creed. The Lambeth Conference of 1978 endorsed this conclusion and requested all member Churches of the Anglican Communion to consider omitting the clause. By 1980 the Church of England had taken no action on the matter.

The Moscow Statement made no reference to the ordination of women, but a note attached to the press communique on the Statement said that the Orthodox members of the commission

---

[14] The clause, 'and the Son', following immediately after the words 'the Holy Ghost who proceedeth from the Father' in the Nicene Creed.

wished to state that if the Anglican Church proceeded to the ordination of women this would 'create a very serious obstacle to the development of our relations in the future'. When in July 1975 the Church of England had agreed that 'there are no fundamental objections to the ordination of women to the priesthood' this caused considerable consternation among the Orthodox and threatened the future of dialogue between the two Churches. When Archbishop Coggan visited the Ecumenical Patriarch, Demetrios I, in Istanbul in May 1977 the patriarch told him that, although he wished well to the theological dialogue, nevertheless 'we do not consider constructive to our efforts the formation of new problems, introducing novelties, entirely foreign to the undivided Church and to its faith and tradition'. He added that the Orthodox Churches 'reject the movement aiming at the ordination of women'. The official joint communique after the meeting spoke of the ordination of women being 'the most specific difficulty during the meeting'. When the Anglican-Orthodox Joint Doctrinal Commission met in Cambridge that year the Orthodox condemned the decision made by certain Churches of the Anglican Communion to ordain women because, in their view, this would have 'a decisively negative effect on the recognition of Anglican Orders'. Such recognition depended upon the Anglican Church having preserved the Apostolic succession, which signified continuity in 'Apostolic faith and spiritual life', and to ordain women was to 'sever themselves from this continuity', The report of the meeting of the Commission the following year was in effect a final appeal to the Anglican Church on the subject of women's ordination and warned that the question had brought Anglican-Orthodox dialogue 'to a point of acute crisis'. It went on: 'In the name of our common Lord and Saviour Jesus Christ we entreat our Anglican brothers not to proceed further with this action which is already dividing the Anglican Communion and which will constitute a disastrous reverse for all our hopes of unity between Anglicanism and Orthodoxy'. When the Commission met in 1980, however, there was a fresh feeling of optimism and it appeared that the talks were once again firmly established. That this was so was greatly to the credit of the chairman, the Bishop of St. Albans (Dr Robert Runcie), who had had meetings with Orthodox leaders in the previous year and had reassured them of the good faith of the Anglican Church.

## 4. 'Partners in Mission'

Mutual Responsibility and Interdependence (MRI)[15] had been the first experience of partnership between the Churches of the Anglican Communion and had led to a new and significant relationship between them. The concept, however, became too largely identified with the MRI Directory of Projects and this in turn led to a 'shopping list' approach to partnership, leaving unchanged the old 'giving-receiving' relationship. In 1973 the Anglican Consultative Council therefore launched 'Partners in Mission', the object of which was 'to develop and foster more effective patterns of consultation and working relationships between the member Churches of the Anglican Communion'.[16] Broadly speaking the pattern of Partners in Mission was that, first, each Church was to work out its priorities in mission for the next five years and produce a plan of where its energies and resources should be concentrated during that period. Next, those plans and the information on which they were based would be shared with a small group of people representative of some of the other Churches in the Anglican Communion, together with some non-Anglicans. Partners in Mission made a halting start and the first two preliminary consultations held in East Africa and Japan revealed that the implications of the exercise had not been fully understood. Three further consultations took place in 1974 in Central Africa, Tanzania, and Uganda which were far more successful. The Church of England had been represented in all these five consultations. By 1980 twenty-six such events had taken place and some of them were already in a second phase. Almost every province except the two provinces in England had taken part in the process. In this country the response to Partners in Mission had been through dioceses and regions and as a result a number of dioceses had become involved in the process. By 1978 it became clear that this was not enough because it did not bring within the process

[15] Cf. above, pp. 183ff.
[16] *Partners in Mission: Anglican Consultative Council. Second Meeting 1973*, 1973, p. 55.

the central bodies of the Church, thus failing to recognize that in this country those bodies were partners in mission with the dioceses. Consequently a consultation for the Church of England was arranged for 1981 which would not attempt the almost impossible task of surveying the whole life of the Church but would concentrate on the work of the central official bodies and the voluntary bodies working at national level. The partners were from seventeen other Churches—nine from the Anglican Communion, four from other Church bodies outside Britain and four from other Churches within Britain.[17]

The principle underlying Partners in Mission that there is *one* mission in the world, shared by the world-wide Christian family, prompted developments in England to improve the relationship between the Church of England, the General Synod, and the various independent missionary societies. The voluntary societies were still the major instruments through which the Church of England shared in the mission of the Church overseas and yet official decisions relating to the Anglican Communion had to be taken by the Church itself through the General Synod. For example, it had not been easy for the Church of England to make a clear response to Partners in Mission because it had been, as it were, at one remove from the involvement enjoyed by the voluntary missionary societies. Furthermore, the new understanding of mission had led to the conviction that those involved in 'home' mission and those concerned with 'overseas' mission must be brought together since both were integral to the one task of 'world' mission. The problem was to establish better co-ordination between the societies themselves and between them and the official Church, as represented by the General Synod, without at the same time squandering the vision, the enthusiasm and the fellowship engendered by the voluntary societies. The solution was the inauguration in 1978 of the Partnership for World Mission, a co-ordinating body bringing together representatives of the General Synod, of the eight 'recognized' missionary societies and of the Church Army and the Mothers' Union. Sixteen other agencies became associate members. The Partnership was to be a forum for co-ordination and joint planning, a source of advice to the

[17] The Report of the Consultation was published in 1981—*To A Rebellious House?*

Church on world mission and evangelism and a body to stimulate prayer and concern for world mission throughout the Church of England.

## 5. Lambeth 1978

The Lambeth Conference of 1978 commended the Partners in Mission concept but encouraged the strengthening of the ecumenical dimension of the consultations. The Conference met for three weeks at the University of Kent near Canterbury. The residential nature of the Conference enabled the bishops to get to know each other better and made possible time for worship and prayer which had been difficult when members of previous Conferences had had to travel to and fro each day. This proved to be a cohesive force among the bishops from a great Communion of sixty-five or seventy million people scattered throughout the world. The harmony that prevailed was to a very considerable extent due to the personal contribution of the Archbishop of Canterbury and to the administrative ability of Bishop How, secretary to the Conference. There emerged a new spirit of confidence in the Anglican Communion which, only ten years before, some had prophesied would disappear in the interests of a wider unity. In its discussions the Conference was well earthed in the realities of the world, being greatly concerned with the exploitation of natural resources and the economic plight of the Third World, while a number of Conference resolutions dealt with the economy, with human rights, and with war and violence. So far as the Church's own life was concerned, the bishops proposed the establishment of an inter-Anglican theological and doctrinal advisory committee and also requested the primates to initiate a study of the nature of authority within the Anglican Communion. The way in which the question of the ordination of women was handled showed wisdom, firmness, and love, and the debate on the subject owed much to the Bishop of Derby, the Right Revd Cyril Bowles, for his chairmanship of the group which produced the final resolution and for his masterly speech which set the tone of the debate. Briefly, the bishops accepted by an overwhelming majority the *de facto* ordination of women in some provinces and, at the same time, affirmed their commitment to the preservation of unity between all member Churches of the Anglican Communion. They recognized the autonomy of each of its member Churches to make its own decisions on the matter, urged all member Churches to continue in communion with one another, and requested those who ordained women to respect the convictions and consciences of those who did not. Finally, they recommended consultation with the entire episcopate, through the primates, before any woman was consecrated to the episcopate, 'lest the bishop's office become a cause of disunity instead of a focus of unity'.[18]

## 6. The Churches and Political Violence

The Church of England's relationship with the World Council of Churches underwent a crisis in 1978. Since the middle of the sixties there had been a shift in the WCC's social concerns and increasing attention had been paid to the widespread violence that was a feature of a world passing through unprecedented social and political change. The main reason for this new preoccupation had been the increasing membership in the WCC of Churches from the Third World. In 1948 the Council had a majority from Churches in North America and Western Europe; by the mid-sixties it had a majority from the Third World Churches, whose concerns were very different from those of the West. Those Churches covered areas where there was famine, political and economic oppression, and where Christians were involved in violent struggles against unjust regimes. Some of those Churches acknowledged that violence produced a moral dilemma for Christians but felt obliged to recognize that in particular circumstances violent action in the cause of justice might be the only available response to an oppressively unjust society. Now it was difficult for members of the Church of England to appreciate the situation of people actively engaged in political struggle in Southern Africa or in South America in circumstances totally alien to those in the West. Moreover, there had been a long period of neglect of the ties between the Church of England and the WCC, with the result that most members of the former were unaware of the radical alteration in the membership of the latter. Consequently, when the

---

[18] *Report of the Lambeth Conference, 1978*, 1978, pp. 45-6.

change in the WCC's social involvement took concrete form in the making of grants to bodies engaged in combating racialism all that many Englishmen saw was what, in their view, was a left-wing organization becoming involved in revolutionary social and political change.

Immediately before the 1968 Assembly of the WCC Martin Luther King, who was to have addressed the Assembly, was assassinated and the reaction of the Assembly was to agree to the need for some action which would decisively align the Churches with people suffering from racial discrimination and would help them in their struggle against it. The following year the Programme to Combat Racialism (PCR) was established, one of the features of which was to discover ways of helping the Churches to reconsider their own involvement in racially discriminatory attitudes. It was the second feature, however, which attracted the most widespread criticism. This was the establishment of a Special Fund to make grants to organizations of the racially oppressed who were working effectively against their oppression. The Fund was entirely separate from the WCC general fund to which member Churches contributed and it obtained its income solely from specially earmarked contributions from Churches, from governments and from numerous private gifts. Grants made from the Special Fund were intended to be a symbol of the Churches' solidarity with groups actively struggling against discrimination. Apart from the requirement that the grants were to be used for humanitarian activities—i.e. social, health, and educational purposes, legal aid, etc.—the PCR refused to exercise control of the manner in which the money was spent, thus reflecting the view of the WCC that people should be trusted to manage their own affairs.

The first grants, made in 1970, produced a critical reaction because they included some to liberation movements fighting the Portuguese in Angola and Mozambique. Criticism came mainly from England and other white nations, such as West Germany, and from the white minority in South Africa. To black Africans, however, the grants were welcome as symbolizing the Churches' identification with the cause of black people in their struggle. When the Anglican Consultative Council met in 1971 it said of the grants 'that in our judgement no public action by the Churches during the past twenty-five years has done so much to arouse public discussion on a moral issue'.[19] As a result of this widespread criticism the WCC initiated a study of violence in the cause of social justice and in due course it commended a statement[20] which made three points. First, there were some forms of violence which the Churches must condemn unequivocally; secondly, the Churches must give more attention to the possibilities offered by techniques of non-violent resistance to injustice; and, thirdly, non-violence itself should not be regarded as uncontroversial because it too could also be highly political and might involve compromise and moral ambiguity.

It was against this background of mounting opposition and suspicion that in 1978 a grant was made from the Special Fund to the Zimbabwe Patriotic Front. The grant was criticized because it involved a political judgement on the part of the PRC that the 'Internal Settlement', under which Bishop Muzorewa and Mr Sithole joined the Rhodesian government, did not amount to a genuine transfer of power to the black majority in Rhodesia and that the Patriotic Front was therefore justified in continuing its guerrilla activities. Another grant was made to SWAPO, the guerrilla movement fighting in Namibia. There was a sharp reaction to these grants. The Salvation Army and the Presbyterian Church in Ireland suspended their membership of the WCC and the Evangelical Church in West Germany expressed severe criticism of the SWAPO grants. In Great Britian the critical response was sharpened because of the many people there who had relations and friends in Rhodesia. To many Britons the action of the WCC appeared to be motivated solely by political considerations and to be a betrayal of the Christian tradition of seeking reconciliation. Many also regarded the actions of the WCC towards liberation movements in Southern Africa and South America as being in sharp contrast to its silence about the denial of human rights in Eastern Europe.[21]

---

[19] *The Time is Now: Anglican Consultative Council,* 1971, p. 18.

[20] *Violence, Non-Violence and the Struggle for Social Justice,* 1973.

[21] An example of this occurred in August 1980 when the WCC was sharply criticized for its silence about the sentence passed on Father Gleb Yakunin, a Soviet dissident. The WCC always answered this charge by saying that delegates from Communist countries are always under pressure and to speak strongly might cause suffering to Christians in the country concerned or Orthodox delegates might not be allowed to continue their association with the WCC, with the result that contact might be lost altogether.

Another criticism was about the lack of consultation with member Churches before the grants were made, with the result that in 1978 the Central Committee of the WCC authorized a process of consultation to begin. Bishops, clergy, and laity in this country were bombarded with complaints and there was a vigorous correspondence in the religious and secular press and much comment on radio and TV. Not all the feeling, however, was hostile. Indeed, after the grant to the Patriotic Front the British Council of Churches received an increased number of donations for the Special Fund.

On more than one occasion the General Synod had been critical of the actions of the WCC, notably in 1974 when it reduced the Church of England's contribution to the WCC by a token sum of £1,000.[22] There was further comment in 1975 when the Synod discussed the forthcoming Assembly of the WCC at Nairobi.[23] In 1978 the grants to the Patriotic Front were debated and, having endorsed the call of the Lambeth Conference for Churches to reaffirm their support for, and to strengthen their understanding of, the WCC, the Synod went on to note that the recent grants had caused controversy in parts of the Church of England. It believed that certain aspects of the Programme to Combat Racism had political and theological implications which urgently required discussion within the membership of the Council and it asked that a delegation should be appointed to take up these matters with the officers of the WCC.[24] Under the chairmanship of the Bishop of Rochester, Dr David Say, the delegation visited the headquarters at Geneva in March 1979. Its task had been widened to discuss relationships between the Church of England and the WCC in general as well as the more specific issue of the Programme to Combat Racism and the Special Fund. The delegation was cordially received at Geneva where staff members accorded it a large amount of time and where Archbishop Ted Scott, Primate of Canada and Moderator of the WCC's Central Committee, made a special visit to meet the delegation. The report of the delegation[25] left no doubt that the strong feelings

[22] *Report of Proceedings*, July 1974, p. 415.
[23] Ibid, November 1975, pp. 210ff.
[24] Ibid, November 1978, pp. 1099f.
[25] *The Church of England and the World Council of Churches*, 1979.

expressed in Britain were communicated to the officials of the WCC and the delegates pressed hard for a fresh examination of the relationship between the Council and its member Churches. On the other hand, the delegation itself had to meet the criticisms that the Church of England's judgement was affected by the continuing family links with people in Southern Africa and by the one-sided reporting of atrocities in Zimbabwe-Rhodesia, that its attitude towards racialism had not changed in the past ten years, and that it lacked the imagination to look at events through the eyes of an oppressed people. What England was failing to do, it was suggested, was to establish a relationship of trust with members of Churches elsewhere in the world.

In its report the delegation reminded people that the Programme to Combat Racism was but one part of the total far-ranging work of the WCC and it gave a full account of its many other activities—in faith and witness, education and renewal, justice and service. The key message of the delegation to the Church of England, however, lay in the first sentence of the Report: 'We belong to the World Council of Churches, and the World Council of Churches belongs to us. With 295 member-Churches, ranging from the Orthodox to the Pentecostals, and with the Roman Catholic Church in close association, it is today a unique meeting place for Christians of all traditions as they seek to carry out their mission to the world. It serves us, the Church, and we cannot do without it.'[26] If that is so, then the Church of England must play its full part in the WCC and must be prepared to take its share of responsibility. 'For too long it has stood back from the WCC and criticised from the wings.'[27] Then the delegation issued a final challenge. 'As far as the Church of England's part in the life of the WCC is concerned, the alternatives are clear. Either it must retain its rightful place in the World Council, which will necessarily involve fuller participation in its work and increasing financial contributions; or it must be prepared to contemplate the honest alternative of withdrawal...To us...withdrawal into ecclesiastical insularity is unthinkable.'[28] As the broadcaster Gerald Priestland commented, the report was 'an indictment not of the WCC's political bias, but of the Church of England's stinginess and isolationism'.[29]

[26] Ibid, Prelude.       [27] Ibid, p. 45.
[28] Ibid.          [29] *Yours Faithfully*, Vol. 2, 1981, p. 96.

The delegation's report was accepted by the General Synod and was commended for study in the dioceses in the belief that this would enable the Church of England's ecumenical commitment to be better understood throughout the Church.

# EPILOGUE

The Church goes on. Assailed it has been on all sides
and on every ground, attacked by some because she
is other-worldly, by others because she is not;
accused in one breath of an insane altruism and in
the next of unworthy egotism; its title-deeds torn
up, its facts disputed, its influence denied! Its
adversaries have demolished it a thousand times in
argument and pronounced the Christian Church a
dead thing, and cried to carry out the corpse, for all
was over but the shouting. And they have betaken
themselves to shouting, only to find when it was over
that the slain hydra had raised a new head, and all
was to do again.

Neville Figgis, *The Gospel, and Human Needs*, 1909

THE DECADE closed with the retirement of Dr Coggan as Archbishop of Canterbury, who, like his two predecessors, was
created a life peer. A man of deep personal piety and possessing
confidence in the Church of England, its ministry and its
people, the size and demands of the highest office in the Church
had stretched him to his limits, although his chronic inability to
delegate was more than matched by his dynamic energy and his
unbounded capacity for hard work. He was a person of great
kindness, with a sincere concern for people, which made him
vulnerable and easily hurt. His scholarship was linguistic rather
than theological and this resulted in a certain lack of theological
awareness which compared unfavourably with that of his predecessor. Yet he was a great teacher, preacher and expositor of
the Scriptures. For him evangelism took priority over the
Church's social witness and this emerged clearly in his Call to
the Nation in 1975 and his strong support of the Nationwide
Initiative in Evangelism at the close of his archiepiscopate. He
appeared to approach social problems more in terms of a failure
in personal religion than as the consequences of the impersonal
structures of society itself, and for him the way to a renewed
social order was through personal evangelism. Dr Coggan has
been described as 'the layman's archbishop', and it is true that
his simple and direct Christianity, which was not unduly con-

cerned with ecclesiastical niceties, was greatly appreciated by many lay people, as were also the puritan streak in his make-up, his stress on personal evangelism and the emphasis he placed on traditional moral standards.

Dr Coggan's primary contribution to the life of the Church was the confidence which he was able to engender after the upheavals and uncertainties of the sixties. He himself was confident in his faith and full of hope, and his desire was that the Church should be confident, faithful, and hopeful too. The radicalism of the sixties was bound to decline in face of the disillusionment of the seventies and Dr Coggan was able to use such inspiration as he possessed to strengthen morale and to enable the Church to recover its nerve. One of the signs of this was the expectation of an increasing number of ordinands and a willingness to plan in faith for this. It may not be realized that it was Dr Coggan personally, and in the face of some reluctance on the part of a number of other Church leaders, who inspired the Church to look forward in hope and confidence to an increase in the ordained ministry.

In September 1979 the announcement was made that Dr Coggan's successor was to be the Bishop of St. Albans, the Rt Revd Robert Runcie. The new archbishop is a marked contrast to his three predecessors. He lacks the administrative flair of Dr Fisher, the deep scholarship, the creative intellect, and the spiritual other-worldliness of Dr Ramsey and the earnest evangelizing spirit of Dr Coggan. Yet he is an able administrator, a person of deep spirituality and committed to the reconciling power of the Gospel. He does not see the Church possessing 'answers to life's problems tied up in neat packages' and is suspicious of 'rigid theology, a judging temper of mind, the disposition to over-simplify the difficult and complex problems'.[1] He has a dislike of 'ringing declarations and general moralizing divorced from a direct experience of the doubts and difficulties of ordinary people'.[2]

Dr Runcie has brought to his new office a breadth of outlook and an uninhibited style of conducting affairs, undergirded by a spirituality rooted in the catholic tradition and by pastoral experience, but with a radical streak which makes him open to

[1] Enthronement Sermon, Canterbury Cathedral, 25 March 1980.
[2] Dr Runcie at a press conference after the announcement of his appointment.

new thought and fresh insights. He has fluency of speech and is an effective communicator and this has been ably displayed in interviews on radio and television and in the sermons at his enthronement, at the service marking the Queen Mother's eightieth birthday, and at the wedding of Prince Charles. He is a committed ecumenist, evidenced by his chairmanship of the Anglican-Orthodox Joint Doctrinal Commission, where his reconciling and diplomatic skills were used to great effect in closing the gap between Anglicans and Orthodox which occurred over the ordination of women. Unlike his two predecessors, Dr Runcie has consistently opposed women's ordination because he sees it as divisive, because he believes the arguments on both sides to be evenly balanced, and because he does not regard the issue as being sufficiently high on the Anglican agenda. He has admitted that he might conceivably change his mind, but that has not happened yet.

When he was appointed Dr Runcie said that he was anxious to avoid getting on 'the archiepiscopal treadmill' and being so overwhelmed with detail that he had neither the time nor the energy to deal with big issues. He wished to see the Church not too preoccupied with its own structures but open to the life and thought of the nation. Unlike Dr Coggan, he believes in consultation and is very concerned to listen to others, including those outside the Church, those engaged in the secular areas of society and those of other religions. It is far too early to pass more than a very superficial judgement on the events of the new archiepiscopate. Dr Runcie has taken steps to avoid some of the 'treadmill' by the establishment of an able and realistic secretariat at Lambeth, under the leadership of Bishop Ross Hook as Chief of Staff, and by the delegation of many of his diocesan responsibilities to his suffragans. He played a notable part on the world stage in connection with the release in 1981 of Dr and Mrs John Coleman and Miss Jean Waddell held captive in Iran. He has made some vigorous interventions in Parliament, has given clear leadership in the General Synod, and has already travelled thousands of miles to visit provinces of the Anglican Communion. The most momentous event of his archiepiscopate hitherto was the historic visit of the Pope to Canterbury Cathedral in 1982.

Although it is too soon to begin to make anything more than a provisional assessment of the history of the last fifty years, certain trends are evident. The period began in a spirit of optimism and, in particular, there were high hopes of ecumenical advance, which received considerable impetus in the sixties from the changing outlook of the Roman Catholic Church. In spite of the opposition which was strong enough to defeat the Anglican-Methodist Scheme there were large numbers in the Church of England willing to embark on Stage One. Much of the ecumenical fervour has been frustrated and the old pioneering spirit and confident hope have been replaced by a more sober and realistic approach to the seemingly intractable problems blocking the attainment of a united Church. The growing relationship between the Church of Rome and the Church of England is perhaps the most pregnant development, but it would be a foolish mistake if the enthusiasm of some misled others to believe that union, or even a covenant, with Rome lies anywhere but in the far-distant future.

The fifties and sixties saw in the Church a demand for radical reform of its structures. This enthusiasm, too, met with frustration, and yet slowly such structural change has occurred that the Church of England is a different institution from what it was in 1945. This has been due to pastoral reorganization, the shortage of ordained clergy, the wider use of lay ministry (including women), the inauguration of synodical government, and a more rational and realistic method of payment of the clergy. The average age of ordinands is higher than at the beginning of the period, more of them are married and have had experience in the secular sphere, and a considerable number have come to Christian faith later in life. This is producing a ministry which is less traditional and less rooted in the past, which can bring new vigour and vision to a parish, but is not free of the possibility of misunderstanding and tension. The relationship between the bishops and their clergy and between clergy and laity in the parish is less hierarchical, more relaxed and uninhibited. Perhaps the greatest change has been in the field of liturgy where there is now a variety of rite and a freedom of expression which would have been unthinkable at the end of the war. The tide of the radical theology of the sixties has receded, leaving some Churchmen as deeply entrenched in conservatism as they were before. For many, however, theology can never again be a neatly packaged bundle of truth to be accepted without question; they may have a dogmatic faith in fewer things, but those fewer things are held with very deep conviction. Christian faith may be less serene and complacent, but it is tougher and better able to cope with questions and is thus experienced as a liberating force. Conservatives and radicals are learning to live side by side and the Church is beginning to reconstruct the faith in the knowledge that some of the certainties of yesterday must be replaced with honest question-marks.

The period has witnessed a deepening gulf between the Church and the nation—that is, between the baptized Englishman, who attends Church irregularly and is not deeply committed to mission, and the regular worshipper who is so committed. The Worship and Doctrine Measure and the Crown Appointments Commission has changed the balance of the Establishment and this appears to have caught many Tory MPs unawares. No state event will ever again be an Established Church event but will involve the participation of the Roman Catholic Church and the Free Churches. The bishops and clergy count for less in the life of the nation unless they win their place on personal grounds. Church appointments are no longer 'news' and ecclesiastical pronouncements count for little. Yet, paradoxically, there has been a greater concern at all levels in the Church about the needs of people, particularly the deprived. There has emerged a new emphasis on the Church as 'a caring community' and many Christians have a deeper understanding of the meaning and mechanism of 'personal relationships'. Synodical debates and the publications of the Board of Social Responsibility indicate the continuing concern which the Church has for the moral problems of industrial and scientific society, together with such issues as nuclear warfare, race relations, abortion, and homosexuality. The Church, taken as a whole, is more 'outward looking' than it was in 1945. This has not produced an influx of new Christians and, indeed, institutional religion has lost much of its traditional roots in the nation. Nevertheless, religious thought, activity, and debate are still vigorous and there are few signs of anti-clericalism or militant atheism.

One of the reasons for the Church's increased concern with

social and economic problems has been the gradual breakdown during these years of the rigid barriers between the sacred and the secular. This is perhaps the most lasting legacy of the radical theologians of the sixties. The danger to which a number of Christians succumbed was to identify the two. When that was avoided Christians came to see that there could be no gospel without mission, no prayer without care and no words without deeds. In 1945 most Christians saw mission in terms of direct personal evangelism; today the Church is aware that personal evangelism cannot be divorced from service to those in need and from the penetration of society and its structures by Christians, and that all three strands constitute the total concept of mission.

We have seen that during this period the evangelical party in the Church of England has become less defensive and more assured and that the anglo-catholic party has declined in strength and influence. A new diversity of opinion has emerged which cuts across former barriers of churchmanship and which can be polarized as radical and conservative, charismatic and non-charismatic, the call for personal evangelism and the challenge of mission to society, the acceptance of change as an invigorating experience and the rejection of change as a threat. Some would see part of the cause of this new diversity to lie in the lack of leadership from the episcopate. The last fifty years have indeed seen a considerable change in the style of episcopal leadership and a greater democratization of the Church. No longer, in any walk of life, do people accept the leader who marches ahead and calls upon his troops to follow, nor are people moved by great oratory and solemn pronouncements. Success in leadership involves consultation, reasoning, and consent. Bishop George Bell, in his life of Archbishop Davidson, wrote nearly forty years ago of the kind of leader

who, having a charge entrusted to him and a body of people at whose head he is placed, rather seeks to act as the interpreter of the best mind that is in them and to give it expression, to discover the *communis sensus* of the society, and to use all the means in his power to give it the opportunity of expression. Such a leader will guide and will show the way, and he will teach and suggest, but he will not be likely to lift his voice from the housetops, and to cry aloud to the laggards to come on at full speed. He will realize the diversity of human nature, of the material with which he has to deal, and will give it, or lead it to, the best and the highest unity of which he believes it to be capable under the given conditions... He will wish to keep the boat even, without endangering the passengers. He prefers peace and agreement before violence and confusion. He runs the risk of misrepresentation, and is unlikely to win great popular applause. But he is not on that account to be dismissed as an unsuitable kind of leader in dangerous and unsettled times.[3]

It is men who see leadership in these terms who have replaced the more autocratic and individualistic bishops of the first half of the century. The new style of episcopal leadership has been emphasized by the theological concept behind synodical government, which sees the Church as a partnership in which bishops, together with the clergy and laity, seek the greater good of the Church.

Ultimately it is neither the policies nor the speeches of its leaders, nor is it the great events, the influential moments, or the leading personalities which determine the health of the Church. There is something more intimate—and fundamental—the inner spiritual life of the Church as this is found in the parishes. The picture here since 1945 is a mixed one. Certain new housing areas and down-town parishes have lacked the resources for mission and care and some country parishes have remained indifferent to the claims of the Church. Congregations elsewhere have been mostly middle-aged or elderly and the Church's ministry to young people has been weak. A number of clergy have feared to share their ministry with the laity and too many churches have failed to respond to such hunger for spirituality as lay around them. In many places congregations have been small, lethargic, complacent, and obstructive to the smallest change. Too often worship has been formal and uninspired and the stranger rejected or ignored. Yet, one of the most remarkable features of our period has been the way in which life in so many parishes has flourished in contrast with the disillusionment experienced in the national life of the Church. Moreover, since the war secularization has accelerated to such an extent that this country has become one of the most secular in Europe. The loss of the sense of God has posed new problems for evangelism because those for whom God is dead, irrelevant, or insignificant, see no need to acknowledge or to worship Him. Yet in spite of this, and al-

[3] Randall Davidson, 1938, p. 1161.

though it has not grown in numbers, the Church has improved in many ways and has produced congregations which are lively and vigorous.

On the whole, church people have become more committed and one of the consequences of this has been a renewal of worship, brought about partly by the liturgical reforms but, in a number of parishes, ministered to by the influence of the charismatic movement, which has deepened spiritual life and met the hunger for spiritual renewal. The Parish Communion or the family service became growth points in the life of many parishes. A second result of the deepening of commitment has been the number of congregations which have become more outward looking, eager to serve society around them, conscious of their membership of a world-wide church, and possessing a deep concern about the plight of the Third World. Walls between the churches have been broken down and, not only in Areas of Ecumenical Experiment but in many other places, clergy and laity of different churches have grown together in understanding and have worked together over a wide range of activities, frustrated only by the constant set-backs to reunion at national level. More care has been taken over preparation for baptism and marriage, which have been seen as opportunities for meeting those who were otherwise cut off from the Church. Increasingly ministry has come to be understood as a shared responsibility between the incumbent and other qualified members of the congregation. Readers, pastoral assistants, lay elders, and other authorized lay ministers have abounded, but also ordinary members of congregations have come to share with the clergy in visiting and in baptismal and marriage preparation. In many parishes house groups for prayer, for biblical or doctrinal study, and for social witness flourish and draw into themselves unbelievers and 'fringers'. Increasing financial burdens have been accepted and Christian stewardship has become a sign of commitment. In evangelical parishes in particular there have been constant efforts 'to take Christ to the people' and it is probably in those parishes, through such organizations as Pathfinders, that work among young people has been strongest and from which many ordinands have emerged. Parish congregations have become more sociable and more caring. An outstanding example is the parish of St. Mary-le-Belfrey, York, which under the leadership of the Revd David Watson, became a stronghold of evangelical revival with large congregations in a church which a few years previously had been on the verge of closure.

This contrasting picture serves only to emphasize that the temperature of the Church of England has to be taken in the parishes, for whatever movement, proposal, or vision emerges within the Church it has no chance of success until it wins the sympathy and earns the commitment of priest and people in the parish.

The real history of the Church of England [wrote Roger Lloyd in 1946] is ... made in its parish churches, and the parish priest is the pivot on which that history turns... The Church might possibly survive a whole generation of impossible bishops and dead cathedrals... But it could not possibly survive a whole generation of bad vicars and lethargic churches. For the parish priest is the centre of the Church's life, and 'the main stream of Anglican piety flows, as it has always flowed, through the parish churches: and therefore it is the parishes that are the exciting thing. For the life of the parish is Church History.'[4]

In spite of the great changes of the past fifty years and in face of the transformation of parochial structures, there is no reason today to question that judgement.

[4] Roger Lloyd, *The Church of England, 1900-1965*, 1966 (first published 1946), p. 23, quoting Charles Smyth, 'The Study of Church History', in *The Priest as Student*, ed. Hubert S. Box, 1938, p. 275.

# BIBLIOGRAPHY

1. GENERAL

BOOKER, CHRISTOPHER. *The Neophiliacs*. 1969.
   *The Seventies*. 1980.
BRIGGS, ASA. *A History of Broadcasting in the United Kingdom*,
   Vol. 4. *Sound and Vision*. 1979.
CALVORCORESSI, JOHN. *The British Experience, 1945-1975*. 1978.
COLVILLE, JOHN. *The New Elizabethans, 1952-1977*. 1977.
CURRAN, CHARLES. *The Seamless Robe*. 1979.
GREENE, HUGH. *The Third Floor Front*. 1969.
LEVIN, BERNARD. *The Pendulum Years: Britain and the Sixties*.
   1970.
MARWICK, ARTHUR. *British Society Since 1945*. 1981.
THOMSON, DAVID. *England in the Twentieth Century*. 1978.


2. ECCLESIASTICAL

(This does not include reports of the Convocations or of the
Boards and Councils of the Church Assembly and the General
Synod referred to in the text.)
*Chronicle of Convocation: Record of the Proceedings of the Con-
vocation of Canterbury*. 1945-1969.
*York Journal of Convocation*. 1945-1969.
*Church Assembly: Report of Proceedings*. 1945-1970.
*General Synod: Report of Proceedings*, 1970-1980.
*Crockford's Clerical Directory*, 1947-1980.
*Church Times*, 1945-1980.


ADAIR, JOHN. *The Becoming Church*. 1977.
BEESON, TREVOR. *The Church of England in Crisis*. 1973.
   *Britain Today and Tomorrow*. 1978.
BOWDEN, JOHN. *Voices in the Wilderness*. 1977.
BULLOCK, F. W. B. *A History of Training for the Ministry of the
   Church of England, 1875-1974*. 1976.
CARPENTER, EDWARD. *Cantuar*. 1971.
COGGAN, DONALD. *Convictions*. 1975.
   *Sure Foundations*. 1981.
COLEMAN, PETER. *Christian Attitudes to Homosexuality*. 1980.
DAVIES, HORTON. *Worship and Theology in England*, Vol. 5:
   *The Ecumenical Century, 1900-1965*. 1965.

DAVIES, RUPERT. *The Church in Our Time.* 1979.
    *The Testing of the Churches, 1932-1982.* 1982.
DE BLANK, JOOST. *The Parish in Action.* 1954.
EDWARDS, DAVID. *Religion and Change.* 1969.
    *Leaders of the Church of England, 1818-1978.* 1971, 1978.
FERRIS, PAUL. *The Church of England.* Revised edition, 1964.
FEY, HAROLD (Ed.), *Ecumenical Advance: History of the Ecumenical Movement, 1948-1968.* 1970.
GARBETT, CYRIL. *In An Age of Revolution.* 1952.
GOODALL, NORMAN. *Ecumenical Progress: A Decade of Change in the Ecumenical Movement, 1961-1971.* 1972.
GUNSTONE, JOHN. *Pentecostal Anglicans,* 1982.
HUNT, G. *About the New English Bible.* 1970.
JAGGER, PETER J. *History of the Parish and People Movement.* 1978.
JEFFREY, R. M. C. *Areas of Ecumenical Experiment.* 1968.
JONES, KATHLEEN (Ed.). *Living the Faith.* 1980.
KENT, JOHN. *The End of the Line: Developments of Theology in the Last Two Centuries.* 1982.
KING, JOHN. *The Evangelicals.* 1969.
LEECH, KENNETH. *Youthquake.* 1973.
    *Soul Friend: A Study of Spirituality.* 1977.
LLOYD, ROGER. *The Church and the Artisan Today.* 1952.
    *The Church of England, 1900-1965.* 1966.
LYNCH, DONALD. *Chariots of the Gospel.* 1982.
MCKAY, ROY. *Take Care of the Sense.* 1964.
MACKINNON, DONALD. 'Justice', in *Theology,* March 1963.
MARTIN, CHRISTOPHER (Ed.). *Great Christian Centuries to Come: Essays in Honour of A. M. Ramsey.* 1974.
MASON, LANCELOT. '"Soldiers" and Bishop Bell', in *Crucible,* March 1969.
NORMAN, E. R. *Church and Society, 1700-1970.* 1976.
PAGE, R. J. *New Directions in Anglican Theology.* 1967.
PATON, D. M. (Ed.). *Essays in Anglican Self-Criticism.* 1958.
PAUL, LESLIE. *The Deployment and Payment of the Clergy.* 1964.
    *A Church by Daylight.* 1973.
PAWLEY, B and M. *Rome and Canterbury.* 1974.
PERMAN, DAVID. *Change and the Churches.* 1977.
RAMSEY, A. M. *Durham Essays and Adresses.* 1956.
    *Canterbury Essays and Addresses.* 1964.
RILEY, J. *Today's Cathedral: Cathedral Church of Christ, Liverpool.* 1978.
ROBINSON, J. A. T. and EDWARDS, DAVID. *The Honest to God Debate.* 1963.

Rose, W. E. *Sent from Coventry*. 1980.
Russell, Anthony. *The Clercial Profession*. 1980.
  (Ed.). *Groups and Teams in the Countryside*. 1975.
Sheppard, David. *Built as a City*. 1974.
Smith, A. C. *The South Ormsby Experiment*. 1960.
Southcott, E. *The Parish Comes Alive*. 1956.
Spence, Basil. *Phoenix at Coventry*. 1962.
Staples, Peter. *The Church of England, 1961-1980*. 1981.
Stephenson, A. *Anglicanism and the Lambeth Conference*. 1978.
Sullivan, Emmanuel. *Baptised into Hope*. 1980.
Tilby, Angela. *Teaching God*. 1979.
Till, Barry. *The Churches Search for Unity*. 1972.
Towler, R. and Coxon, A. P. M. *The Fate of the Anglican Clergy*.
  1980.
Vidler, Alec. *20th Century Defenders of the Faith*. 1965.
  'The Limitations of William Temple', in *Theology*, Jan. 1976.
Walton, Mary. *A History of the Diocese of Sheffield, 1914-1979*.
  1981.
Wand, J. W. C. *Recovery Starts Within: The Book of the Mission
  to London*. 1949.
Wedderspoon, Alexander (Ed.). *Grow or Die: Essays on Church
  Growth*. 1981.
West, Frank. *The Country Parish Today and Tomorrow*. 1960.
Wickham, E. R. *Church and People in an Industrial City*. 1957.
Williams, H. C. H. *Twentieth Century Cathedral*. 1964.

3. BIOGRAPHY AND AUTOBIOGRAPHY

Barnes, John. *Ahead of his Time: Bishop Barnes of Birmingham*.
  1979.
Barry, F. R *Mervyn Haigh*. 1964.
Brabazon, John. *Dorothy L. Sayers: The Life of a Courageous
  Woman*. 1981.
Brown, Leslie. *Three Worlds: One Word. An Account of a Mis-
  sion*. 1981.
Collins, L. John. *Faith under Fire*. 1966.
Daniels, Robin. *Conversations with Coggan*. 1983.
De Blank, Bartha. *Joost de Blank: A Personal Memoir*. 1977.
Dillistone, F. W. *C. H. Dodd: Interpreter of the New Testament*.
  1977.
  *Into All the World: A Biography of Max Warren*. 1980.
  *The Life of Joe Fison: A Fire for God*. 1983.
Dunstan, Alan and Peart-Binns, J. S. *Cornish Bishop: a Biography
  of J. W. Hunkin*. 1977.

EDWARDS, DAVID. *Ian Ramsey.* 1973.

FFRENCH-BEYTAGH, G. A. *Encountering Darkness.* 1973.

GRUBB, KENNETH. *Crypts of Power.* 1971.

GUMMER, SELWYN. *The Chavasse Twins.* 1963.

IREMONGER, F. A. *William Temple.* 1948.

JAGGER, P. J. *Bishop Henry de Candole.* 1975.

JASPER, RONALD. *George Bell.* 1967.

KEMP, E. W. *Life and Letters of Kenneth Escott Kirk.* 1959.

*Spencer Leeson: A Memoir by Some of his Friends.* 1958.

LINDSAY, DAVID. *Friends for Life: A Portrait of Lancelot Fleming.* 1981.

MATTHEWS, W. R. *Memories and Meanings.* 1969.

MOULE, C. F. D. (Ed.). *G. W. H. Lampe.* 1982.

PACKARD, KENNETH E. *Brother Edward: Priest and Evangelist.* 1955.

PEART-BINNS, J. S. *Ambrose Reeves.* 1973.

*Eric Treacy.* 1980.

PURCELL, WILLIAM. *Fisher of Lambeth.* 1969.

SLACK, KENNETH. *George Bell.* 1971.

SMYTH, CHARLES. *Cyril Foster Garbett.* 1959.

SPROXTON, VERNON. *Teilhard de Chardin.* 1971.

STACEY, NICHOLAS. *Who Cares?* 1961.

STOCKWOOD, MERVYN. *Chanctonbury Ring: An Autobiography.* 1982.

TRACEY, MICHAEL and MORRISON, DAVID. *Whitehouse.* 1979.

VIDLER, ALEC. *Scenes from a Clerical Life.* 1977.

WAND, J. W. C. *Changeful Page.* 1965.

WARREN, MAX. *Crowded Canvas.* 1974.

WEST, FRANK. *FRB: A Portrait of Bishop Russell Barry.* 1980.

WHITEHOUSE, MARY. *A Most Dangerous Woman?* 1982.

WILLIAMS, H. A. *Some Day I'll Find You.* 1982.

# INDEX